The Madness of It All

The Madness of It All

Essays on War, Literature and American Life

W.D. EHRHART

McFarland & Company, Inc., Publishers
Jefferson, North Carolina, and London

Library of Congress Cataloguing-in-Publication Data

Ehrhart, W.D. (William Daniel), 1948–
   The madness of it all : essays on war, literature and American
life / W.D. Ehrhart.
      p.   cm.
   Includes bibliographical references and index.
   ISBN 0-7864-1333-6 (softcover : 50# alkaline paper) ∞
   1. Ehrhart, W. D. (William Daniel), 1948–   2. Poets, American—
20th century—Biography.   3. Vietnamese Conflict, 1961–1975—
Veterans—Biography.   4. United States—Civilization—20th
century.   I. Title.
PS3555.H67 Z464   2002
811'.54—dc21   2002006104

British Library cataloguing data are available

Manufactured in the United States of America

*McFarland & Company, Inc., Publishers
   Box 611, Jefferson, North Carolina 28640
   www.mcfarlandpub.com*

For Anne
and for Leela

ACKNOWLEDGMENTS

These essays first appeared in the following publications: "If This Be War"—*Philadelphia Inquirer*, February 10, 1991; "To Hell with Them All"—*Philadelphia Daily News*, February 11, 1991; "Partytime in the U.S.A."—*Philadelphia Inquirer*, July 4, 1991; "'We Must Have This'"—*Virginia Quarterly Review*, v.68, #1, Winter 1992; "Who's Responsible?"—*Viet Nam Generation*, v.4, #1/2, Spring 1992; "Why My Daughter Won't Grow Up in Perkasie"—*Viet Nam Generation*, v.4, #3/4, Fall 1992; "Forever Gone"—*San Jose Mercury News*, December 2, 1992; "On Common Sense and Conscience"—*Los Angeles & San Francisco Daily Journal*, January 15, 1993; "On the Virtues of Dishonesty"—*Philadelphia Inquirer*, February 5, 1993; "An Encounter with the IRS"—*Philadelphia Inquirer*, March 5, 1993; "Alive with Pleasure"—*Philadelphia Inquirer*, June 17, 1993; "On Being the Last True Superpower"—*Chestnut Hill Local*, June 24, 1993; "On the Sad Fate of American Doctors"—*Baltimore Sun*, September 10, 1993; "Why Didn't You Tell Me?"—*Studies in Education* #66, Winter 1994; "The Vietnam War and the Academy"—*VVA Veteran*, February 1994; "No Facts, Only Perceptions"—*Virginia Quarterly Review*, v.70, #3, Summer 1994; "The War That Won't Go Away"—*VVA Veteran*, August 1994; "I Could Not Help My Friend"—*Virginia Quarterly Review*, v.70, #4, Autumn 1994; "This Is All We Wanted"—*Washington Post*, April 23, 1995; "Freedom Is Cigarettes and Beer"—*Manoa*, v.7, #1, Summer 1995; "A Letter from Robert Redford"—*London Free Press* (Ontario), December 20, 1995; "The Summer I Learned to Dance"—*War, Literature and the Arts*, v.8, #2, Fall/Winter 1996; "Tugboats on the Delaware"—published in two parts in *New Jersey Waterways*, v.1, #3, September 1996 & v.2, #1, March/April 1997; "What Grace Is Found in So Much Loss?"—*Virginia Quarterly Review*, v.73, #1, Winter 1997; "On Inflammatory Rhetoric"—*Mt. Airy Times Express*, April 16, 1997; "A Modest Proposal"—*Republic Monitor*, April 17, 1997; "Indecent Techno-assault"—

Philadelphia Forum, v.2, #25, July 24, 1997; "Military Intelligence"—*Swarthmore College Bulletin*, v.XCV, #3, December 1997; "Soldier-Poets of the Korean War"—*War, Literature, and the Arts*, v.9, #2, Fall/Winter 1997; "I Want to Try It All Before I Go: The Life and Poetry of William Wantling"—*American Poetry Review*, November/December 1998; "Howard Fast's 'Korean Litany'"—*War, Literature, and the Arts*, v.12, #1, Spring/Summer 2000; "From the Halls of Montezuma to the Chosin Reservoir"—*Marine Corps Gazette*, v.84, #6, June 2000; "Pennridge High School and the Vietnam War"—*The Vietnam War on Campus*, Marc Jason Gilbert, ed., Praeger, 2001; "The Poetry of Bullets, or: How Does a War Mean?"—*Proceedings of the Center for the Study of the Korean War*, v.1, #1, April 2001; "Setting the Record Straight: An Addendum to the Life and Poetry of William Wantling"—*Poetry Wales*, v.37, #1, July 2001; "'In Cases Like This, There Is No Need to Vote': Korean War Poetry in the Context of American Twentieth Century War Poetry"—*Colby Quarterly*, v.37, #3, September 2001; "'The Madness of It All': A Rumination on War, Journalism & Brotherhood"—*Virginia Quarterly Review*, v.78, #1, Winter 2002; "Drawbridges on the Delaware"—*Virginia Quarterly Review*, v.78, #4, Fall 2002; "Where Do We Go from Here?"—*VVAW Veteran*, v.32, #1, Spring/Summer 2002.

Howard Fast's "Korean Litany" is reprinted from *Korean Lullaby* (New York: American Peace Crusade, undated) by permission of the author.

W.D. Ehrhart's "The Teacher" and "Beautiful Wreckage" are reprinted from *Beautiful Wreckage: New & Selected Poems* (Easthampton, Mass.: Adastra Press, 1999).

CONTENTS

Acknowledgments vii
Preface 1

———— The Essays ————

A Line in the Sand 9
If This Be War 10
To Hell with Them All 12
Partytime in the U.S.A. 14
"We Must Have This" 16
Who's Responsible? 21
Why My Daughter Won't Grow Up in Perkasie 31
Forever Gone 37
On Common Sense and Conscience 40
On the Virtues of Dishonesty 42
An Encounter with the IRS 44
Alive with Pleasure 47
On Being the Last True Superpower 49
On the Sad Fate of American Doctors 52
Why Didn't You Tell Me? 54
The Vietnam War and the Academy 59
Sticks and Stones 64
No Facts, Only Perceptions 69
The War That Won't Go Away 74

I Could Not Help My Friend 79
This Is All We Wanted 87
Freedom Is Cigarettes and Beer 89
A Letter from Robert Redford 95
Shaking Hands with Abe Lincoln 97
The Summer I Learned to Dance 99
Tugboats on the Delaware 105
"What Grace Is Found in So Much Loss?" 116
On Inflammatory Rhetoric 127
A Modest Proposal 129
Indecent Techno-assault 131
Military Intelligence 133
Soldier-Poets of the Korean War 141
"I Want to Try It All Before I Go": The Life and Poetry
    of William Wantling 173
Howard Fast's "Korean Litany" 182
From the Halls of Montezuma to the Chosin Reservoir 188
Tarnishing the Glory of the Corps 192
Pennridge High School and the Vietnam War 195
The Poetry of Bullets, or: How Does a War Mean? 205
Setting the Record Straight: An Addendum to the Life
    and Poetry of William Wantling 217
"In Cases Like This, There Is No Need to Vote":
    Korean War Poetry in the Context of American Twentieth
    Century War Poetry 222
"The Madness of It All": A Rumination on War, Journalism
    and Brotherhood 241
Drawbridges on the Delaware 255
Where Do We Go From Here? 262

Military History of W. D. Ehrhart 265
About the Author 267
Index 269

PREFACE

I cannot begin to count the number of times over the past 37 years that I have wished I had never heard of Vietnam, let alone fought in the Vietnam War. That experience has haunted my days. It has troubled my nights. It has shaped my identity and colored the way I see the world and everything in it. As I wrote in a poem called "For a Coming Extinction":

> Vietnam. Not a day goes by
> without that word on my lips.
> I hear the rattle of small-arms fire
> when I tuck my daughter in,
> think of the stillborn dreams of other men
> when I make love to my wife,
> sharp snap of a flag in high wind—
> blood, stars, an ocean of ignorance.

In a very real and personal way, as the title of one of the essays in this collection says, it's "The War That Won't Go Away."

Moreover, it has shaped and colored not only the way I see both myself and the world, but also the way people see me. Such public reputation as I possess is almost entirely bound up in the Vietnam War and by the fact that I have written five books, multiple essays, and dozens of poems about the war. I am regularly asked to read or speak about the war to audiences ranging from high school and college classes to church congregations to conferences of scholars and academics. Frequently, I'll find myself standing in front of a group of high school kids or junior college teachers or whatever, talking about the war, while in another part of my mind I'll be thinking, "Geez, Ehrhart, why are you still talking about this? Get a life!"

But I have a life. I've been married over 20 years. We've been living in the same house for 16 years. I have a teenaged daughter with whom I

1

just went to a 10-hour rock festival (*that's* love). As a favor to a friend, with only 36 hours' notice and under very difficult circumstances, I recently spent five months teaching Melville and Crane and Fitzgerald, Sillitoe, and the English Romantics to high school junior and senior boys at the Haverford School—a favor that has led to my returning to fulltime teaching. I vote in every election, even primaries. A poem of mine about the beech tree in our back yard was published not long ago in a nature anthology, and another about my days as a merchant seaman was included in an anthology about Portland, Oregon.

Many of the essays in this collection reflect a range of interests that goes far beyond the Vietnam War or even war in general. Among the many shorter essays, "On Common Sense and Conscience" considers the American legal system and the right of jury nullification; "On the Virtues of Dishonesty" reflects upon the kinds of examples contemporary American culture and society offer to young people today; "Shaking Hands with Abe Lincoln" challenges the isolation of American presidents, and "Alive with Pleasure" looks at the tobacco industry. "On Inflammatory Rhetoric" grapples with the delicate subject of race in America while "A Letter from Robert Redford," "Indecent Techno-assault" and "An Encounter with the IRS" are (I hope) amusing reflections upon some not so amusing aspects of American life. "On the Sad Fate of American Doctors," though dated, turns out to have been quite prescient, considering the campaign promises of then-candidate Bill Clinton and the subsequent fate of health care reform in America. "A Modest Proposal" may yet turn out to be just as prescient.

Among the longer essays, both "The Summer I Learned to Dance" and "Why My Daughter Won't Grow Up in Perkasie" are set in the small town in which I grew up. The first is a story of foolhardy bravado while the second explores national mythology and self-deception in small-town America. "Tugboats on the Delaware" and "Drawbridges on the Delaware," as their titles suggest, deal with various aspects of life on the Delaware River, which forms one boundary of both the city and the state in which I live.

The essay on the tugboat *Teresa McAllister* and its crew may be the best single piece of writing I've ever done. It is certainly my favorite piece, barring perhaps only a handful of my poems. And the research I did on the Tacony-Palmyra Bridge was far and away the most challenging I've ever undertaken, requiring me to be on call 24 hours a day, seven days a week for more than five weeks, to drop whatever I was doing (including sleeping) and get myself to the bridge whenever there was an opening regardless of the time of day or night, and even to board a moving freighter from the deck of a moving pilot boat in the middle of the river by means of a 30-foot rope ladder hanging down the side of the freighter's cold steel hull, all of this in the rain at 3:30 A.M. Try that one if you want to get your heart rate up.

All of these essays notwithstanding, however, my lifelong preoccupation with war and its consequences, precipitated by my youthful encounter with the Vietnam War, is readily apparent in many other essays of the included in this collection. The first four essays, all written between the fall of 1990 and the summer of 1991, came in response to the Gulf War against Iraq. "We Must Have This" deals with the Palestinian *Intifada* of the late 1980s and early 1990s, and is especially disturbing to me because both it and the book which prompted it read as if they were written yesterday, not a decade ago. "The Vietnam War and the Academy" and "Pennridge High School and the Vietnam War" deal with various aspects of that war, as do "Forever Gone" and "The War That Won't Go Away."

A number of other essays are harder to categorize because they deal with multiple wars or with war in more general or oblique ways. "Who's Responsible?" was prompted by Bobbie Ann Mason's post–Vietnam War novel *In Country*, but talks at length about the Gulf War and other American wars as far back as the Civil War. "Sticks and Stones" (as in "sticks and stones may break my bones, but words will never hurt me") begins with the Balkan wars of the early 1990s, but ranges from the American Plains Indian wars to the wars of the Haitian, Salvadoran and Guatemalan governments against their own people.

But if war has been a lifelong preoccupation of mine, so has literature, and those two threads are woven together over and over again in many of these essays. "We Must Have This," "No Facts, Only Perceptions," "I Could Not Help My Friend," "This Is All We Wanted," "Freedom Is Cigarettes and Beer," "From the Halls of Montezuma to the Chosin Reservoir," and "Tarnishing the Glory of the Corps" are all, in essence, book reviews. "What Grace Is Found in So Much Loss?" is a follow-up to an essay on Vietnam War poetry I wrote in the mid–1980s called "Soldier-Poets of the Vietnam War." "Who's Responsible?" and "The Madness of It All" began as book reviews but quickly became much larger essays.

I feel compelled to point out, moreover, that all of this focus on war in one form or another is not entirely my doing. Once people begin to think of you in a certain way, that tends to have a self-reinforcing effect. Of the eleven essays I mention in the preceding paragraph, for instance, eight of them were solicited by other people, not initiated by me. This is true of many of the other essays in this collection as well. I could decline such requests, I suppose—in fact, increasingly, as often as not, I do. But it's hard to say no when the person asking has done favors for me in the past, or is a friend, or comes at me from an angle that catches me with my guard down, or waves money at me, or whatever. I can't always say no, and don't always care to.

A case in point explains why so many of the essays toward the end of this collection deal with the literature, especially the poetry, of the Korean War. Way back in 1986, I met a professor, a man about my age named Phil Melling, at a conference at the University of Manchester in England. Two years later, he and his colleague Jon Roper invited me to the University of Wales at Swansea. They invited me again in 1994. I love Swansea Bay and the Gower Peninsula. Dylan Thomas called Swansea "the Graveyard of Ambition." Apparently, the town fathers took umbrage at this, but I think what Thomas meant was that once you get there, you don't want to leave. Certainly I didn't. So in late 1996, when Phil and Jon asked me if I might be interested in taking an appointment as a research fellow in American studies, I readily agreed.

They assumed that I would research and write about the Vietnam War, since that is the context in which they knew me and my work. When I told them I was kind of tired of the Vietnam War after 30 years, they asked me what else I might be interested in working on. Not, at that time, possessing a Ph.D., I had to stay within the bounds of American war literature, where I have established some expertise and credibility because of the work I've done on literature, especially poetry, of the Vietnam War. I said maybe I'd see what I could find on American poetry of the Korean War.

I am sure that to many people who know me, my writing about the Korean War was perceived as "Ehrhart doing his war thing again," but for me it was like being on vacation. I don't even remember the Korean War. I was not yet five years old when the truce was signed. I have only a vague recollection of watching my older brothers and some of their friends playing "war" in our backyard, and an even more vague memory of the enemy being "the Commies." I might have been three or four or five. And that's it: my only real-life connection to the Korean War. I've no axe to grind, no agenda of my own, no baggage to haul around.

And it turned out to be a great subject to research. Little has been done on any aspect of the Korean War, and nobody even knew there was such a thing as Korean War poetry until I began to find and elucidate it. Moreover, slowly but surely, word of my new expertise began to spread. I was invited to speak on Korean War literature at the Dwight D. Eisenhower Library in Abilene, Kansas (I even wore a suit for that one). I was invited to give the keynote speech at a conference in Missouri on war and memory in which I was able to bring to bear my previous knowledge of Vietnam War literature, my growing knowledge of Korean War literature, and other knowledge I've gathered about war and literature over the years, and you end up with my essay "The Poetry of Bullets."

Or take "Military Intelligence": the editor of *War, Literature, and the Arts* sent a copy of their 1996 special issue on my writing to the editor of my college alumni magazine. The editor of my college alumni magazine thought it very odd that a journal coming out of the Air Force Academy would focus on a decidedly antiwar writer like me. I started to explain how this had come about, but after a few minutes he stopped me and asked if I would write it all down in the form of an essay. Left to my own devices, it never would have occurred to me to write such an essay, but it makes a good story.

Each of these essays, in fact, has a story of its own. My two essays on the poet William Wantling are a powerful demonstration of the dangers of publishing too quickly. "Why Didn't You Tell Me?" is at least partly responsible for prompting a woman to write a book about survivors of rape and those who love them. The author of *Achilles in Vietnam*, a man I had never met in my life prior to his thrusting the unbound page proofs into my hands at a conference at Notre Dame in 1993, begged me to review his book, then attacked me in print and on the internet when he didn't like what I wrote.

Hey, you don't want my opinion, don't ask for it. Speaking of which, "Tarnishing the Glory of the Corps" was commissioned and accepted by the outgoing editor of the *Marine Corps Gazette*, then promptly killed by the incoming editor, who decided he'd rather displease me than displease a columnist at *Parade* magazine. And speaking of displeasing people, "The Madness of It All" seems to have greatly displeased a man I deeply respect and had become very fond of in recent years, proving once again that writing about one's friends is always a dangerous undertaking.

It's much safer to take on faceless bureaucracies that nobody likes. "An Encounter with the IRS," which appeared originally in the *Philadelphia Inquirer*, was eventually published in the *Sacramento Bee*, the *Cleveland Plain Dealer*, the *Chicago Tribune*, the *Houston Post*, *Reader's Digest*, and—most astonishing and delightful of all—*Newsbreak*, the monthly internal publication of the Internal Revenue Service's Adjustment/Correspondence Branch in Ogden, Utah. When the woman from the IRS office in Ogden called and sheepishly asked permission to reprint my essay, I told her I'd made over $2,000 on it, I'd paid my taxes on the money I'd earned, she was welcome to reprint my piece, and could she arrange for the IRS to fine me on an annual basis since we all seemed to come out ahead in the end.

"An Encounter with the IRS," like many of the very short essays in this book, was originally written as a newspaper commentary. Back in the early 1990s, freelance syndicated graphic artist Barrie Maguire saw one of my commentaries, liked it, and offered to do illustrations to go along with my commentaries. We collaborated on a number of pieces that ran in publications from the *San Diego Union-Tribune* and the *San Jose Mercury-News* to the *Vancouver Sun* and the *London Free Press* (Canada, that is, not England). I am grateful to Barrie for allowing me to include some of his illustrations in this book.

There are other stories, too. As I said, just about every essay in this collection has a story to go with it. But in the end, the essays themselves—like poems or any other writing, I suppose—must stand on their own or not stand at all.

A Note on the Text

Some of these essays originally appeared under different titles. Those titles were determined by the editors of the publications in which they appeared, not by me, and I have therefore replaced these externally imposed titles with titles of my own. In a few cases, I have reinserted material that was included in my original manuscripts but deleted by editors for reasons of space or whim.

Some of these essays have appeared in multiple versions. Where this has been the case, I have usually chosen to include the original version except where a later more complete version better reflects the manuscript version I wrote in the first place.

I have tried to keep actual revisions to a minimum, rewriting only when the original text demanded it for reasons of style or logic. Some of the later essays, written originally for scholarly or literary publications, were highly footnoted; I have removed almost all—not quite, but almost all—of these footnotes in the interest of making the essays more accessible for general readers. (If you want all the technical stuff, you can always go to the original sources in which those essays were published.) Except in the few places noted in the text, however, I have made no attempt to update facts and references which may now be out of date. While specific facts and references may be dated, the general sense of what I wrote in each essay remains true.

In the Acknowledgments, I have indicated only the publication in which each essay first appeared. The essays are mostly arranged in their chronological order of publication except for "A Line in the Sand," "Sticks and Stones," "Shaking Hands with Abe Lincoln," and "Tarnishing the Glory of the Corps," which are here published for the first time and placed in accordance with when each was written.

W.D. Ehrhart
April 2002

THE ESSAYS

A Line in the Sand

As I write this, 100,000 U.S. military personnel are deployed in the desert of Saudi Arabia while the Iraqi army of Saddam Hussein occupies Kuwait. Cocked and pointed at each other like the frightening collection of loaded weapons that they are, both sides wait to see what the other will do. How did it come to this?

In 1973, the United States received a message that we really ought to find a way to better manage our consumption of energy, so that we would not have to depend upon undependable external sources of oil. We ignored that message. In 1979, we got an even more pointed message. We ignored that one, too.

If we now find ourselves with no option but to risk the lives of our children in a desert wasteland far from our own shores, that is hardly the fault of Saddam Hussein, a tyrant by any reasonable definition, but a tyrant our government fostered and fed almost up to the very eve of his invasion of Kuwait.

Of course, no one in Washington, D. C., is particularly eager these days to own up to the fact that for nearly a decade after our man the Shah of Iran was overthrown by his people, we figured we could bribe, cajole and manipulate Saddam into being our new man in the Middle East.

While the folks in Washington insist with stern-faced sobriety that Saddam's international lawlessness in invading Kuwait cannot be allowed to go unpunished, those same folks made not a peep when the same man openly invaded the Ayatollah Khomeini's Iran in 1981.

When it appeared that Iran might not only withstand the Iraqi invasion, but might actually win that war, we proceeded to provide Saddam with vital satellite intelligence on Iranian troop movements while holding our silence in the face of incontrovertible evidence that Saddam was using chemical weapons.

When an Iraqi Exocet missile killed 37 U.S. sailors aboard the U.S.S. *Stark* in the Persian Gulf, the U.S. Navy proceeded to blow the Iranian navy out of the water.

That's not a typographical error: Iraq killed our sailors, so we attacked Iran. And just for good measure, we then shot an Iranian civilian airliner out of the sky, killing all 299 people aboard.

That shootdown, of course, was an unfortunate accident—though when the Soviets shot a Korean civilian airliner out of the sky several years earlier, it had been an act of murderous barbarism. But that was when the Soviet Union was still the Evil Empire.

Now the Soviets are on our side in this war-waiting-to-happen with

Iraq. So are the British and the Argentinians, who fought a war with each other only eight years ago.

Meanwhile, Iran and Iraq, mortal enemies who only recently concluded their bloody eight-year war against each other, now jointly condemn the current deployment of U.S. troops, while another one of *our* allies in this current showdown is that mentor and benefactor of extremist terrorists suddenly turned good guy, Syria's Hafez Assad.

The Israelis are pointing to Saddam while shouting at us, "We told you so," and our old Middle Eastern pal King Hussein of Jordan sits on the fence not knowing what to do.

Just last week, columnist George Will suggested, as Saddam claimed when he invaded Kuwait, that the Kuwaitis may indeed have been slant-drilling into Iraqi oilfields and stealing Saddam's oil after all. But our "line in the sand" is okay anyway, says Will, since the real issue is neither international lawlessness nor cheap oil, but rather Saddam's potential nuclear, chemical, and even biological weapons capabilities.

Never mind that U.S. and other Western European companies are the ones who provided Saddam with such potential. Never mind that Will's call to put American service personnel in harm's way comes from a man who was prime meat during the Vietnam War, but managed neither to volunteer nor to get drafted into military service.

I hope we will all somehow manage to wake up from this nightmare before it turns deadly. I hope all our brave young men and women come home safely, their rifles clean, their ammunition unused. Whoever "wins" a shooting war—with or without chemical weapons, with or without nuclear weapons—a lot of people are going to die. Some of them will be our sons and daughters.

How will those young Americans feel if they ever discover that they have sacrificed so much in defense of a family oil business with a seat in the United Nations so that the rest of us Americans, most of whom will have sacrificed nothing, can continue to drive our cars to the mall on Saturday night?

❖ ❖ ❖

If This Be War

While the New York Giants and the Buffalo Bills battled it out in a close and hard-fought Super Bowl XXV, our brave men and women in the

Middle East were waging a real battle. But our troops were never far from our thoughts, right? The players had U.S. flag decals on their helmets. The halftime show was a rousing patriotic extravaganza of children and music and red, white and blue. Television viewers were even treated to videotape of U.S. soldiers enthusiastically watching the game in Saudi Arabia.

But it occurred to me that, for all our heartfelt thoughts and gestures of support for the troops, this war isn't really costing most of us very much. We got to see our football game. We'll all get up tomorrow and go to work or school or whatever. We'll all talk about what we did over the weekend, and maybe talk a bit in quiet tones about the latest news from the war zone, and then we'll go home and do it all again the next day. And the day after that.

Aren't we supposed to be at war? Don't 87 percent of the American people support this war? Talk's cheap. It's easy to support a war that doesn't cost you anything. It's easy to tie a yellow ribbon to the front lamppost and say you are behind the troops all the way. But if this is war, we ought to behave as if it is. All of us should be making sacrifices. I have a few suggestions:

• Cancel all sporting events for the duration of the war. In spite of the stirring halftime footage, most of our troops in the Persian Gulf didn't get to watch the Super Bowl. We shouldn't have either. In fact, we should cancel all television programming except news. Every time we turn on the TV, we'll be reminded of the sacrifices our brave young men and women are making for us. Life should not be comfortable in wartime.

• Shut down all colleges and universities for the duration of the war. What good are future literature majors and chemists and doctors if we lose this war to a man our own president has described as worse than Adolf Hitler? Moreover, all otherwise eligible students from schools of higher learning should be drafted into the military. Why should only those too disadvantaged or too poor to go to college bear the entire responsibility for defending all of us? And besides, if half a million soldiers are sufficient to defeat the Iraqi army, surely 2.5 million soldiers would virtually overwhelm them.

• Outlaw all nonessential travel for the duration of the war. Our brave men and women in the Middle East can't hop in the car and drive over to the Smiths to play bridge or take a ride to the Poconos to go skiing. Why should we? Essential travel should be regulated through a voucher system and it should be enforced by military police officers. Our troops are dying for the oil we need. We ought to be willing to need less of it.

• Shut down all nonessential industries and businesses for the duration of the war. We don't need party hats and video games and bubblegum during wartime. People need jobs, of course, but we're going to need a lot of military police officers to enforce travel restrictions.

• Reduce all Americans' pay to the level of the military pay scale for the duration of the war. Chief executive officers, for instance, could be given generals' pay. Supervisors would get sergeants' pay. New employees would receive privates' pay. What we would have received in excess of our new military pay could be donated to the federal government to eliminate the national debt. What better way to show our support for the troops than to unmortgage their futures even as they fight and die to defend ours?

Maybe you think I'm kidding about all of this, but I'm not. Super Bowl I was played while I was fighting in Vietnam. I was lonely and frightened, living like an animal. The patriotic halftime show didn't make me feel any better about it. I didn't see the halftime show. I didn't see the game. You could have tied up all of Manhattan Island with a huge yellow ribbon, and I wouldn't have cared. I just wanted to come home fast and in one piece. War is a miserable place to grow up.

We have been told by our government that the only way to peace in the Middle East is through this war. Okay, let's go to war then. All of us. Every last one of us. Let's start making some sacrifices around here. If we all pitch in, we might end this war that much sooner. If the rest of us have to pay even a fraction of the price being paid by the young men and women of our armed forces, the war might be over by tomorrow.

❖ ❖ ❖

To Hell with Them All

The other day I was standing in line at the supermarket, and I couldn't help overhearing part of a conversation between the checkout clerk and the woman in front of me. "If I could just get my hands on Saddam, I'd castrate that butcher," the checkout clerk said. "And *then* I'd torture him! That's what he deserves. He isn't human." He said this with a straight face, and the woman nodded in apparent agreement. He could have been anywhere between 28 and 43 years of age. He was wearing a yellow ribbon and a Red Cross pin on one lapel, a U.S. flag patch on the other.

He then explained that his brother is in Saudi Arabia, and that he himself is a Red Cross volunteer. He said that he might be called to the Middle East by the Red Cross once the ground fighting begins. "I wouldn't mind going," he said. "I'll do anything I can for our soldiers. But I'll be damned if I'll lift a finger to help an Iraqi soldier. To hell with all of them."

By itself, the incident would be only a fleeting if chilling anomaly. But if that checkout clerk's views are perhaps on the extreme side, they are by no means anomalous. In the past few weeks, I've heard an otherwise sane housewife describe Saddam Hussein as a madman, a friendly postal worker wish for the utter destruction of Iraq, and a high school teacher suggest that we should drop a nuclear bomb on Baghdad.

It is often said that war brings out the best in people, that it inspires heroism, self-sacrifice and camaraderie, and this is true. But war also brings out the worst in people. Otherwise rational and caring people tend to stop thinking in war. We want to believe that what is happening is not a nightmare so horrible we would never sleep again if we once paused to reflect upon it, and so we do not pause to reflect.

We do not want to imagine that Saddam Hussein—however different from us he may be, however incomprehensible—is, like us, just a human being. We do not want to believe that the soldiers of Iraq, let alone its people, are human beings who hope, strive, suffer and feel just as we do. We hold our children in our arms and wish to protect them from harm, and if we ever thought about those Iraqi parents and children who are helpless beneath our bombs, it would drive us mad. And so we listen to our civilian and military leaders speak glibly of "collateral damage," and we feel reassured, and we do not stop to consider how cold and detached our language has become.

In short, we demonize the enemy so that we can go on living with ourselves. It happens in every war. The Germans become Huns. The Russians become Reds. The Chinese become chinks. The Koreans, and in turn the Vietnamese, become gooks. And now the Iraqis are barbarians. How can people capable of disconnecting Kuwaiti babies from their respirators and firing missiles into Tel Aviv be like us? How can they be human? Obviously, they can't be.

And so it is all right for us to kill them. How can anyone even begin to equate our "smart bombs" and "surgical strikes" to the indiscriminate use of SCUD missiles or the release of millions of gallons of oil into the Persian Gulf? The comparison is ludicrous. We are different from them. We are human. We have no choice except to defend ourselves and our way of life from the barbarian onslaught—but we at least, unlike the Iraqis, are waging war responsibly, humanely, indeed morally.

Some things can't be avoided, of course, no matter how careful we are. By way of acknowledging, however obliquely, that innocent civilians *are* dying in Iraq in spite of all our sophisticated technology, General Norman Schwarzkopf recently said that "war is a dirty business." But even that statement is a reassuring euphemism. War isn't really a dirty business. It is a cruel and bloody and violent business, and it drags down all who are a part of it—those in the war zone and those at home—into the mire of savagery. Once the shooting starts, the line between who is behaving humanely and who is not becomes a matter of salving one's conscience by ignoring the truth.

Will that Iraqi father holding his dead child feel grateful that our pilots are taking extra risks in order to minimize collateral damage? The Emir of Kuwait said recently that a destroyed but liberated Kuwait is better than a largely whole but occupied Kuwait. I wonder if his subjects will agree.

And if that checkout clerk at the supermarket does end up in the Middle East, and Iraqi prisoners of war do end up under his care, I wonder what those who survive will say to their families and friends about the true character and soul of the American people.

❖ ❖ ❖

Partytime in the U.S.A.

Ever since the end of the Gulf War in late February, it's been partytime in the U.S.A. We've had the Nashville Tribute to Desert Storm and the Bob Hope Tribute to Desert Storm and the *People Magazine* Tribute to Desert Storm. General Norman Schwarzkopf's ruggedly cherubic visage has graced the cover of every magazine in the land, Stormin' Norman look-alikes have been showing up in advertisements and commercials more often than Michael Jordan, and Desert Storm trading cards can be found right next to those of Orel Hershiser and John Kruk. Our nation's capital spent $12 million on a Welcome Home Desert Storm parade, and one small town in western Massachusetts even held a parade for a local doctor and reservist who spent six weeks in Germany dutifully awaiting casualties that never arrived.

There were American casualties, of course. Not many, but every once in a while I've wondered if the families of those casualties are enjoying the celebration as much as the rest of us. And I find it ironic that we managed to inflict more casualties upon ourselves than the Iraqis managed to inflict on us. But nobody likes a wet blanket, so let's not think about those things.

After all, Kuwait has been liberated. The Emir is once again safely ensconced on his gold toilet, and the al-Sabah family is back in charge of a country where two-thirds of the inhabitants are neither citizens nor have any prospect of ever becoming citizens, where legitimate political opposition is treated as treason, and where nowadays one can be shot for exercising poor taste in the choice of one's T-shirt.

Anyway, we kicked Saddam Hussein's butt. We bombed him back into the pre-industrial age. We blew up his airplanes, and shot down his missiles, and finally caught his army fleeing north by the thousands on a highway so gridlocked it looked like the Los Angeles Freeway at rush hour. We strafed and bombed those hapless, helpless, unresisting columns with the fury of God's avenging angels.

Never mind that Saddam Hussein himself didn't actually sustain so much as a skinned knee. Never mind that he's not likely to die of the cholera and typhoid that are killing Iraqi civilians because we bombed military targets like power plants, water pumping stations and sewage treatment facilities. Never mind that he's still firmly in control of what is left of Iraq, and still spouting the same garbage he was spouting all through the decade during which the U.S. and many of the rest of our coalition partners sold him technology, weapons and food, sure that he was the perfect counterweight to the ayatollahs.

Never mind that we explicitly urged Iraqi Shiites and Kurds to rise against Saddam, then stood idly by—often within sight and sound of the carnage—while Saddam butchered the Shiites and chased the Kurds into the mountains of Turkey to die of starvation, disease and exposure.

At least it was the cleanest and most humane war we ever fought. We watched the videos on TV of all those smart bombs sliding down chimneys and bursting through doors with the precision of neurological surgeons. Never mind that ninety percent of the bombs we dropped were the same old iron clunkers we were dropping on Japan and Germany fifty years ago. Never mind that our high-tech airplanes often couldn't tell the difference between an Iraqi tank and a Bradley Fighting Vehicle. Never mind that falling pieces of Patriot missiles killed and injured at least as many people as the SCUDs they were sent aloft to intercept. Never mind that, by the Pentagon's own admission months after the fact, seventy percent of all the bombs dropped on Kuwait and Iraq failed to hit their targets, hitting instead such things as baby formula factories, civilian bomb shelters and residential neighborhoods, reports of which were dismissed at the time as nothing more than Iraqi propaganda.

Well, in any case, we've now inaugurated the New World Order. Never mind that we had to bribe, bully or bludgeon most of the rest of the United Nations to go beyond the use of economic sanctions against Iraq. Never mind that we had to go begging with hat in hand to get our allies to contribute a minesweeper here or a medical team there, a single squadron of airplanes or a little spare change to buy our own troops bottled water. Never mind that our military chaplains were not permitted to wear the insignia of their calling, or that the Saudi Arabian religious police are once again accosting women for daring to appear unveiled in public.

Never mind that after a short-lived and tense period of minimal cooperation between Israelis and Arabs at the height of the war, the attitudes and rhetoric of the various Middle Eastern camps are as intransigent and antagonistic as ever. Never mind that instead of a comprehensive regional peace conference, we are witnessing a new round of arms sales throughout the Middle East that makes all previous sales look prudently restrained.

And never mind that we've just been subjected to the most thorough censorship and restraint of free information in the history of our nation, or that the major media, without exception, willingly became nothing more than shills and cheerleaders for the government while we ourselves lapped up the sanitized pap they served us like eager puppies.

Meanwhile, it's been months since anyone has even mentioned the ongoing savings and loan bail-out that is bankrupting not just us, but our children and their children as well. And matters like the continuing plight of the homeless, the still-growing AIDS epidemic, festering race relations, the collapse of our cities, the decay of our educational system, and the failure of the War on Drugs can only spoil the mood, so let's not think about those things either.

After all, it's great to feel like a winner, and we haven't gotten to feel like winners in a long time, so let's just enjoy it while we can. Never mind what we've won or lost. Everybody loves a party.

Well, almost everybody.

❖ ❖ ❖

"We Must Have This"

It is a cruel irony that Gloria Emerson's *Gaza: A Year in the Intifada* (Atlantic Monthly Press, 1991) should make its appearance at a time when sympathy for the plight of the Palestinian people is hard to come by. On August 2, 1990, the army of Saddam Hussein invaded and occupied Kuwait. The United States, and much of the rest of the world, took exception. Saddam said he would negotiate a withdrawal from Kuwait if Israeli occupation of Palestine were also up for negotiation. Yasser Arafat, the Palestine Liberation Organization, and many ordinary Palestinians openly sided with Saddam. After a brief and brutally one-sided little war, Iraq lay in ruins. So did Palestinian hopes. And the Palestinian cause.

"If it is permissible to support Saddam Hussein," wrote Yossi Sarid, a member of Israel's Knesset who had long advocated Palestinian self-determination, "then perhaps it is not too bad to support the policy of Mr. Shamir, Mr. Sharon and Mr. Rabin."

In truth, Palestinian support for Iraq was disastrous. This was not the work of a solitary bomber or gunman, or even a small cabal of determined zealots. The Palestinians themselves, so it seems, the whole people, supported Saddam openly and brazenly. Even for someone utterly repulsed by the hypocritical rhetoric and high-tech butchery of George Bush, it was hard to fathom the passionate enthusiasm with which Palestinians embraced a man about whom nothing kind can be said. It seemed madness.

Now this book appears, so soon after the last bodies have been dragged from the terrible carnage of that superhighway running north from Kuwait City that the stench still lingers. So soon—and yet, one fears, too late. Who will read it now? *Gaza?* Those Palestinians? The ones who chose Saddam Hussein? Who cares about them? They're crazy. They get what they deserve.

And that is sad because to read *Gaza* is to understand that Palestinian support for Saddam in the recent Gulf War, like the Intifada itself, was not an act of madness but of desperation. Almost unimaginable desperation. Almost, but not quite. Because Emerson is the writer she is, the human being she is, she makes it possible to imagine the desperation of the Palestinians. We ignore or dismiss that desperation at peril of our own souls.

Raji Sourani "was blindfolded and hit and beaten every half hour…. When he complained, a lit cigarette was pressed into his hand." Sourani, a prominent Gazan lawyer, was shackled to "an iron door with bars, one arm manacled high above his head and the other arm below his waist so the body could not be straightened. 'They put this hood on your head, saturate it with water and close it,'" he told Emerson, "'They expel tear gas inside it too.'" The hood smelling of old sweat and old vomit.

Aoun Shawa, a Gazan businessman, was accused of withholding taxes from the Israeli Civil Administration, which regulates most aspects of the lives of Gazans. "They bullied me terribly," Shawa told Emerson, "Four or five men jumping from a jeep and one car, *civilians with machine guns*, charging into this office, taking all my papers, saying 'Come with us.'"

Naela Zaquot, arrested by the Shin Bet, Israel's state police, "wanted to tell one of the women among her captors that she was pregnant but was told she was not allowed to speak…. She was hooded…. She began to

hemorrhage.... 'You must talk if you want a doctor,' said the guard....
During the miscarriage she [lay] in clotted blood and said aloud her husband's name."

There are dozens of stories like these. Hundreds of them. Emerson hurls them at you like rocks, a withering fusillade of misery, the rage and helplessness of the Palestinians palpable, Emerson's own outrage barely under control. Of General Amram Mitzna's defense of the conduct of Israeli Defense Forces after it became known that Israeli soldiers had tried to bury alive four young Palestinians, she writes: "He spoke like a civilized man." She calls the duel between Israeli interrogators and Palestinian prisoners "the terrible and uneven match." She notes the "fierce, stupid contrasts of any war: herds of dark brown and white goats on the same streets as soldiers with the AR-15, with the Uzi, and the greatest swagger that any army ever chose to have."

Emerson knows well the "fierce, stupid contrasts" of war. A highly respected journalist who has covered four wars, she earned a National Book Award for her brilliant portrait of the American war in Vietnam, *Winners and Losers*. But though she is no stranger to war, it is one of her singular graces that she has never become familiar with it.

Gloria Emerson, journalist, war correspondent, and author of *Winners and Losers, Some American Men, Gaza,* and *Loving Graham Greene*. (Photograph provided by Gloria Emerson)

"One American," she wrote in 1972, "was picked up with a head wound and lay on the floor, not dead or not alive. The medic could not stop the bleeding.... It all becomes normal, the other correspondents, men, would say. In time, you'll see. They lied."

Nearly two decades later Emerson writes, "The Israeli Defense Forces maintained the position that consideration was always given" to Palestinian women, "but the witness knows better." And the witness is Emerson, who describes "a group of middle-aged women, their bodies shaped like old pillows, another choir of grief," who are charged by soldiers whose faces reflect "high glee, as if now they were playing a favorite game and certain to win."

At a conference in western Massachusetts in the winter of 1988, the redoubtable Colonel Harry Summers, Jr. (Retired) told an audience that the U.S. government had played no part at all in the 1963 overthrow of Ngo Dinh Diem. Emerson bluntly asked Summers to explain, then, why Lucien Conein, the veteran CIA operative, had told her that he had said to the Saigon generals who subsequently deposed and executed Diem, "If you don't get rid of Diem, we'll do it ourselves." Taken aback, Summers ponderously launched into a long-winded and convoluted response, but Emerson cut him off sharply. "How can you lie to all these people?" she asked, gesturing around the room. The moderator intervened, and Summers must have thought he had dodged a bullet, but later Emerson collared him in a corridor and continued to dog him with such tenacity that one almost felt sorry for the man.

It is one thing, however, to take to task a retired army colonel-turned-academic, quite another to take on the state of Israel. Surely Emerson must have known, even before she had written the first word of this book, before most people in the U.S. had ever heard of the al-Sabah family, when the U.S. government still thought Saddam Hussein was manageable and Emerson herself could not have imagined the disaster that was coming, that she would be inviting ridicule and vituperation, accusation and anger. There are certain things one must not do. One of them is to suggest, however politely, that the people of Palestine and the PLO are, for all practical purposes, one and the same. Another is to suggest that Israeli treatment of Palestinians in the Occupied Territories is a moral, legal and physical crime.

One can hear the pacemakers changing gears even as one writes these words. Yet Emerson does not hesitate. She tells what she saw and what she heard during her year in Gaza in the midst of the intifada (which in Arabic means "shaking off"). We seldom hear the voices of ordinary Israelis. Of the West Bank we hear only occasionally and from a distance. She spent her time in Gaza and the Strip (she never calls it, as most westerners do, the Gaza Strip; there is the city of Gaza, and there is the territory that surrounds it). It is the Palestinians of Gaza we hear. It is their story she tells.

Under such circumstances, terms like anti–Semitic and anti–Israeli insinuate themselves into the discussion, though Emerson is neither. She never questions the legitimacy of the state of Israel. She writes with feeling about such Israelis as Leah Tsemel and Tamar Peleg, lawyers who, in the face of a rigid and foreordained Israeli judicial system, tirelessly labor year after year defending Palestinians, usually without even knowing the charges. We hear of "the gentle officer," embarrassed by the soldiers who do not obey him, who shakes Raji Sourani's burned and shackled hand and tells him, "We will someday sit together and live in peace."

Nor are the faults and fantasies of the Gazans ignored. "The intifada began with a careless Israeli truck driver," Emerson explains, "although Gazans will tell you he committed an act of revenge." Of the refugee camp where the intifada began she says, "Jabalia ... thought the world knew of its existence. Gazans knew little about the old war in Southeast Asia, only who had won.... More than that did not seem to matter." In one of the most brilliant sections of the book, she deflates a "dignitary" of Hamas, the Palestinian Islamic fundamentalist movement, with a precision that is both funny and merciless: "'We *respect* women!' Hamas said, leading me to the kitchen to meet his wife.... Here was Hamas' example of the happy, dutiful, devout woman, proof of all that her husband believed and admired, and at last able to put dinner on the table."

But Emerson does attack, without apology, Israeli policy in the Occupied Territories, the conduct of the IDF in the Occupied Territories, the torture, the utter absence of due process, the economic restrictions, the beating of six-year-old boys, the shooting of 13-year-old girls, deportation, demolition of homes, and a host of other evils for which she provides compelling testimony: names, dates, places. These are facts. These things happened. Never mind your excuses and justifications, as if two wrongs make a right. This is happening now. It cannot be explained away.

And in this Emerson is right, though it speaks ill of all of us, Israelis and non–Israelis alike. What we see, one-sided, biased, loaded, whatever it may be, is finally not what Emerson believes, but what the people of Gaza believe. And what they believe can be dismissed only with extreme prejudice.

In her massive and convincing history of Palestine, *From Time Immemorial*, Joan Peters debunks the notion that Palestinians have a claim to the land of Palestine that rivals the claim of the Jews, a commonly heard argument among Palestinians and their supporters. What Emerson does, in effect, is to say: so what? What difference does that make now, in the closing years of the 20th century?

Consider that Palestinians living in the refugee camps have been there since 1948. Consider that Gaza and the Strip, along with the West Bank, have been under Israeli military occupation since 1967. No Palestinian refugee under the age of 42 can remember anything but the threadbare, overcrowded camps. No Palestinian under the age of 24 can remember a time when Israeli soldiers did not kick down doors in the middle of the night, slapping mothers to the floor and dragging children into the darkness. That adds up to a lot of Palestinians.

Historical claims, whatever their spiritual power or physical authority, have no meaning to the woman whose fiancé has been paralyzed for life by an Israeli bullet, to the family whose home is demolished on an hour's notice, to the grower who is not permitted to replace the orange and lemon trees dying in his grove, to the doctor who is fired and then imprisoned for expressing sympathy to hospital staff members whose children have been killed in the intifada.

One can argue the fine points and not-so-fine points of history, but such is academic in the worst sense of the word. Whoever wins the debate, whoever is most clever and facile and witty, the Palestinians will not go away. There will be no peace unless the Palestinians are addressed. And Emerson makes it perfectly clear that only two choices are available: listen to what they are saying or exterminate them. As it was for Americans with the Vietnamese, you will not subdue them. You will only have, as you have had for half a century and more, perpetual war, perpetual hatred and violence, perpetual shame. This Emerson is saying not just to Israelis, but to the conscience of the world, to each of us alone and together.

One hopes, as the yellow ribbons occasioned by Desert Storm begin to fade to dirty brown, that thoughtful people will consider Gloria Emerson's book and the people about whom she writes with such riveting skill. "After two years or ten years that's okay," a Palestinian fisherman told Emerson of his hopes for an independent state, "But it must come. We must have this." After reading Emerson's *Gaza*, it is hard to disagree.

❖ ❖ ❖

Who's Responsible?

[Originally given as a talk to the Freshman Forum at La Salle University, Philadelphia, Pennsylvania, October 15, 1991. All of the students participating in the forum had read Bobbie Ann Mason's novel *In Country*.]

If you look at the copyright page of Bobbie Ann Mason's *In Country*, you will find the following sentence: "Special thanks to W. D. Ehrhart for helpful advice." That acknowledgement came about in the following manner:

In the winter of 1984, I got a telephone call from Mason. She explained that she had heard of me through a colleague of her husband's at Rodale Press, where I had worked the previous year. Her husband had told his colleague that she was working on a novel about the Vietnam War, and the colleague had told him about me and suggested that she read my book *Vietnam-Perkasie*. She told me she had indeed read the book, along with a great many other books about the Vietnam War, but that she was still fearful of getting the story wrong.

She of course had not been in Vietnam or in the military, and the war and its attendant domestic repercussions had largely passed her by. Now she was worried that she might embarrass herself, introduce military terminology or hardware that was not appropriate to the Vietnam War, or create scenes or situations that were not possible in reality. The bottom line was a polite, almost timid request that I read her manuscript with an eye toward technical accuracy.

I had never heard of Bobbie Ann Mason before this phone call came out of the blue, and I was a little skeptical, in those days, of a nonveteran expropriating the experience of Vietnam and making it her own. But I was flattered that she thought well enough of my own book to ask me for help, and having been the recipient over the years of a lot of help from others acting under no obligation but generosity, I told her I'd do it. And I did.

For the most part, I liked the story very much, and I was deeply impressed by the obvious fact that Mason had done her homework. I don't recall the specific errors I brought to her attention—small things like the wrong kind of rifle here, the misuse of a term there—but they were very few and very far between. I remember that Mason had been especially concerned about the veracity of the white birds Emmett remembers so wistfully, but she needn't have been. She had given me, it turned out, a very easy and enjoyable task as well as a bit of an honor: I don't suppose there are all that many people who can claim to have read a bestseller before it is even published.

Being the opinionated fellow I am, however, I could not resist the temptation to exceed the parameters of my charge and offer her some advice concerning the shape and substance of the story itself. Two elements of the narrative did bother me, and I told her so.

The first is the absence of any significant Vietnam veteran who has not been, in one way or another, visibly and permanently damaged by his collision with the Vietnam War. Emmett Smith can't hold a job or open himself to the attractive and nurturing Anita Stevens. Tom Hudson is sexually impotent. Earl, who is not given a last name, is belligerent and confrontational. Pete Simms fires his shotgun at nothing and wallows in the delusion that some nebulous "they" wouldn't let "us" win. The one man who appears to have his life together, Jim Holly, subsequently discovers that his wife has left him.

Vietnam veterans, as a group, *have* had a tough time. The statistics on suicide, incarceration, divorce, unemployment and other indictors of trouble have been widely broadcast in the years since the war ended. You can look them up easily enough. The Vietnam War was a very peculiar war in many ways, and some of the burdens Vietnam veterans have had to cope with are rare in the American experience. But the truth is that, in many significant ways, we have had it no tougher than veterans of any war, a historical fact that has been lost amid popular mythology that has risen up since the early 1970s. Read MacKinlay Kantor's *Glory for Me*, or Paul Fussell's *Wartime*, if you don't believe me. War is a brutish and vile business. It does things to the lives of those who survive it, and to their souls.

It is also true, as a corollary, that most Vietnam veterans, whatever specific baggage we may be lugging around, have come to a workable accommodation with our experience and gotten on with our lives. We may be scarred, but the overwhelming majority of us are functional and productive. I can no longer count the number of Vietnam veterans who serve in the halls of Congress (though one might argue that such is neither functional nor productive). Two Vietnam veterans have already won the National Book Award—three if you count Gloria Emerson, and one ought to. A Vietnam veteran founded Federal Express.

As for myself, not a day passes of which the Vietnam War is not a part, if only in thought, yet I have been happily married for eleven years, I own my own home, I have consistently plied my trade as a writer for over two decades, my students are convinced that I give too much homework, and my daughter thinks I'm a pretty nice guy at least some of the time. Pity the poor Vietnam veteran, a refrain much in evidence during the recent Assault of the Yellow Ribbons occasioned by Desert Stomp, is largely a misplaced sentiment.

If you read *In Country* carefully, you will notice that Mason tacitly acknowledges what I am saying. Along with Emmett and Tom and Pete, there is Allen Wilkins, owner of a menswear store and Little League coach, and Larry Joiner's acquaintance "who's got a good job in public relations," and Dawn Goodwin's cousin who "was in Vietnam, but you'd never know it." But Allen makes only a few cameo appearances, Larry's acquaintance is worth only a paragraph, and Dawn's cousin gets three brief sentences; we never meet these last two men, who are not even given names.

Thus I suggested to Mason that she include at least one "healthy" Vietnam veteran among her more important characters. Mason didn't go as far as I would have liked, but in the novel you read, there is at least the suggestion that Jim and his wife might yet work things out. The manuscript version offered no such hope. Whether Mason made this change on my recommendation or not, she has never told me and I have never asked. So long as I don't know, I can always take credit, in my secret heart, for Jim and Sue Ann's possible future happiness together.

The other element of the narrative that bothers me is the ending: the scene at the Vietnam Veterans Memorial (which almost immediately after its creation became known as "the Wall"). And the Wall has become an awful cliché. Photographs of the Wall adorn the jackets of dozens of books about the Vietnam War. Mention of that somber recitation of names, both visual and verbal, has come to substitute for substance and fact, as if the Wall says it all when in truth it tells us only what each of us chooses to hear. It precludes discussion or critique or wisdom, as though its dark polished face is all we will ever need to know, or ought to know, about the Vietnam War.

This is very convenient for those in whose interest it is not to raise such questions as: Why did all those people die? Who offered them up for slaughter? What was accomplished for the price of so much blood? How was it permitted to go on for so long? Where are the names of the three million dead of Indochina? Be moved by the terrible beauty of your own reflection in the silent, smooth granite. Consider the wonder of so many young men, and women too, willing to give everything for their country. Notice the little offerings—the flowers, the handwritten notes, the high school yearbook photos—left in the cracks of the Wall by parents and children, lovers and friends still grieving after all these years.

That the Wall has become such an intoxicating and misleading artifice is no fault of Mason's. At the time she was writing *In Country*, the lawn surrounding the Wall was still mostly mud. Her use of the Wall as a literary and cultural symbol was, as far as I know, an original and even prescient choice. It is others who are the copycats.

But it was apparent, even then, that the Wall was going to become what it has in fact become: a moving and inarticulate substitute for accountability. And indeed, at the end of *In Country*, as Sam ponders the mystery of that other Sam A. Hughes chiseled onto the Wall and Emmett's face "bursts into a smile like flames," we can't help feeling like everything is going to come out okay after all. We like stories that end that way. We like wars that end that way.

But real stories seldom end so neatly, and wars never do. Not even Desert Storm. Ask the Kurds. Thus, I strongly urged Mason to find another venue for her conclusion. Your having read the book, you know how persuasive I was. I console myself with the knowledge that had I been playing baseball instead of offering literary criticism, I'd still be batting better than Ted Williams, and he's in the Hall of Fame.

My criticisms notwithstanding, however, I retain a healthy respect for *In Country* and teach the book regularly in courses of my own. I am teaching it this fall at Bucks County Community College. Mason does a number of things very well, and I would like to examine some of them.

To begin with, Mason doesn't try to think like a veteran. The story is told not through Emmett's eyes, but through Sam's. This is a coming-of-age story, finally. Whatever else is going on, Sam is a child, a teenager, trying to find the right way to be a woman, an adult. She is intelligent, funny, endearing. She thinks going to the mall in Paducah is big league excitement, but in the end we know she is going to college in Lexington, and it's not hard to imagine she'll grow beyond Hopewell one day. Much of what we see in Sam is us, what we are or used to be when we were younger: awkward and antsy, confident, fiercely naive. It's fun to watch her growing up. We like Sam.

Another thing I like is the way in which Mason turns the entire narrative into one long exercise in American popular culture. She captures effectively the homogenization of America, a depressing evolution for those of us who grew up in a nation where regional and local differences still abounded, but the way things are, like it or not. While we know that Hopewell is a small town in rural Kentucky because we are told as much, there is little to set Hopewell apart from the mass culture that has absorbed it: Doritos and Pepsi and Music Television, *Pac-Man*, Home Box Office, McDonald's, Bruce Springsteen and 7-Eleven. It is culture reduced to the lowest common denominator, which is what our culture has come to. I happen not to like that fact, but it's Sam's world nevertheless, and I like the way Mason handles it. Sam could be any kid in Anytown, U.S.A.

Into this universal story, the Vietnam War is introduced as naturally as if it came with the territory, which it does. There is nothing contrived about Sam's curiosity about her father and the war that denied him to her, about her attraction to a handsome older man, or even the trip to the Wall. Since 1965, the Vietnam War has become a constant companion to millions of Americans. Millions more, the young who remember nothing, wonder what strange power this word "Vietnam" has on those who remember. And indeed, like the fictional Sam, there are real children, now adults themselves, who do not know their fathers because of the American War in Vietnam.

That war, in fact, is the quintessential American experience of the second half of the 20th century, the stamp of a generation, equaled only by the civil rights movement. To write about the United States in the second half of the 20th century is to write about the Vietnam War. It can be avoided only with effort.

But there are a lot of books about Vietnam. David A. Willson, the librarian at Green River Community College in Auburn, Washington, and author of the wonderful Vietnam War novel *REMF Diary*, has a collection of several hundred pornographic novels using the Vietnam War as the backdrop. Danielle Steele has written a Vietnam novel. The use of Vietnam in literature, as in most other facets of our culture, is frequently contrived. It's all in how one handles it.

Mason handles it very well. Emmett, for all that he is clearly a very troubled man, is also a nice guy, a caring man. He's fond of Moon Pie the cat, he loves his niece, and he is touchingly solicitous of Mamaw Hughes. There isn't a mean bone in his body. He isn't scary. None of Mason's vets is. They may be floundering, but they're not dead weight. Mason's portrayal of veterans is sympathetic without being lurid or romantic.

Her depiction of the war itself, and the antiwar movement it spawned, are also handled well. Dwayne Hughes's letters to his young wife ring true, as do the vignettes and descriptions offered by the survivors. And Mason offers a gentle view of the hippies and protesters, some of them, like Emmett, former soldiers themselves. In an age in which the war has been hideously transformed into a noble cause lost, at least in part, because of an antiwar movement frequently portrayed as an irresponsible exercise in immaturity, it is worth noticing that Emmett and most of the other vets have nothing good to say about the war. Those that do, like Pete, are otherwise discredited by their own subsequent words and actions. Emmett may not have flown any Viet Cong flags from the top of the courthouse lately, but he never even hints at any remorse for having done so when he was younger. And Irene still remembers her hippie boyfriend fondly. Like Sam Hughes, we see only fleeting and frustratingly incomplete glimpses of those times, but what we see is neither gloss nor fantasy.

It is Sam who has the fantasies. She thinks the sixties were a lot of fun and going home with Tom is like walking point. Her efforts to understand what the Vietnam War was really like are almost comical, and here what I said earlier about pop culture becomes especially cogent, for Sam has no point of reference to use as a touchstone except *Born in the U.S.A.*, *Apocalypse Now* and reruns of *M*A*S*H*. Even after she realizes, on one level at least, that "whenever she [has] tried to imagine Vietnam she [has] had her facts all wrong," she still urges Emmett, with absolute sincerity, to "do the way Hawkeye Pierce did when he told about that baby on the bus." For her, the Watergate scandal that resulted in the resignation of a sitting president for the first time in U.S. history was only "a TV series one summer," and she thinks C-47s with Gatling guns—devastating killing machines, I can tell you from experience—are "wonderful" aircraft.

In this, Sam is much like each of you, like virtually every student and young person I've spoken with in the last fifteen years. I can't tell you how many times I've been asked, "Was it really like *Platoon*?" (Or *The Deer Hunter*, or *Full Metal Jacket*, or whatever Vietnam War movie happens to be hot at the box office that year.) Not long ago, a 13-year-old boy asked me, "Did you really go on patrols and do stuff like in *Tour of Duty*?" It was clear from his voice, his posture, his saucer eyes, that he thought it must have been wonderfully exciting. Real was what he had seen on television.

But the young cannot know unless someone teaches them, and the entertainment industry is not in the business of education. The poem I read to that boy and his junior high school classmates, Bryan Alec Floyd's unrelentingly graphic and horrifying "Sgt. Brandon Just, U.S.M.C.," got those kids thinking hard, at least for a while.

Dwayne's diary, with its "dead gook rotting under some leaves" and Darrel's blood "shooting out of his back and mouth," gets Sam thinking hard. So does Emmett's collapse into tears, his sorrow "full-blown, as though it had grown over the years into something monstrous and fantastic." And Irene challenges Sam's romanticized notions of the sixties: "It wasn't a happy time, Sam. Don't go making out like it was." However imperfectly, by the end of the story, Sam is beginning to replace her fantasies with something approaching understanding.

I like other things in this story, too: Mamaw Hughes, who says that her son died "fighting for a cause," though she makes no attempt to explain what that cause might have been, no doubt because she doesn't have an explanation; she has only her memories and her grief. Lonnie Malone, poor Lonnie, who "fished from a pontoon boat and roasted wienies at a campfire" while Sam's father had eaten "ham and beans from a can and slept in a hole in the ground," and who hasn't got a chance in hell of competing with Tom Hudson in Sam's imagination. Mason's relentless excoriation of the U.S. government in general, and the Veterans Administration in particular (now called the Department of Veterans Affairs), for poisoning its own soldiers with dioxin and then refusing to accept even the slightest responsibility, a fact which remains largely true to this day.

There is more I could talk about, if time permitted. But I want now to turn to a few more general thoughts. I made passing reference earlier to the fact that Vietnam veterans are not unique in the burdens they have had to bear. Yes, we lost our war, which is a rare burden indeed in the American experience, but it is not unique: for all practical purposes, we lost the War of 1812, too, our capital taken and burned to the ground, the only land battle of any significance that we won taking place after the treaty to end the war had already been signed, facts that may not have been fully emphasized in your high school history classes. About the best you can say of the Korean War is that it was a draw. And of course, half the United States, more or less, lost the Civil War.

And yes, we were often treated in less than kindly fashion after we came home, though you might stop to consider that World War One veterans who came to Washington at the height of the Great Depression to ask for help from the government they had served were chased out of town with machine guns and cavalry.

And yes, a great many people opposed the war openly and vehemently, but the Mexican War was none to popular either; Henry David Thoreau went to jail, for instance, rather than pay taxes to support that war, and his essay on civil disobedience has become a model for war resisters from Mohandas Gandhi to Martin Luther King, Jr.

So you must understand that neither the particular political or military circumstances surrounding the Vietnam War, nor the way in which U.S. soldiers were treated when they came home, can account for the behavior of the veterans you find in *In Country*, a notion you might implicitly assume given the times in which you've lived. The veterans you have read about, most of them, to a greater or lesser degree, like many actual veterans of the Vietnam War, are suffering from what is now called post-traumatic stress disorder. PTSD for short.

During the recent lunacy in the Persian Gulf, we were urged over and over again to get behind the government and support the troops, not to let the Desert Storm soldiers suffer the same fate as Vietnam War veterans, as if Vietnam veterans suffer from PTSD because we were not supported and appreciated enough. Somebody made a hell of a fortune manufacturing and selling yellow ribbons last fall and winter, but the fact is that PTSD does not result from lack of appreciation or support; it results from being subjected to the almost unbearable terrors of the modern battlefield.

PTSD comes from being 18 or 19 or 20 years old and finding yourself in an environment where every blade of grass and chirping bird is potentially deadly. It comes from living in abject fear day in and day out for months on end, never knowing if the next breath you draw may be your last, if the next step you take may dismember you. It comes from seeing the boy who was your friend a moment ago lying on the ground at your feet with half a head and no arms and his belly split open like a butchered pig. It comes from inflicting that sort of punishment on other human beings.

Moreover, PTSD is not a phenomenon limited to Vietnam veterans or unpopular wars. In the American Civil War, the first truly modern battlefield in the military sense, where weapons of mass destruction obliterated the old virtues of skill at arms, courage and honor, bringing death down equally and at random upon the brave and the fearful, the skilled and the inept, PTSD was mistaken for cowardice or "nerves." In World War One, it was called shell shock. In World War Two and Korea, it was known as combat fatigue.

What the medical community finally began to realize in the last stages of the Vietnam War, though they did not put it all together until nearly a decade later, and then largely due to the refusal of Vietnam veterans to slink away in silence, is that in the face of the lethal pressures of the battlefield, apparently aberrant behavior is a perfectly normal response, even years after the fact. Not that the behavior is normal, of course, but that it is predictable and to be expected under the circumstances. PTSD is how normal people react to abnormal stress.

All wars have produced men like Emmett Hughes and Tom Hudson and Pete Simms. The only way to prevent PTSD is to keep young men, and women too, away from battlefields. (I am less concerned about old men. They are usually the ones who start the wars in the first place, then they send the young ones off to die.) And if the soldiers who fought in the Persian Gulf this past winter don't end up with the kinds of problems Vietnam veterans have had, it will only be because, in the words of Captain LeAnn Robinson, a Persian Gulf veteran, "This sure as hell wasn't much of a war."

Another thought this book brings to mind is how Sam's yardstick for judging the past has become our yardstick for judging the present. What I mean is this: when Sam thinks of Vietnam, she does so in terms of movies, television and music. She can conjure her own history, for the most part, only through popular culture—and the results are hardly satisfactory. We can see this because we are outside the book looking in. We know that Emmett and his friends are not Eddie and the Cruisers. We know that Cawood's Pond is not Dak To. And if Sam eventually comes to know it, too, or begins to, it is because Emmett and Irene and her own dogged determination to understand force her to get beyond her illusions.

Now consider the recent Gulf War. George Bush boasted of "kicking butt" as though he were a high school football coach. Others explicitly likened it to the Super Bowl. For months on end, we read in the newspapers and heard on the radio and saw on television only what the government wanted us to read and hear and see. We watched those nifty videos of smart bombs dropping down chimneys and tank shells obliterating enemy targets that looked like blips on an Atari screen. Many of the pilots and gunners explicitly likened what they were doing to playing video games. Meanwhile, the troops—all but the very few who actually saw any combat—wiled away the hours playing handheld video games. Shall I say "real" video games, as opposed to the fake video games that only killed people instead of blips on a screen? And now the Pentagon is making, for free distribution to all Desert Stomp soldiers and their families, an actual video of the Persian Gulf War, complete with rock-and-roll soundtrack. Maybe we'll all get to see it on MTV.

What we didn't get to see, and most of us never will see, are the stinking, broken bodies of anywhere from 100,000 to 200,000 dead human beings—no one knows for sure, or at least no one is telling. What we didn't get to see is what happened to the Kurds and Iraqi Shiites George Bush publicly incited to rebellion, only to stand idly on the sidelines insisting it was not our responsibility while Saddam Hussein butchered them. We didn't even get to see the flag-draped coffins of our own dead soldiers, let alone their mangled, lifeless remains.

And we didn't get to see where all those dumb bombs landed. Oh yes, there were a lot of stupid bombs dropped on Iraq and Kuwait. Nobody told you that at the time because they didn't want you to think we might actually bomb, even by accident, civilian shelters or baby formula plants, but over 90 percent of the bombs dropped during Desert Storm were dumber than stumps, the same old iron clunkers that got dropped on Vietnam and Korea and Germany and Japan. More than 70 per cent of them missed their targets. Even the smart ones missed, as often as not.

But we didn't get to see any of those things. And most of us never considered what we might not be seeing or reading or hearing. It never even occurred to us to wonder. We just sat there glued to our television sets, transfixed by all those wonderful bombs miraculously dropping down those impossibly narrow chimneys and thinking, "Golly damn, that's amazing." And then we were told that we'd won, and there were a lot of parades and celebrations, and everybody got to feel good about America. Like Sam Hughes's Watergate, the Gulf War was just a series we saw on TV. Who is outside of our book looking in? Who will be our Emmett and Irene? Who will teach us the difference between imagination and fact, illusion and reality?

There is one more thought I would like to share with you. Did it sink in just how young Dwayne and Emmett and the others were when they went to war? Mason tells us that Dwayne was 19. Emmett couldn't have been much older. The average age of American soldiers in Vietnam was 19 and a half, and that includes all those generals and crusty old sergeant majors. I was 17 when I enlisted in the Marines. I went to Vietnam when I was 18. I had three stripes, a Purple Heart and a ticket home before I turned 19 and a half. Like Emmett, I didn't know beans when I went. Like Dwayne, I discovered that Vietnam was not what I had imagined it would be. I have been paying ever since, and will continue to pay until the day I die, for having been so ignorant.

Is there anyone in this room who is not at least 17 years old? How many of you supported the U.S. war in the Persian Gulf? How many of you had ever heard of the al-Sabah family before August 1990? How many of you can write a paragraph or two describing the system of laws and institutions governing Saudi Arabia? How many of you can find Kurdistan on a map? How many of you can detail the interactions between the United States and Iraq between 1980 and 1990? Doubtless, few of the young men and women who were deployed to the Persian Gulf would fare any better than you on these questions, yet they went, most of them willingly, some of them eagerly. They didn't know beans, but they went because they love their country and they trusted those who were sending them. So did I when I went.

Most of them were lucky. If we build a Gulf War Veterans Memorial, it won't be much bigger than an expensive headstone. But will we be so lucky the next time, or the time after that? If you think the Vietnam War was a fluke, you ought to read more history. Emmett tells Sam that the study of history teaches only that you can't learn from history. I don't happen to believe that. I'm not convinced that Emmett does either.

The Vietnam War didn't just happen. It didn't gather cosmic dust somewhere out in the universe until it gained enough mass to come crashing down on Planet Earth like some sort of random bad luck. United States involvement in Vietnam, what we call the Vietnam War, happened because distinct individuals made distinct choices over a discrete period of time—and Jane Fonda wasn't one of them. Virtually all of those decisions were wrong.

If you actually study the history of the Vietnam War, what you will learn is a valuable lesson in the way the U.S. government and the various individuals who constitute that government at any given time actually work. You will learn that our government is capable of profound arrogance, willful self-deception, and deliberate lying. You will learn that what is done in the name of liberty, freedom and democracy is often none of these things.

The study of history, of course, can be boring as all get-out. As Sam discovers, all the names run together. Ngo Dinh Diem. Bao Dai. Dien Bien Phu. Ho Chi Minh. You get bogged down in manifestos and State Department documents. It's more fun to play hoops, or go dancing, or eat a cheese steak. It's more fun to read a book like *In Country*. And *In Country* is a wonderful story to read.

But it's not the whole story. Not by a long shot. The poet John Balaban, in his book *Remembering Heaven's Face*, tells of a saying he learned from Vietnamese peasants in the Mekong Delta: "Go out one day, and come back with a basket full of wisdom." Unless you are willing to open your minds and set aside the things you believe only because you have heard them all your lives, unless you are willing to acquire knowledge, you will be forever at the mercy of those who depend upon your ignorance. You will be Emmetts and Sams and Irenes, just waiting to happen.

❖ ❖ ❖

Why My Daughter Won't Grow Up in Perkasie

Bob Gillman glared at me, his face red with too many highballs and his eyes full of tears. *What am I doing here*, I thought. *I should have known better.*

I had grown up in this town. Then I had joined the Marines, fought in Vietnam, and discovered that the world was not what the people of Perkasie thought it was. The town looked different when I came back, but it wasn't.

I had wondered then how I could have missed it. These people had misled me. And they had done this not out of malice or greed or spite, but out of willful and studied ignorance. They believed everything they had taught me.

I drifted in and out of town after I got out of the Marines. My father was a Protestant minister, and my mother was a public school teacher. I'd come home for a month here, six weeks there, three or four months sometimes, between semesters or travels, a succession of jobs and apartments.

My mother didn't understand what had happened to me, but she knew something had happened. My father didn't have a clue, but I worked at liking him, and we managed. I slowed down after a while, enough to understand that they were who they were, and I was not likely to teach them much by shouting.

I kept to myself when I was home, reading and writing in the front room of the third floor under the eaves. I had little contact with the people of Perkasie who had sent me off to kill and die and had thought it a fine thing. I could see soldiers burning their houses, raping their daughters, shooting their sons and husbands, their wives and mothers, churning their tree-lined streets to rubble. But the people of Perkasie could not see what I saw.

When I first came home, I tried to renew old friendhsips, but my peers were busy with college or families or just trying to earn enough money to go to the East Rock Hill Tavern on Saturday night. They couldn't see it either.

Sometimes I would not come back for a year or more. I worked on an oil tanker. I drove a forklift, roofed houses in Chicago, loafed in Miami, taught school in Maryland. A new apartment building went up down by the covered bridge (they called it the Covered Bridge Apartments), and a traffic light was installed at 5th & Market, but the town didn't change.

By the Twin Bridges over Branch Creek (folks always called it Lake Lenape, though it wasn't a lake), I could sometimes see Jeff Apple, Maynard Hager and me chasing painted turtles through the lily pads at the east end of the island, but there was no going back to that. Maynard was dead, having survived more than two years in Vietnam to die one night while riding his motorcycle at high speed without a headlight or helmet. His name should have been on the Vietnam Veterans Memorial in Washington, but it wasn't. Jeff, who had flunked second and fifth grades and had been written off as a dummy by the Pennridge School District, owned his own home and business in Fort Lauderdale.

Rev. John H. Ehrhart, the author's father, in front of St. Stephen's United Church of Christ in Perkasie, Pennsylvania, where he was pastor from 1955 to 1984. Rev. Ehrhart died in 1988. (Photograph provided by the author)

Then I got married. My parents were very fond of my wife. After a year in Maryland, we moved to Newtown, thirty miles from Perkasie, then to Doylestown, only fifteen miles away. I always thought it a coincidence, a matter of chance job opportunities, but maybe it was a cosmic practical joke on me.

One day in 1985, I got a call from Don Davis. He'd known my older brothers, had been a classmate of one of them. He was program director of the Perkasie Rotary Club. He'd heard I'd published a book, and wanted me to come and talk at the next monthly meeting.

"Have you read the book?" I asked. He hadn't. "You ought to," I said.

"Hey," he said. "You're a hometown boy. You've accomplished something. You got written up in the *Inquirer*. That's good enough for me."

"What do you want me to talk about?" I asked.

"Anything you like," he said.

I thought of my mother.

One day—this was before I got married—I had been sitting in the living room watching the news with her. It was late 1979 or early 1980, during the first few months of the Iran hostage crisis. They were showing videos of the hostages and talking about the harsh conditions under which the hostages had to live.

"But think of what the Shah did to his own people," my mother had said. "And we supported him all those years."

She wouldn't have said that ten years ago, I had thought.

"Okay," I told Don Davis.

In the twenty years since I'd joined the Marines, no one in Perkasie had ever asked me what I thought. I knew the audience would be filled with the fathers of kids I'd grown up with, people in whose homes I'd spent many hours and many days, men who attended my father's church and played golf with him.

Left to right: Anne, Bill and Leela Ehrhart in Perkasie, Pennsylvania, for the funeral of the author's mother, Evelyn, 1990. (Photograph provided by the author)

"All of us here desire peace," I began. "Some of us have seen war first-hand. Others have lost loved ones to it. We want no part of it. If we some-times appear belligerent, we must believe it is only a necessary response to the provocations of others. We are peacekeepers."

The audience stared at me.

"Thus we explain the invasion of Grenada," I said, "the U.S. Marines in Lebanon, U.S. soldiers in Honduras, our war against Nicaragua, our military aid to El Salvador, and our deployment of Pershing II and cruise missiles to Europe."

I looked at Frank Grossinger, vice-president of Bucks County Bank & Trust Company, whose daughter I had launched on her college career, but he would not make eye contact with me.

I spoke about the Vietnam War, describing the Vietnamese struggle for independence, the venality of the Saigon regime we'd invented, the killing reality of American troops in the ricefields and hamlets of Vietnam.

"But when the war finally ended," I said, "we were content to let it slip away, and then to reconstruct it as the noble cause we would like it to have been."

From another room, I could hear the dull thump of a heavy object falling, followed by curses.

"Therein lies the tragedy of the Vietnam War: our failure to confront it. Thus, when the Russians shoot down a civilian airliner, we call it an act of barbarism, but when we bomb a civilian mental hospital, it's a mistake. When the Cubans send military advisors and medical personnel to Nicaragua, we call it Soviet expansionism, but when we send combat troops to Hon-duras, it's a training exercise. When the Russians send troops into neigh-boring Afghanistan, we call it an invasion, but when we invade a Caribbean island 1500 miles from our shores, it's a matter of national security."

The slow rustle of bodies ponderously shifting. The clink of silverware and glass.

"How many more Vietnams will it take?" I said. "How many more times will we send our sons and brothers and fathers off to die in places like Lebanon and Grenada before we learn that the world will not conform to what we imagine it should be? Even now, American warships—"

"Who do you think is keeping the Free World free?" shouted Art Fralich, the plumber, who lived just across the street from my parents. I looked at Mr. Fralich. He looked back at me as if I were dog shit he'd just stepped in.

"What do you mean by the Free World?" I replied. "Do you mean South Africa? Chile? How about Saudi Arabia, where they execute unmar-ried women for having sex? Do you mean like South Korea, where it's trea-son to organize a labor union? How about Zaire? There's a lovely place."

Left to right: **Anne, Bill and Leela Ehrhart in Philadelphia, 2001. (Photograph by Renni Conti.**

"What the hell do you know about it?" Wilson Scheller called out. He owned the hardware store. I looked at Don Davis, but he wasn't looking at me. He seemed to be looking nowhere at all.

"Well, I've read a few books about it," I said.

"You believe everything you read?" sneered Mr. Scheller.

"I believe what I see," I said. "I know what I saw and did in Vietnam. I've been to Nicaragua. I've been to Honduras. Where have you been? Plumsteadville? Quakertown?"

"Why don't you go to Russia if you don't like it here?" said John Sterner, the pharmacist.

"That's the only answer you've got?" I said. "That's the best you can do? Why don't I go to Russia?"

"My boy died for his country!" Bob Gillman shouted, his voice on the edge of breaking. "Your father would be ashamed of you!"

David Gillman had become a helicopter pilot. His chopper had crashed and burned. What was sent back to Perkasie didn't fill a grocery bag, but Mr. Gillman had put it in the ground and put a headstone over it. He believed his son had died for a reason. It kept him going. Without it, he would have to face his insatiable grief. He glared at me, his face red with whiskey and his eyes full of tears.

What am I doing here, I thought. *I should have known better.*

"I'm sorry about your son," I said. "My parents risked three sons in Vietnam. By the grace of God, they got all three of us back. I'm sorry you weren't so lucky. I don't think my father's ashamed of me. Why don't you ask him yourself?"

I don't suppose he ever did. A few years later my father died. During the eulogy, Rev. Tim Dewald, a man my age who had been my father's assistant pastor for some years, noted that while the spines of all of the other books on my father's church office desk were placed so that my father could see their titles, one book faced the opposite way so that people entering his office could read its title. It was my first book of poems, *A Generation of Peace.*

A few years later, my mother died. I put the book in her casket. My mother and father are buried side by side at the top of Market Street, on the ridge overlooking the town. You can see the whole Branch Valley stretching away in three directions. You can see the school where my mother taught, and the creek where I used to play, and the steeple of my father's church.

❖ ❖ ❖

Forever Gone

Trying to prove what happened to U.S. servicemen missing in action from the Vietnam War is like trying to prove how many angels can dance on the head of a pin. It can't be done. In the end, it's a question of faith.

Logic dictates that no MIA survived. Ugly things happen to human bodies in modern war. Napalm reduces corpses to the size and consistency of burned-out campfires. Box mines leave not enough to fill a shoebox. White phosphorous melts everything.

Add to that the fact that 81 per cent of the missing were pilots or air-crew, most of whom went down in remote tropical terrain where human remains vanish utterly in weeks, and even steel and aluminum are swallowed by jungle growth in a few months.

Add to that the fact that 1,101 of the 2,273 missing Americans were known to have died at the time they were reported missing, and were listed as missing only because their bodies were not recovered. (It's tough to recover a body from the wreckage of an F4C Phantom fighter-bomber that collides with the earth at 400 miles per hour in the middle of nowhere.)

Then consider that the Second World War left 78,750 Americans missing (19.4 per cent of total fatalities) and the Korean War left 8,177 Americans missing (15 per cent of total fatalities), while only 1,172 Americans remain missing from the Vietnam War (roughly 2.5 per cent of total fatalities).

Given the awful confusion of battle, the effect of combining high explosives with high technology, and the intractability of the geography, it is nothing short of a wonder that so few U.S. casualties from the Vietnam War remain unaccounted for.

As for the Vietnamese who are said to be holding our missing men in secret captivity to use as a bargaining chip to gain concessions from the U.S. government, can you imagine the effect it would have if the Vietnamese finally tried to cash in that bargaining chip after denying the existence of these men for the past twenty years? Whatever your opinion of the Vietnamese, they are not that stupid.

On the contrary, the Vietnamese have repeatedly assisted U.S. recovery teams over the past ten years. In one instance in the mid–1980s, an entire Vietnamese hamlet was bulldozed at Vietnamese expense to excavate a crash site. What few bone fragments were found could not be positively identified even as being human. That's what happens to human bodies in modern war.

Now imagine what you would think if the Vietnamese demanded an accounting from us for their own missing soldiers, estimated at 200,000 to 250,000. What you imagine is what the Vietnamese think of our demands. They have no more idea what happened to our men than we have of what happened to theirs.

Most compelling of all, in spite of years of rumors and headlines, in spite of the standing million-dollar reward for live Americans or even hard evidence of live Americans, in spite of several actual rescue attempts, not one American serviceman missing in action in Southeast Asia has turned up alive.

What we have is what we've always had: rumors and headlines. Twenty years is a long time. A million dollars is a lot of money. Logic dictates that no one has collected the reward because there is nothing and no one to find.

But logic has no place in the hearts of those who believe an infinite number of angels can dance on the head of a pin. It is perhaps the saddest legacy of our saddest war.

Therein, I think, lies the secret to the terrible power of the myth of U.S. MIAs in Southeast Asia. Those missing men represent the fate of a generation, or at least that part of my generation that went to Vietnam believing in the rightness and invincibility of our country, our government and our leaders only to find all three wanting.

We were asked to fight a dirty little war that had no discernible point except to heap unspeakable misery upon the people we were supposed to be saving, a war that transformed us from bright-eyed teenagers into hollow-eyed survivors.

Neither our nation nor our government has ever accepted responsibility for what happened to us when we were young and vulnerable. What we've gotten instead are excuses: the liberal press lost the war; the meddling politicians lost the war; the antiwar movement lost the war. Everybody's been pointing fingers every which way since even before the war ended.

And we got left holding the bag. It hurt then, and it still hurts. And no stone wall with the names of our dead buddies carved into it, no parade, no *Rambo* movie can ever make that hurt go away.

But it's damned hard to stare into the mirror and accept the fact that your country and your government and your leaders just plain screwed up, and don't care enough about you to admit it, and never will.

Some people won't or can't take that kind of hurt. If what we suffered—and I include here the families of the missing—wasn't for something worthwhile, wasn't an act of sacrifice for a higher cause, then what was all that suffering for? That's too much hurt for some people to bear.

So they go on fighting the war, refusing to abandon their missing comrades as they themselves have been abandoned, holding on because there is nothing else left to hold on to. They believe that someday they'll be vindicated, someday they'll prove the justice of their cause.

I mean no disrespect to them or to their missing comrades, but it's time and long since time for the rest of us to come to terms with reality: those American servicemen missing in action in Southeast Asia are dead. God rest their souls, and the souls of those who mourn for them.

❖ ❖ ❖

On Common Sense
and Conscience

Recently I was called for jury duty by the Pennsylvania Court of Common Pleas. Few people I know enjoy jury duty, but most people do it because it is part of our responsibilities as citizens in a free society.

I was placed on a jury panel, and we were taken to a courtroom where the trial judge asked us a number of questions to help him decide which of us would actually be chosen to hear that particular trial, a process known as *voir dire*.

Most of the questions were pretty simple: do you know anyone involved in this trial? Would jury duty be a hardship? Then the judge asked, "Can you set aside your own feelings and allow me to direct you in matters of law?"

I wasn't sure I'd heard him correctly, so I asked for a clarification. "In other words," he said, "your job will be to decide the facts. Mine is to decide the law."

I raised my hand.

"You can't do that?" the judge asked.

"I can't swear to it, your honor," I said.

"You can't allow me to interpret the law?" he asked, his voice rising a little.

"I can't swear to it, your honor," I said.

"And what is it in your experience," the judge said, peering at me over the top of his half-glasses, "that qualifies you to interpret the law better than me? I've been an officer of the court for forty years. Who are you that you know better than the Supreme Court of the state of Pennsylvania how to interpret the law?"

I was about to explain myself, but the judge never gave me the opportunity. "Now I'll ask you again," he continued without so much as a blink or a pause, "Can you set aside your own feelings and allow me to direct you in matters of law?"

"No, sir, I can't swear to that," I said.

"Sit down," said the judge, shaking his head in what could only be understood as a gesture of extreme disgust, as if to say, "Why do they send me wiseacres like this?" I was subsequently excused from the panel.

But I'm not a wiseacre—or at least I wasn't being one in this instance—nor was my intention to shirk my civic duty. The judge asked me a question, and I gave him an honest answer. I'm sorry the judge wasn't interested in hearing my explanation.

I would have told him that when I was a young Marine in Vietnam, I committed murder, attempted murder, arson, burglary, robbery, assault and battery, assault with a deadly weapon, aggravated assault and malicious mischief. But the people who sent me to Vietnam did not use those names for what I did. They gave me a bunch of medals and promoted me to sergeant, and it was all perfectly legal.

I would have reminded the judge that within his lifetime and mine, black people who tried to get a cup of coffee at Woolworth's were assaulted, beaten and arrested. Sober judges would then preside over trials in which these people were found guilty of disorderly conduct and criminal trespass while those who beat them were never charged with any crime, let alone tried and convicted. And it was all perfectly legal.

I would have said to the judge that while the United States and Nazi Germany may have little in common, the Third Reich nevertheless had a proper piece of paper for every corpse in Auschwitz, Dachau and Bergen-Belsen. It was, by German law, all perfectly legal.

One needs only a cursory knowledge of history and a little common sense to understand that what is the law and what is just sometimes diverge.

This being so, it seems imprudent for any thoughtful person to swear away his or her right to trust one's own conscience. And it seems an injustice in itself for any judge to ask a person to do so.

All of this is manifest in the Nuremberg Principles, which demand adherence to conscience above all else, and which are by treaty part of the law of this land.

Moreover, the right of jury nullification, whereby a jury can ignore the law and heed their conscience, has a long tradition in Anglo-Saxon jurisprudence, dating back to 1670 when a London jury refused to convict William Penn of "unlawful, seditious, and riotous assembly" for preaching Quakerism.

Indeed, the jury's right to decide the law as well as the facts has been reaffirmed repeatedly, in this country as far back as 1734.

John Adams, our second president, said that juries should decide guilt or innocence according to their "own best understanding, judgment, and conscience, though in direct opposition to the direction of the court."

Much more recently, Supreme Court Justice Oliver Wendell Holmes said that juries have the power "to bring in a verdict in the teeth of both law and facts."

Such a position may not be the dominant legal opinion, but it is supportable both by logic and by precedent, and my response to the judge's question was neither frivolous nor perverse.

If jury duty is one of the responsibilities of citizens in a free society, so too is the obligation to exercise one's brain.

When you take away the right of the people to think for themselves, what remains is not a free society.

❖ ❖ ❖

On the Virtues of Dishonesty

Recently, one of my 10th grade English students missed class on a day when a major paper was due. When I later asked him why he'd been absent, he told me he'd been in the nurse's office, but when I checked with the school nurse, he hadn't been there. Then his math teacher told me that he'd been in the computer room working on his paper that period.

When I confronted the student with what I'd discovered, tears welled up in his eyes, but even then he wouldn't admit that he'd lied to me. He only lapsed into sullen silence. I gave him an unexcused absence for the class, automatically dropping his quarterly grade by a point, and failed his paper without reading it.

I did these things because I am a teacher, and I want my student to learn that honesty still counts in this world. But as he left my classroom, head down and shoulders bent, I could not help considering what he has probably already learned: that if honesty counts for something in this world, it counts for very little.

Boxes of pudding mix announce that the contents make four generous portions, but neglect to mention that this applies only if those eating the pudding are no larger than hamsters. Advertisers tell us that we can be virile men pursued by the Swedish bikini team or alluring women pursued by Tom Cruise look-alikes if we drink their brand of beer or use their

perfume. Janitors are sanitation engineers, and employees are associates.
And when hundreds of "associates" are
permanently laid off from their jobs,
their former employers call it down-
sizing and speak boldly of the company's bright future while voting
themselves fat bonuses.

The American Medical Association
buys full-page ads in national magazines
to disguise its sustained resistance to
health care reform as "defend[ing]
patients' rights." The Pentagon press
secretary shows videotapes of smart
bombs ringing doorbells in Baghdad,
omitting the fact that 92 per cent of the
bombs dropped during the Gulf War
were the same old iron dumbos we were
dropping on Germany in 1944.

At every level of government, politicians insist they are vigorously
waging war on drugs while in my student's neighborhood, in the course of
his young life, the drug gangs have graduated from switchblade knives to
Uzi submachine guns, and no one is doing a thing to correct the circumstances that lead young men to live fast and die violently.

From the frivolous to the fatal, lies are the currency of our culture.
Why should my student fess up to what he's done when college football
coaches promise their players they'll stick with the team through thick and
thin only to move on the next day to another university offering a higher
salary? When tobacco companies continue to insist, in the face of overwhelming evidence, that no link has been established connecting smoking
with death and debilitating disease? When a president nurtures a despica-
ble tyrant year after year, then sends the children of others into harm's way
when the tyrant turns on his benefactor, only to claim the result as a great
victory and go unchallenged in that claim?

Why should my student worry about the consequences of his dishonesty when a major league owner is suspended from baseball for life
only to be reinstated after a few years? When a convicted junk bond king
serves less than two years of a ten-year sentence and emerges from prison
in possession of $500 million? When a Secretary of Defense lies under oath
to Congress and is pardoned even before he stands trial?

My students and I are studying William Shakespeare's *Macbeth* at the
moment. It's a play about a man who will stop at nothing to get what he

wants, wreaking bloody havoc during his short reign as the illegitimate king of Scotland. At the end of the play, however, the rightful king is restored to the throne, saying, "What needful else that calls upon us, by the grace of Grace we will perform in measure, time, and place."

What Shakespeare means, in his elegantly flowery language, is that evil has been vanquished and God's justice will henceforth prevail. My students are struggling hard to fathom the archaic imagery of Elizabethan English, and often don't get the meaning until I explain it to them in patient detail.

But no amount of explanation can get them to comprehend that in Shakespeare's day, people really believed that evil would ultimately be punished and good would be rewarded. For my students, such is the stuff of fantasy, what happens on prime time television, in grade-B thrillers, or in stupid plays they have to read in English class. It does not happen that way in the world in which they are trying to find their place.

Thus I sometimes glance up to find a student nervously gazing at me, a sure sign that he or she would dearly like to take a look at a neighbor's paper if I would only mind my own business. And sometimes I find answers on quizzes from adjacent students that are too similar to be coincidental. Once in a while, I even catch someone with a hand in the cookie jar, as I did that student who hadn't the forethought to consider that his dishonesty would easily be detected or the instinct to grasp that I would take it seriously.

As I watched my student walk away, I wanted to feel as though I'd taught him something of value that day. I had a fleeting fantasy of my own: that somewhere down the years my student would come to understand what I had done and why, and that in that moment of recognition, he would thank me in his heart for being firm with him.

But then I thought of Lady Macbeth's advice to her husband: "Look like the innocent flower, but be the serpent under't." And I can't help wondering if the only thing of value my student learned that day was not to get caught unless you are rich or powerful or famous.

❖ ❖ ❖

An Encounter with the IRS

I got a letter from the Internal Revenue Service recently and discovered that I'm a fraud.

It was quite a shock, let me tell you. I had no idea. I pay my taxes religiously. I even report the $25 personal checks I occasionally get for doing poetry readings or lectures. Nobody reports stuff like that, but I do. I don't want trouble.

I have a terrible fear of running afoul of the IRS. I've heard about tax audits: having to drag years and years of boxes full of yellowed receipts you can't even read anymore down to some interrogation center where you have to explain each and every scrap of paper hour after hour for days on end to a bored civil servant who doesn't believe anything you say.

I've heard about tax court, where black-robed judges hand your house over to the local sheriff or garnish your wages for the next thirty years. No, thank you. I don't need any of that sort of thing. I'm as honest as the day is long.

At least I thought I was. Then I got this letter: "Fraud Penalty Added –See Code 05 on Enclosed Notice: $6.00." I immediately read Code 05. It said, "A penalty has been added for fraud." Well, that's pretty straightforward, I thought.

There was no explanation *why*, however, but there was an 800 telephone number, so I called it. It was answered by—let's call her Mrs. Service. I asked Mrs. Service how I could have committed $6 worth of fraud, but she didn't know.

I asked her who I could talk to that might know. She said that if I disagreed with the statement, I could contact the IRS Adjustment Office. I would have to write a letter describing the entire circumstances of my claim, she explained, and include a complete copy of my income tax return.

"That seems like an awful lot of work for $6," I said. "Can't you just give me the telephone number?"

"I don't have that," Mrs. Service replied.

"You don't have a phone number for the adjustment office?"

"No," Mrs. Service replied.

"Don't you have a phone book you can look it up in?" I asked.

"I'm sorry, no."

"But it's only $6," I said. "I only want to know how I could have committed $6 worth of fraud. Can you give me a hint?"

"I'm sorry," she said. "I don't know."

"Who can I talk to that might know?"

"My supervisor might know."

"Can I please talk to your supervisor?" I asked.

"She's not available," Mrs. Service replied.

"When will she be available?" I asked.

"I don't know," Mrs. Service replied.

"Could I have her name and telephone number?" I asked.

"I don't have that," Mrs. Service replied.

"You don't know the name and phone number of your own supervisor?"

"If you'll give me your name and number, I'll have her get back to you."

"How can you have her get back to me if you don't know who she is?" I asked.

"If you'll give me your name and number," Mrs. Service replied, "I'll have my supervisor get back to you."

"Really?"

"Yes," Mrs. Service replied.

"Today?"

"Yes."

So I gave Mrs. Service my name and telephone number. This was at 8:45 A.M. I sat by my telephone for the rest of the day, but Mrs. Service's supervisor never called.

At 5:01 P.M., I picked up the Scarlet Letter: "Fraud Penalty Added – See Code 05 on Enclosed Notice: $6.00. You may avoid additional interest and penalties if you pay the amount you owe by March 18th."

Additional interest and penalties. That sounded ominous. Would Mrs. Service's supervisor call me before March 18th? Mrs. Service had assured me that her supervisor would call me today, but she hadn't.

Did I want to call tomorrow and try again with Mrs. Service? There didn't seem to be much promise in that.

Should I write to the IRS Adjustment Office? How many hours, how many drafts, how many days would it take me to write down the entire circumstances of my claim? What *were* the circumstances of my claim, anyway? I had no idea. None whatsoever.

I could hire an attorney to pursue the matter, but how much would that cost? Even at a modest $60 an hour, a lawyer would have to solve the mystery in less than six minutes for me to come out ahead.

So much for my options. Recalling that old adage about death and taxes, I wrote out a check for $6 to the IRS.

I still don't know, and never will know, why or how I'm a fraud, but I know there are something like 250 million taxpayers in this country. Let's say the IRS does this sort of thing to only one percent of the taxpayers each year. At $6 each, that's $15 million.

Now let's say that Mrs. Service makes roughly $25,000 a year to answer that telephone number I called. That means the $15 million the IRS collects every year from frauds like me can pay the salaries of 600 employees like Mrs. Service who cannot or will not answer the questions of those who call the number provided by the IRS to answer taxpayers' questions.

And the IRS says I'm the fraud. Don't you just love it?

❖ ❖ ❖

Alive with Pleasure

Want to hear a good joke? The other day I passed a colorful billboard advertising cigarettes: two very attractive young people—a handsome man and a beautiful woman—were laughing and having a wonderful time together, and in large letters the billboard proclaimed, "Alive with Pleasure."

Don't you get it? Let me give you a hint. Tobacco, mostly in the form of cigarettes, kills 434,000 people every year. Think about that slogan. Think about that young, attractive, healthy couple in the picture. Now do you get it?

How about this one? I recently heard a tobacco industry spokesperson say that if taxes on cigarettes are raised, cigarette consumption will drop, and that will put a lot of people out of work, people like tobacco industry workers and convenience store clerks.

You don't get that one either? I'll give you another hint. Think about the people that tobacco industry spokesperson didn't mention: all those doctors and nurses who treat smokers while they're dying, the claims adjusters and clerical staff, the people who make medical tubing and intravenous needles and all the other paraphernalia smokers dying of lung cancer and emphysema and heart failure need before they actually die.

Of course, that tobacco industry spokesperson also neglected to mention that a lot of people would *keep* their jobs if cigarette consumption were reduced—namely the 434,000 smokers who lose their jobs every year because they die—but if he'd mentioned that part, it would have spoiled the joke, and who wants to spoil a good joke?

No, but seriously, folks, don't you think it's funny that so addictive and deadly a drug is perfectly legal and readily available? Don't you think it's funny that every citizen of this country subsidizes the tobacco industry through farm price support payments, tax write-offs for cigarette manufacturers, and increased insurance premiums and health care costs?

Can you imagine buying a vial of heroin over the counter at your local 7-Eleven, or a few hits of LSD at the corner gas station? How about public television underwritten by the Medellin cartel, or a tennis tournament sponsored by the Opium Growers Association? Yet for all the hype and hoopla about crack cocaine, reefer madness, and holes in daddy's arms where the money goes, tobacco is the undisputed heavyweight champion of drugs, killing more people each year than heroin, cocaine, alcohol, automobile and airplane accidents, homicide, suicide, and AIDS *combined*.

Read that list again. Read it slowly.

And tobacco is virulently addictive. I know because I've been addicted to it for 29 years. I started smoking when I was 15. I thought it was cool. (Tobacco industry spokespeople tell you that the $3.3 billion they spend each year on advertising and promotion—a tax-deductible business expense—is not intended to induce young people to take up smoking, but if you believe that, you wouldn't know a good joke if it walked up and shoved a whoopie cushion under your backside.)

In the ten years after I began smoking cigarettes, I also tried marijuana, cocaine, methamphetamines, barbiturates, LSD and PCP. (Well, it *was* the sixties, after all.) I enjoyed some of those drugs more than others, but the only drug I ever became addicted to was tobacco.

And oh, how addicted I became. By the time I was 42, I had a constant hacking cough and a 4-year-old daughter who would say every time she watched me light up another cigarette: "Please stop smoking, Daddy; I don't want you to die." And I'd say, "I'll quit soon, sweetheart," but the thought of living without cigarettes terrified me more than the thought of dying before I got to see her grow up, and after a while my daughter began to understand, even at her age, and she gave up asking.

Then one day this past winter, in a completely spontaneous fit of sanity, I flushed my tobacco down the toilet. It's hard to explain why. Suffice

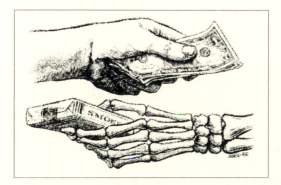

it to say that I had just finished yet another temporary job and found myself, in the dead of winter, middle-aged, unemployed, and feeling as if my life were totally out of my control; I just had to take control of something, and my tobacco was the first thing I could get my hands on.

For the next few days, I couldn't sit still and I couldn't sleep; I wandered aimlessly through the house all day and all night, periodically bursting into tears for no apparent reason. After three days, I stopped crying and began sleeping, but I could do no work that required mental concentration. In fact, though I am a writer and poet with more than a dozen books published in two decades, I was not able to write for over three months. In nearly three decades, I had never written a word when I wasn't high on nicotine—pen in one hand, cigarette in the other—and as the weeks passed, I began to fear that I might never write again unless I gave in to my addiction.

I've won that particular skirmish, but my battle will never be over. I tried to quit after six years, and again after 15 years, and both times I failed. I know a man who quit for 13 years, but couldn't stay clean. I might stay clean, and I might not. And maybe I've already planted the seeds of my own premature death, even if I never take another puff. Maybe I'll live to see my daughter grow up, and maybe I won't.

"God damn the pusher," sang a band called Steppenwolf when I was in college. "God damn the pusher." I've had plenty of occasion to remember those words down all the long years since. And the next time you see a sleek, slick, sexy ad that says "Alive with Pleasure" or "You've come a long way, baby," the next time you see an exhibition at the Metropolitan Museum or the National Gallery sponsored by one of those big, rich, respectable cigarette manufacturers, you too might take a moment to remember those words: "God damn the pusher."

Hell of a punchline, isn't it?

❖ ❖ ❖

On Being the Last True Superpower

Now that the Soviet Union has been relegated to the ash heap of history, the United States is readily acknowledged as the world's only superpower. Indeed, a great many people in and out of government have begun to use our unique superpower status as the foundation for any number of arguments, most recently that we can and must intervene militarily in Bosnia. To cite a typical example, one national news weekly recently editorialized that "our status as the last true superpower demands that we be prepared to use force not only in our own defense but also in defense of international law and democratic values."

The logic puzzles me. If we are obligated to use our super power in defense of international law and democratic values in Bosnia, why aren't we obligated to use it for exactly the same reasons and purposes in Sudan, Angola or Cambodia, each of which would seem to be equally worthy of our attention?

Such speculation, however, obscures an even more important question, perhaps the most fundamental question of the post-Cold War era: What exactly does it mean to be a superpower?

Not long ago, I got a letter from an Austrian friend who lives in Klagenfurt, a city just over the mountains from what used to be Yugoslavia. In his letter, he argued quite eloquently that the United States has a moral obligation to intervene in Bosnia, with force if need be, to stop what he called "the worst European barbarity since the end of World War Two."

In that same letter, my friend also wrote: "Both of my parents are ailing, but I was able to arrange a 26-day cure in a spa for them, which our splendid health care system will largely finance." Would you use the word "splendid" to describe our health care system? Even after whatever reforms the Clinton Administration makes are actually made, will you or your ailing parents ever get to "take the cure" for a month at a mountain health spa, compliments of a splendid health care system? What most of us are going to get, in one form or another, are even higher costs for medical care than we're paying now.

I've been to Klagenfurt and three other major Austrian cities. Only one beggar panhandled me during my entire visit, and I saw no one sleeping in doorways or over steam grates or on park benches. Moreover, Austria's city streets are clean and properly paved, parks are maintained, public spaces are safe and tidy and friendly. Can any of these things be said about our cities?

What can be said about my city—Philadelphia—is that the parking lot of the train station my wife uses to commute to work is littered with crack vials and used hypodermic needles, and the tunnel underpass between the platforms has been sealed shut with cinderblocks because it had become a haven for drug dealers and prostitutes and drunks who needed a place to urinate. There have been drive-by shootings in my neighborhood, a firebombing, rapes, assaults, and all manner of mayhem including the occasional murder—and I don't even live in a bad neighborhood. In the bad neighborhoods, such things occur not weekly or monthly, but daily.

Where my Austrian friend lives, such things occur almost never. Of course, the Austrians don't have a fleet of space shuttles or a superconducting supercollider or even one nuclear submarine armed with enough missiles to destroy several dozen cities the size of Klagenfurt. Their contribution to Operation Desert Storm consisted of 200 volunteer medics, nurses and doctors. They certainly aren't capable of deploying a half-million soldiers halfway around the globe, complete with all their armaments and equipment. They have neither an army that size nor the planes and ships with which to transport it.

The last true superpower, on the other hand, has all these things and more. We've got more guns—legal and illegal—in the hands of private citizens than any other country on earth, along with an astonishing propensity to use those guns on each other. We've got the highest rate of incarceration of any country on earth. We've got the worst public education system in the developed world. An appalling number of our schools are frightening places where cops patrol the halls, metal detectors adorn the entrances, and the only meaningful test each day, for students and teachers alike, is survival.

Then there's our crumbling system of highways, railways, bridges, water and sewer works, and other assorted necessities of civilization collectively called our infrastructure. And the impossibly soaring cost of higher education. And the mass flight of manufacturing jobs to countries with armies far less impressive than Austria's. And our never-ending war on drugs. I could go on, but you get my point.

President Clinton, like other presidents before him, says that we can solve these problems, but most of them have gotten steadily worse while politicians do nothing to address them except posture and gesture and flap their lips endlessly.

None of this strikes me as being particularly super, so what does it mean to be a superpower? I'm truly sorry about the terrible suffering in Bosnia. But I keep wondering why the suffering in Bosnia is more worthy of our attention than the suffering in Sudan or Angola or Cambodia. I keep wondering if the people of Lebanon and Grenada and Panama are any better off than they were because of our military interventions in those countries. And I keep thinking about that other superpower that projected global military might for over half a century while perpetually neglecting the quality of life of its own citizens until it was too late to matter.

❖ ❖ ❖

On the Sad Fate of American Doctors

While I'm hoping for the best from President Clinton's long awaited and much delayed health care reform plan, a recent conversation I had with an old college friend leaves me feeling none too optimistic about the prospects for any serious reform of the U.S. health care system.

My friend, an eminently successful surgeon I'll call George, spoke with unbridled animosity about the increasing intrusion of government into the medical profession since he began practicing 18 years ago. "It's impossible for doctors to make it in this country anymore," he said, blaming the sad fate of American doctors on "socialized medicine."

The Clinton Administration, George is certain, will only make things worse. It was hard enough to make a decent living under Republican administrations "with all the paperwork and regulations," George told me, but Clinton's tax policies "are destroying the incentive and initiative of the people who make America go."

I've known George for 24 years. He works very hard. He has three different practices in two cities, and he also teaches at a major university medical school. When he speaks of our college swimming coach, long dead now, he gets tears in his eyes. He's been married to the same woman for 16 years, and together they are raising two obviously much-loved children. George is a good and caring man. A decent man.

He is also a man with a lakefront home built to his specifications. Tied to the dock in front of the house are his houseboat, his ski boat, his fishing boat, and his runabout. His children go to private school. He drives a Mercedes Benz. He belongs to an exclusive country club. His wife just bought a $2,000 coat. I don't know what his annual income is, but I know it's well in excess of $250,000. It might be double that, or more.

During our conversation, George made multiple references to the *Wall Street Journal* and *Forbes*, explaining to me that "*Forbes* is a magazine that CEOs and other important businessmen read." He made no references to the *Journal of the American Medical Association* or the *New England Journal of Medicine*, but he did advise me to invest in mutual funds rather than certificates of deposit.

He also told me that health maintenance organizations "don't give people any choice" and that HMOs "are denying people medical care they need." When I asked him to give me an example of someone who was denied needed medical care by an HMO, however, he replied that it was hard to give a specific example. I repeated my question several times, and each time he was equally evasive.

I suspect he was embarrassed to give me an example of what he meant because the kind of choice—the necessary medical care—he has in mind is high-priced elective cosmetic surgery. Indeed, a very large portion of George's income derives from making people look better. I'm not necessarily talking face lifts here, but neither do lives hang in the balance when George wields his scalpel. Let me give you an example:

When I was a teenager, I went through the windshield of a car. I got cut up pretty badly, and I've got some pretty ugly scars on my face and neck that are still visible 30 years later. George knows how to remove scars like that, considers their removal a medical necessity, believes he is performing a humanitarian service for which he deserves to be amply rewarded, and doesn't wish to hear that my scars and I have grown quite fond of each other over the years.

I don't mean to make George look bad. I've encountered doctors who are truly mercenary, like the one who charged $475 to examine my niece's broken collarbone for 15 minutes, and then prescribed a brace for her that turned out to be too small, causing my niece days of unnecessary pain. I don't believe George is that unscrupulous or that incompetent. I do believe, somewhere under all the years that have passed between us, there is still the decent man I met my first week at college.

That's what's so depressing about the conversation I had with him. Here's a decent man who earns year after year *at least* ten times what I've ever earned in the best of times, and he thinks he isn't making it; who believes that by performing expensive, esoteric surgery, he's helping to "make America go"; who sounds more like a stockbroker than a caregiver; who seems frighteningly incapable of looking beyond the needs and wants and desires of his own immediate family.

I realize that one doctor does not a survey make, nor are doctors the only factor in the equation of health care reform. But I can't imagine that hospital bureaucracies, health insurance companies, or pharmaceutical manufacturers are any more eager for genuine health care reform than George is, or any more capable of imagining what life is like for the vast majority of Americans who are truly struggling to make it.

Meanwhile, George has got a hell of a lot of disposable income to spend in defense of what he perceives to be his self-interest, he's adamantly opposed to any kind of health care reform that will damage his perceived self-interest, and he has working for him one of the most powerful lobbies in the United States.

I'd say George has a lot more reason to feel optimistic about the ultimate outcome of Clinton's health care reform plan than I do.

❖ ❖ ❖

Why Didn't You Tell Me?

Having taught at three different Friends schools in the past fifteen years, I think it safe to say that in such a context I am, if not unique, at least unusual: an ex-Marine sergeant and a war veteran. The discovery of my decidedly un-Quakerly background has raised more than a few pairs of eyebrows among my colleagues, accompanied by the implicit and sometimes explicit question: How did you end up here? A fair question, but for me there is no contradiction between what I was and what I am. Indeed, I doubt that I would ever have become a teacher at all had I not first been a Marine.

When I volunteered for the U.S. Marine Corps at the age of 17, I believed absolutely that I was doing the right thing, a good thing, my duty. It was the spring of 1966, and there were already 200,000 U.S. soldiers fighting in Vietnam. Lyndon Johnson had solemnly warned us that if we did not stop the Communists in Vietnam, we would one day have to fight them on the sands of Waikiki. In the small semi-rural white Protestant community in which I grew up, Memorial Day was a very public ritual, and there were no antiwar demonstrators. My photograph appeared in the local weekly newspaper, announcing my enlistment, and most of my teachers heartily congratulated me, stopping me in the halls to pump my hand. Thus armed with the confidence of youth, the clarion call of my president, and the benediction of my community, I went to war.

On my third day in Vietnam, I watched as fellow Marines tossed a score or more of civilians—old men, women, children, all of them bound hand and foot with communications wire—from the tops of two amphibious tractors onto the ground nine feet below. I could actually hear bones snapping and joints dislocating amid the cries of fear and pain rising from that awful pile of humanity. I had never seen or heard anything like it, and I had to concentrate hard to keep my knees from buckling and my stomach from divesting itself of its contents.

But that was nothing, it turned out. Six months later, the sight of a mortally wounded woman holding a dead child in her arms hardly received a second glance as I paused just long enough to shift the weight of the weapons and equipment I carried before plodding on through what had long since become a lethal nightmare.

I knew by then that what was happening around me had nothing to do with what I had been led to believe by my teachers and my president and the *New York Times*, but I did not understand how or why this had come to be, or how I had become something ugly and evil. The questions that arose were as ugly and evil as I had become, and there were no answers but the ones I had been given in advance, and those lay discarded amid the rubble and misery I had helped to create. I no longer dreamed of medals and parades and hometown girls kissing the returning hero. I dreamed of survival.

I came home at the age of 19 with a Purple Heart, two Presidential Unit Citations, a Navy Combat Action Ribbon, and a wound in my soul that would not heal. Elsewhere I have written at great length about what happened to me in Vietnam and in the years immediately thereafter, so I will not take the time here to go into detail. Suffice it to say that after a long and painful journey of self-education and self-discovery, I came to a number of conclusions, among them:

That governments, including our own, are not only capable of lying, but can be relied upon to do so at every available opportunity; that Vietnam was neither a mistake nor an aberration, but rather the logical and deliberate extension of policies and practices dating back at least to the arrival of the first English colonists on this continent; that all wars are perceived and explained by those who wish to wage them as just and unavoidable; that the roots of war can almost invariably be found not in the justifications offered by politicians and generals, but in the inequitable distribution of the world's wealth and resources and the greed and arrogance of human beings powerful enough to pass themselves off as principled and honorable; that war neither enlarges nor ennobles the human spirit, but debases and diminishes any and all who come into contact with it; and that while there are many things in this world worth dying for, there is precious little worth killing for.

I came to believe that I and my entire generation had been betrayed by our elders. That sense of betrayal only deepened when I learned that my father's generation, which had fought what has come to be known as the "Good War" in Europe and the Pacific only a few years before I was born, had summarily executed German prisoners and boiled the flesh from the heads of Japanese soldiers to make the skulls into souvenirs, and that they had suffered the same debilitating emotional damage as a result of their encounter with war that had for more than a decade after the Vietnam War been said to be the sole province of Vietnam veterans.

Why hadn't anyone told me? Why had they deliberately hidden the truth and told me instead that war would make a man of me? Those people who were responsible for my education, in both the narrowest and broadest senses, sent me off to war profoundly ignorant and utterly defenseless. It remains a wonder to me that anyone can live with the anger such a betrayal engenders and not be consumed by it.

That I can and was not has to do with three lucky breaks I got: I had parents, especially my mother, who never closed the door on me, though they must have been as thoroughly confused as I was in those early years after I had come home to them a stranger; I had some friends in college who didn't care if I'd been to Vietnam or Borneo or Mars; and I could write.

I'd begun writing in my last two years of high school, but after I got out of the Marines and started college, I began to write about the war. I didn't know it then, but the writing was a way to get at what had happened to me and why and how I felt about it. I began to articulate my soul and the wound it carries. I found a way to try to tell people what I have learned and what I have paid for that knowledge. I found the voice that had been taken from me in the ricefields and hamlets of Vietnam.

Though I have written about a great many subjects over the years, I always come back to the war, or rather to what I learned as a result of the war, and to what it cost. My writing has been for me a continuing education, as I hope it is for those who read it. Somewhere along the way, I came to understand that I have been an educator all my adult life.

I came to the profession of teaching, however, rather later than some, and not entirely willingly. After knocking about for several years after college, I went to graduate school because it was something to do. I had no money, but they told me I could buy my master's degree by teaching first-year undergraduate composition. I'd already been a merchant seaman, a forklift operator, a legal aide, a reporter and a roofer, but being a teacher had never occurred to me, and being a teacher of composition sounded particularly dull. But my options were limited: take the offer or go find a real job. So I took the offer.

And I discovered that I liked teaching. I liked being around young people. I liked watching them learn and grow and discover good things in themselves that they hadn't known were there. They made me feel like I was doing something worth doing. I hadn't imagined myself capable of touching lives without hurting them. That I could do it, and do it well, made the wound in my soul a little smaller, though I approach the melodramatic to say so.

My college roommate was teaching at a small Quaker school in Maryland when I finished graduate school, and with his help I was able to land a job teaching history and English there. I had a terrible first few weeks. I thought 15-year-olds deliberately forgot to bring their notebooks to class just to spite me. Every day was a struggle. My newfound confidence was badly shaken. I wasn't as good at this as I had thought. One sleepless night I got up and wrote this poem:

THE TEACHER

A cold moon hangs
cold fire among the clouds,
and I remember colder nights
in hell when men died
in such pale light as this
of fire swift
and deadly as a heart of ice.

Hardly older then
than you are now,
I hunched down shaking
like an old man
alone in an empty cave
among the rocks of ignorance
and malice honorable men
call truth.

Out of that cave I carried
anger like a torch
to keep my heart from freezing,
and a strange new thing called
love
to keep me sane.

A dozen years ago,
before I ever knew you,
beneath a moon not unlike
this moon tonight,
I swore an oath to teach you
all I know—
and I know things
worth knowing.

It is a desperate future
I cling to,
and it is yours.
All that I have lived for
since that cold moon long ago
hangs in the balance—
and I keep fumbling for words,
but this clip-clapper tongue
won't do.

I am afraid;
I do not want to fail:

I need your hands to steady me;
I need your hearts to give me courage;

> I need you to walk with me
> until I find a voice
> that speaks the language
> that you speak.

The next day I read it to the students in assembly. When I finished, no one said a word. Then two or three students started clapping. And then the whole place erupted. I could have cried. Actually, I think I did. And the very next day, Jay McIntyre forgot to bring his notebook to class, but it was okay.

Since then I've lived a schizophrenic and harrowing life trying to balance my need to write with my love of teaching without having my house repossessed. It's wild. If I teach, I don't get any writing done, and then I get crazy. If I don't teach, I miss the energy and hopefulness of young people, and then I get sad. So I teach a little here, and write a little there, and worry a lot about making ends meet.

But that's okay. I've had it worse. I've got a wife who loves me, and a daughter who is precious beyond words, neither of which was even remotely imaginable for many years after I came back from Vietnam. I have this pen, which gives me my voice. And every once in a while, I have the good fortune to get my hands on a classroom full of kids. And let me tell you, that's fun.

My students may well be surprised to hear me describe what I do with such enthusiasm. Things come to teachers' ears, and it has come to mine that I am sometimes perceived as a stern taskmaster. That's okay, too. Though I sometimes overshoot the mark, I know a little something about what one can endure when one has little choice, and I believe it more often better to ask for too much than to ask for too little because a day may come—in war or in peace, in marriage or in work, in the myriad ways and settings and circumstances that arise in the course of a life—when they will have to endure more than their young minds can now begin to think possible.

So I like to push them. I like to make them haul stuff out of themselves that leaves them positively astonished. And I like them to push back. They drive me nuts. I can't get them to shut up and pay attention. I dress them down, and they all sit there like chastened angels, hang-dog and sorrowful, and ten minutes later they're babbling away again. It keeps me fresh. And if it doesn't exactly keep me young, it keeps me a lot younger than I was 25 years ago.

And every once in a while I even get the chance to say a word or two about what's waiting for them out there in the world. I just have to do that. I can't help myself. My deepest fear as a teacher and as a human being is that one day some student of mine will point an accusing finger back across the years and cry out in anguish: "Why didn't you tell me?"

❖ ❖ ❖

The Vietnam War
and the Academy

The first time I encountered the Vietnam War as grist for the academic mill, I spent three days walking around Manchester, England, with my mouth hanging open, my chin somewhere down around my knees. The occasion was a 1986 conference at Manchester Polytechnical Institute entitled "Cultural Effects of Vietnam," and I had been invited to give a poetry reading, an offer I had gladly accepted because nobody I know turns down a free trip to England.

I had never been to an academic conference before, however, and I was not prepared for what awaited me. Over the course of those three days, panel after panel—each consisting of two to five presenters—covered topics like "Rockin' Hegemony: West Coast Rock and the Vietnam War," "John Wayne in a Modern Heart of Darkness," and "Puritanism in Film and Fiction: from *The Scarlet Letter* to *Apocalypse Now.*"

I didn't even know what "hegemony" meant. I kept pinching myself and asking the air, "Are they talking about the Vietnam War that happened on *this* planet? The war *I* was in? The one with all the dead people and stuff I have nightmares about?" It all seemed so bloodless, so empty of passion, so—well, so academic. It was as if they'd stolen some very personal thing and made it into a coffee table curiosity.

Much of my response, I eventually came to understand, was actually a kind of territorial imperative: the war was mine, it happened to me, and therefore it belonged to me and my comrades, not to a bunch of intellectuals who hadn't been within eight thousand miles of a shot fired in anger. What authority could possibly equal "I was there"?

I was also, I think, having difficulty coming to terms with the fact that what still seemed so fresh and vivid to me had already become history. The conference was a rude reminder that time was racing by at alarming speed, that I was no longer a young man. I used to think "first you get old and then you die" was a clever expression, but by the time I left Manchester, it had lost much of its charm.

Fortunately, for there is no telling how badly I might have behaved had it been otherwise, my shock was largely dulled by a severe case of jet lag; for most of those three days, all I could do was gape and scratch my head. And once I got back home and had time to ponder what I'd just survived, I began to consider the conference and what it represented somewhat differently than I had while it was right there in front of my dangling lower jaw.

Left to right: Novelist John Clark Pratt and poet John Balaban, at the Conference on Cultural Effects of Vietnam, Manchester Polytechnical Institute, Manchester, England, 1986. (Photograph by W.D. Ehrhart)

Firstly, while many of the presenters at Manchester were indeed pure intellectuals whose interest in the war seemed almost by definition academic, others were either Vietnam War veterans like retired air force pilot turned English professor John Clark Pratt, or committed activists like Don Luce, who had spent fourteen years in Vietnam until he was expelled by Nguyen Van Thieu for helping to expose the infamous "tiger cages" of Con Son Island. Larry Heinemann read from his not yet published *Paco's Story*, and John Balaban read his own poems along with Vietnamese folk poems which he read in both Vietnamese and English.

Secondly, while there were presentations that ought not to have been allowed out except after dark and then only on thick short chains with choke collars, there were others that were quite stunning in their clarity and intelligence and perceptiveness. College librarian, novelist and Vietnam veteran David A. Willson gave a hilarious and brilliant paper on the cover art of Vietnam War paperback books. Austrian scholar Adi Wimmer demonstrated how *Rambo: First Blood, Part Two* transforms Sylvester Stallone into the Viet Cong and the Vietnamese into the U.S. Army, thereby turning historical reality inside out. And Pilar Marin of the University of

Seville gave so lucid a paper on Lloyd Little's *Parthian Shot* that I have stayed in touch with her ever since.

Wimmer and Marin, obviously, are not Vietnam veterans and have no direct knowledge of the war in Vietnam, yet both of them taught me a great deal about something I had up until then considered exclusively mine, which brings me to a third observation: If personal witness is the only legitimate lens through which to see the Vietnam War, what happens when all the witnesses are dead? That question had not occurred to me prior to Manchester, but like it or not, "I was there" only goes so far. Ask any veteran of the Spanish-American War. Oops, you can't because they're all dead. Likewise, sooner or later, the only people writing and talking about the Vietnam War will inevitably be those who have no direct knowledge of it. Shall we veterans encourage and assist them in their efforts while we still can, or shall we be hostile and exclusionary and petulant?

I have come to understand, in fact, that we need the academy very much. In a world where actors make multi-millions fighting in Hollywood the war I fought in the ricefields for $121 a month, where POW/MIA flags fly over every rest stop on the New Jersey Turnpike and *Miss Saigon* is all the rage on Broadway, one of the only places young people have any chance of learning anything of value about what actually happened in Vietnam and why is in colleges and universities where reside those very professors and scholars I first encountered in Manchester.

Indeed, I have come to look forward to the opportunities I occasionally get to participate in such conferences. True, there are always moments of sheer lunacy, like the time in Toronto in 1990 when some professor gave a paper on the social class differences between officers and enlisted personnel, using Bob Mason's *Chickenhawk* as her model for officers. When I pointed out to her that Mason was a warrant officer/pilot, a flying bus driver with neither social standing nor command responsibility, she smiled brightly and replied, "Oh! I didn't know that."

But there are also moments of sheer delight, like the time at the same conference in Toronto when Professor Paul Lyons of Stockton College revolutionized my understanding of the so-called Vietnam Generation in the space of twenty minutes, convincingly demonstrating that most male members of our generation neither fought nor protested the war, but legally and effortlessly sidestepped it *à la* Dan Quayle and Bill Clinton and went on about their lives with hardly a pause.

Thus, when Professor Robert Slabey of the University of Notre Dame invited me to participate in the conference he was organizing, "The United States and Viet Nam: From War to Peace," I eagerly accepted the invitation. And a fine conference it turned out to be. The moments of sheer lunacy were mercifully few, and the moments of sheer delight were plentiful.

Consider this, if you will: I got to hear readings by Pulitzer Prize winner Robert Olen Butler, National Book Award winner Heinemann, and National Poetry Award winner Balaban, all in the space of a single afternoon.

Or this: the next afternoon, I joined Balaban, Butler and Heinemann on Marc Leepson's panel, "The Arts of War and Peace." Meanwhile, among the audience were Lynda Van Devanter (*Home Before Morning*), Gerald McCarthy (*War Story*), Larry Rottmann (*Voices from the Ho Chi Minh Trail*), John C. Schafer and Dale Ritterbusch (contributors to *Carrying the Darkness*), and Willson (*REMF Diary*), along with H. Bruce Franklin (*M.I.A., or Mythmaking in America*), Arnold R. Isaacs (*Without Honor*), and Elliott Gruner (*Prisoners of Culture*), any of whom could easily have taken my place on the panel.

Indeed, though the academics were mostly a serious and thoughtful lot—some of the very best in the field, many of them Vietnam veterans, others bright young scholars like Vince Gotera, whose study of American veterans' poetry, *Radical Visions*, is destined to become the definitive text—Slabey went to considerable lengths to make sure this would not be merely a gathering of academics.

Rottmann, for instance, brought his seven-member road crew from the Southeast Asia-Ozark Center at Southwest Missouri State to perform a somber version of his *Voices* book. And that apparently indefatigable personality Thi Thanh Nga (a.k.a. Tiana) treated us all to a dose of *From Hollywood to Hanoi*, two segments of which were well worth having to sit through the rest of the film. In the first, two Vietnamese-American teenagers struggle to answer the question: "Are you Vietnamese or American?" Each answers, changes the answer, again changes the answer, finally replies, "I don't know." In the second, William Westmoreland, wearing one of those conical Vietnamese hats, tries to explain away what he'd said to a previous filmmaker some twenty years ago about Orientals not valuing life the way "we" do.

Much of the real value of conferences, of course, lies outside the formal program: the chance to renew old friendships and make new ones, the chance to recharge one's emotional batteries, the chance (okay, I admit it) to stay up late drinking beer in the hotel bar listening to David Willson skewer some unsuspecting novice with his rapier wit (a cliché, but no less true for it).

Each night, in fact, I stayed up later than the night before, which made each morning's 7 A.M. jog around the Notre Dame campus that much harder than the previous morning's run. Once you got going, however, it turned out to be a special time. In South Bend, on the western fringe of the eastern time zone in December, it's still pitch dark at 7 A.M., and on two mornings it was raining to boot, making it even darker. The ducks on the lake were just beginning to stir at that hour, a mist still lay on the water, and the easy conversation between jogging partner Paul Lyons and me ranged from the rigors of boot camp to the failures of the antiwar Left. Two of the four mornings (when it wasn't raining), Marc Leepson even joined us, making himself a better man for his trouble.

Here are some other things that were special:

During a coffee break, Skip Isaacs, a former *Baltimore Sun* reporter, told me about a young man he had interviewed on the steps of the Capitol during Vietnam Veterans Against the War's "incursion into the country of Congress," Dewey Canyon III, in April 1971. The man was about to throw away a Silver Star, and this disturbed Isaacs, who had tried to talk him out of it. But the young vet had told him, "I'm not proud of what I did," and he had tossed it over the cyclone fence Congress had erected to keep America's sons at bay. "I've never forgotten that man," Isaacs said. "I've often wondered what became of him."

"I know what became of him," I said. "His name was Ron Ferrizzi, wasn't it? He and his wife have a picture framing shop two miles from my house, they're raising two fine sons who just graduated from college, and as far as I know he's never regretted tossing that medal over the fence, so there you are. For once, a happy ending."

Former Marine and Oklahoma State English professor Peter Rollins was almost as amazed as Isaacs had been when I pointed to his miniature ribbon bar and correctly identified his Expeditionary Medal. Not many people know that the first Marines sent to Vietnam received not the Republic of Vietnam Service Medal, but the Expeditionary Medal instead. Rollins and I disagree on just about everything to do with the Vietnam War, but the conversation we struck up that afternoon did much to humanize the distance between us.

It was my turn to be amazed when Professor Catherine Calloway of Arkansas State showed up at the conference with a dozen copies of *Unaccustomed Mercy*, an anthology I'd edited. She had brought them because her students wanted me to sign them, and when I did, she acted as if *I* were doing *her* a favor when in truth she and her students were paying me a compliment I'll remember all my life.

For me, in fact, the whole conference seemed filled with compliments most writers get only rarely in a lifetime, if at all. Certainly nothing quite like it has ever happened to me before. It's a very strange feeling—wonderful, but strange—to sit in an audience listening to some scholar say flattering things about your work, and this happened not once but twice in a single morning. Sitting next to Balaban, who was in the same awkward position I was in, I stared at my feet a lot, feeling pleased and embarrassed, thinking, "Geez, I'm not even dead yet." That afternoon I gave a reading to an audience of which the majority not only knew who I was, but had actually read me. *That's* never happened to me before, either.

On our last morning trot around the lake, the conference having officially closed the night before, I found myself thinking back to that earlier conference in Manchester. What a bizarre experience it had been—not strange, like listening to Lorrie Smith's paper about Balaban, Bruce Weigl and me, but truly bizarre—as if I had stumbled into someone else's dream. It had left me ill at ease and befuddled, not knowing quite what to make of it until well after the fact. This time, seven years later, I felt positively exhilarated. What was the difference? What had changed?

Me, I suppose. I've mostly come to terms with my own advancing years. I'm unavoidably middle-aged now, my hair is graying, my joints are stiff, and I can't arrest or change any of that. I've had to come to terms with myself in ways that occasionally even take on a passing resemblance to wisdom. I know that all of us who lived through the Vietnam War years really *are* history to kids who would likely have a difficult time explaining the difference between the last U.S. helicopter out of Saigon and Custer's last stand.

Neither Hollywood nor Madison Avenue nor Music Television is ever likely to teach them the difference, and you and I aren't going to live forever, so if they're ever going to learn anything worth knowing about the war in Vietnam, it will be people like the ones I met at Notre Dame who will teach them.

I guess that's why I came away feeling so exhilarated. It was a pretty good crowd. Nice bunch to spend a few days with. I wouldn't mind *my* kid taking a course or two with folks like that.

❖ ❖ ❖

Sticks and Stones

At the very beginning of the agony of the former Yugoslavia, in early June 1991, I received a passionate letter from a young Slovene professor of American literature whom I'd met two years earlier during a visit to Ljubljana. Slovenia, like several other republics in the Serbian-dominated Yugoslav Federation, had recently voted to secede from Yugoslavia and become an independent nation, and the secession was to take effect at the end of June. But the Serbs were making no secret of their displeasure with this, and the Yugoslavian national army, even more so than the national government, was dominated by Serbs.

Indeed, the rising tensions of imminent war had been painfully visible in Uros's recent letters. "In times of great political turmoil and danger," he had written the previous December, "one barely finds a moment of happiness to think of one's friends somewhere far, far away." Six weeks later he had written, "The political situation here is severe, with aggression constantly in the air. The secessional war hasn't really broken out yet and I hope it never will, but it's very hard to say what will happen next. We're living in a state of uncertainty, from one threat to another—either from the army or the Serbian government, which is really the same thing."

But the letter I got in early June was the one that broke my heart. "Just a few days ago," Uros wrote, "a 60-year-old civilian was killed when run over by an army vehicle, while several unarmed people were shot at and one of them seriously wounded. June 26th is supposed to be the day of Slovenia's secession from Yugoslavia, but in view of the threats and the constant aggression, we are getting more and more frightened as the day approaches.

"Bill, please do something to help open the eyes of the American people and of your government. Perhaps you could give a lecture or write an article about 'the Yugoslav truth.' If America is really such a democratic and tolerant country, as it claims to be, such information will quickly and widely spread. We are on the verge of collapse. Rumors that the Austrians and Italians are preoccupied with building refugee camps are no comfort to us."

All of this was happening during and just after Operation Desert Storm. Uros had heard and read the American president's firm and repeated declarations that aggression would not be tolerated, that a New World Order had begun, and he had seen the United States send half a million soldiers thousands of miles from our shores to back up that assertion. He believed that if the American people and the United States government only understood "the Yugoslav truth," surely we would readily defend the Slovene people against Serbian aggression.

I have never had to write a more difficult letter than the one I wrote in reply to Uros's plea for help. I have seldom been so ashamed to be an American. I had to explain to this newly married young man awaiting the arrival of his first child that there would be no help for him or his country from the self-proclaimed leader of the New World Order, that when the president of the United States had said Americans were fighting Iraq in order to thwart aggression and liberate an oppressed people, he had not really meant it, but had come to the aid of Kuwait only because Kuwait

had large quantities of oil upon which the United States is foolishly depen-
dent, and because it seemed an easy opportunity to liberate not Kuwait but
the United States "from old ghosts and doubts" created by a failed war
twenty years earlier. I had to explain that most Americans could not find
Slovenia on a map and did not much care what happened there, that no
one would publish my article if I wrote it, or come to my lecture if I gave
it, and that it would change nothing if anyone did.

Try explaining all of that to someone who's never spent a day in the
United States, whose knowledge of America is derived entirely from secondary sources like the Declaration of Independence, *The Grapes of Wrath*,
and Cable News Network.

Fortunately for Uros and his country, after some border skirmishes
and several Serbian bombing raids on Ljubljana, the Serbs chose to attack
elsewhere instead: first Croatia, then Bosnia. In all the long nightmare that
was once Yugoslavia, Slovenia alone is the one bright hope, the only break-
away republic that just might survive intact and unbloodied.

I had the good fortune to visit Ljubljana for a second time this past
November [1993]. This time my passport was stamped "Slovenia" instead
of "Yugoslavia," and this time I got to meet Uros's wife, Barbara, whom
he had married only after our first meeting, and his daughter, Alma, now
almost two. It was also the first contact I'd had with Uros since I'd sent
that terrible letter two and a half years earlier; he had never replied to it,
nor to two other letters I'd sent subsequently.

Throughout his long silence, mutual friends kept assuring me that
Uros was not angry with me, only busy with his job and his new family,
but I knew he must have been deeply hurt by my response to his plea for
help, and the moment our eyes met, even before he spoke, I knew I had
been right.

"I was very angry," he said. "Kuwait had been stealing Iraqi oil, and
we had stolen nothing from anyone. Kuwait is a feudal sheikdom, and we
are a western democracy. Kuwait is rich, and we are poor. Yet you helped
Kuwait, but would not help us. I felt betrayed by America." He paused.
"And you are American," he added almost apologetically.

Uncomfortably mindful of my old drill instructor's colorful adage—
"Excuses are like assholes: everybody's got one"—I pointed out to Uros that
while all of this was true, none of it had been my idea, trying again to
explain a country I have a good deal of difficulty explaining even to myself.

Later, in a very different context, I used a variation of the expression
"to stand someone up," as in: "We had a date, but she stood me up." Uros
was not familiar with that American idiom, and when I explained that it
meant to make an appointment or commitment and then fail to keep it,
he replied, "Oh, like you stood me up when I asked you for help." From

Uros Mozetic (*second from right*) with colleagues from the University of Ljubljana (*left*) and the author (*far right*), Slovenia, 1993. (Photograph by Adi Wimmer)

the way he smiled at me, it was impossible to tell if he had misunderstood my explanation of the idiom, or my explanation of the letter—or if he had understood both explanations all too well.

I am not suggesting here that the United States should or should not have offered assistance to Slovenia, nor am I suggesting that the U.S. ought or ought not to intervene elsewhere in the Balkans. Interesting questions, these, but part of a different discussion.

My immediate concern is not with what we as a nation do and don't do in the world, but rather with the language we choose to explain it to ourselves and others. By the grace of God, faith in the promise of America ended up costing the Slovene people very little. But how many Croatians and Bosnians voted for secession from Yugoslavia believing that the leader of the New World Order would never allow Serbian aggression to go unchallenged? Hadn't he said as much when he challenged Saddam?

And what of Iraqi Kurds and Shiites who took a U.S. president at his word and rose up against a tyrant, only to have that same president and the military he commanded and the nation he represented stand idly by— often within sight and sound of the slaughter—while Saddam Hussein's still-quite-functional army crushed their uprisings?

What of all those Vietnamese banging desperately at the gates of the U.S. embassy compound the morning the last U.S. helicopter lifted out of Saigon? Or even of Ho Chi Minh, who traveled to Versailles in 1919 believing that

Woodrow Wilson was telling the truth when he said that all nations and all peoples have the right to self-determination? How different all our lives might have been had Wilson taken both his own words and that skinny little man from French Indochina more seriously.

What of Chief Black Kettle of the Cheyenne, who flew the American flag while Colonel John M. Chivington attacked his helpless village at Sand Creek, butchering hundreds of unarmed women, children, and old men because Abraham Lincoln had told Black Kettle that so long as he flew that flag, he and his people would be safe?

Trusting the words Americans use to explain themselves can be, and often is, a fatal exercise in naivete. From the days of John Endicott, governor of Massachusetts Bay Colony, who demonstrated his interest "in the welfare of the better type of American Indian" by endeavoring to kill every male Indian on Block Island, to the day this past October when U.S. soldiers attempted to fulfill their humanitarian mission in Somalia by attacking a hotel in downtown Mogadishu, there has often been a very large gulf between American words and American deeds.

I'm not surprised that those in power seek to put their decisions and their actions in the best possible light, even if they have to dissemble to do so. Power is inherently dishonest, and powerful people neither obtain nor maintain power by being honest. And I'm not surprised that the mass media report what powerful people say without ever seriously challenging what is said. After all, freedom of the press means only that those who own the presses, the radio and television stations, are free to say what they like, and those who own the presses, the radio and television stations, are powerful people.

What surprises me is the continuing willingness of ordinary Americans to go along with, and even buy into, the perpetually bogus explanations we get for what is being done under our flag, in our names, with our tax dollars, and often with the lives of our sons and daughters.

Consider, for instance, the inscription beneath the Statue of Liberty: "Give me your tired, your poor, your huddled masses yearning to breathe free." All through the 1980s, our government sent back almost every refugee fleeing the oppression and violence of El Salvador, Guatemala and Honduras, claiming that these people were economic refugees who had no legitimate reason to fear for their lives, and almost nobody in America seemed to care. Now in the 1990s, we are turning back nearly every Haitian who manages to set sail for our shores. The U.S. Coast Guard carries them right into Port au Prince and turns them over to an illegal government of thugs and murderers; the president says we're sending these people back to Haiti for their own safety and well-being, and almost nobody in America seems to care.

Well, why should we? Times are tough all over. Heck, we're not so gullible, anyway, are we? Do we really believe that poem about the huddled masses? Did we ever believe that Ngo Dinh Diem was the Winston Churchill of Asia, or that Roberto D'Aubuisson gave a hoot about democracy in El Salvador? It's fun to imagine we're as swell a bunch of folks as our junior high history books tell us we are, but does any American smarter than a fire hydrant actually believe it? Does anyone believe the U.S. government or the people it represents really give a flying fig about tyranny or human rights or unprovoked aggression?

Unfortunately, time and again, we the people demonstrate that we do indeed believe our own rhetoric. People old enough to have read *The Pentagon Papers* and *All the President's Men* willingly send their sons, and now their daughters too, off to places like Lebanon and Grenada and Panama and Kuwait and Somalia without even asking, let alone demanding of those who are doing the sending, "Is this *really* necessary?"

Moreover—and this is the unconscionable part, the part that really embarrasses me—truly oppressed and downtrodden people all over the world also believe our rhetoric, and are often willing to hazard everything including their lives on the strength of their faith that the United States of America will not let them down. When the tanks rolled into Tianenman Square and crushed the Chinese democracy movement a few years back, hundreds, perhaps, thousands, of young Chinese died within sight of their own homemade replica of the Statue of Liberty. Ponder that one, if you dare.

I'm deeply relieved that my friend Uros survived his misplaced faith in America. But I'm just as deeply ashamed that many millions of others have paid so dearly, and continue to pay, for theirs. If we as a nation can't or won't deliver on our explanations of who we are and what we represent, we ought at least to have the decency to be more careful about the language we use to explain ourselves.

❖　❖　❖

No Facts, Only Perceptions

The most persistently nettlesome legacy of the Vietnam War is the belief that U.S. servicemen missing in action are still alive in Southeast Asia. So powerful is this belief that no U.S. president since Richard Nixon—

who is largely responsible for creating it in the first place—has dared to suggest to those who believe that what they believe is a fantasy.

Indeed, no successful politician at any level of government has dared to say such a thing in public, and people who have—H. Bruce Franklin, for instance, in his cogently argued *M.I.A., or Mythmaking in America*—have been ignored, vilified, or marginalized. Aging men in camouflaged jungle uniforms incongruously bedecked with medals and ribbons maintain a permanent vigil for our MIAs at the Vietnam Veterans Memorial in Washington, D.C., and the black-and-white POW/MIA flag—the only flag besides the Stars and Stripes ever to fly atop the White House—adorns state and local government flagpoles from Massachusetts to Montana.

And it doesn't end there. Thanks to Sylvester Stallone, Chuck Norris, Tom Selleck and other Hollywood war heroes who never got within 5,000 miles of Vietnam during the war, an entire generation of Americans who weren't even alive during the war take as a given that MIAs are still alive in Southeast Asia. This cross-generational transmission of belief ensures that the ghosts of the MIAs, if not the MIAs themselves, will end up outliving the rest of their generation, both those who served and those who didn't.

Moreover, these ghosts are an exceedingly effective weapon with which to punish the Vietnamese for having had the audacity to embarrass and humiliate the United States. Ronald Reagan used the MIAs to justify continuation of the economic and diplomatic embargo of Vietnam that has been in place since 1975. Recent attempts by the Bush and Clinton administrations to end that embargo have each been thwarted by the sudden appearance of dramatic new evidence supporting the existence of living MIAs: in 1991, photographs of three aging U.S. prisoners being held in Laos; eighteen months later, a Soviet copy of a Vietnamese politburo memo dating from the war and claiming that Vietnam held over twice as many U.S. prisoners as it has ever admitted to.

It matters not at all that these and every other sensational lead on MIAs are each time quickly and conclusively demonstrated to be bogus: those POW/MIA flags still fly above every rest stop on the New Jersey Turnpike, the National Park Service still allows those middle-aged warriors to haunt the Vietnam Veterans Memorial, Congressional committees still spend millions of dollars on one investigation after another, and millions of schoolchildren still believe America's bravest sons wait forlornly in bamboo cages for rescue that never comes. One cannot kill a myth. Ghosts are immune to facts.

"There are no facts," says Jake Loman in Wayne Karlin's new novel *Us* (Henry Holt, 1993), "only perceptions." Take pretty Kitty of the front desk at the Miami Hotel in Bangkok who spies for Aung Khin, the Kuomintang warlord who controls much of the opium trade in the Golden Triangle of Laos-Thailand-Burma (now Myanmar). Kitty turns out to be Sadong, who's really spying for the Burmese rebel Taksin, Aung Khin's most bitter enemy, who's actually Dr. Dawee of Thailand. But Sadong turns out to be Aye Than, who might or might not be Aung Khin's daughter, or lover, or both. Maybe she's Taksin's lover, too. Maybe not. Meanwhile, Taksin appears to be a man but turns out to be a woman, while Taksin's lieutenant, Auntie Soe, appears to be a woman but is actually a man. "There are no facts," says Loman, "only perceptions."

It's the early 1990s in Karlin's novel, and Loman is a three-tour Vietnam veteran who owns the Naga Queen, a bar in Bangkok where Fat Al, Chuckie's-in-Love, and Helicopter Harry pass the time telling war stories to tourists and carrying on with Loman's prostitutes as if they were still on R&R from Vietnam, which in a perverse sort of way they are. Into Loman's bar, in rapid succession, come a scar-necked man with Montagnard bracelets on his wrists who stabs a German tourist menacing Loman with a broken beer bottle before hissing the word "Us" at Loman and disappearing into the night; Charlene and Usama, documentary filmmakers who tell Loman they have information about "sightings of MIAs, possibly the ones who call themselves Us, with the Taksin group"; Congressman Elliott Mundy, who tells Loman he has "confirmed sightings, eyewitness accounts of Westerners who meet the age requirements [for MIAs] working with Aung Khin's band"; and Arthur Weyland, an ex-CIA officer (or is he ex-?), who tells Loman, "You'll do what I want because I have my connections and because you have a bar you'd like to keep."

Helicopter door gunner Wayne Karlin, U.S.M.C., Vietnam, 1967. (Photograph provided by Wayne Karlin)

Loman himself has always wanted to believe that the MIAs are alive,

Novelist and short story writer Wayne Karlin in 2000 during shooting of the Vietnamese feature film *Song of the Stork* in which Karlin plays a former soldier returning to postwar Vietnam. He also wrote part of the script and served as a consultant on the film. (Photograph provided by Wayne Karlin)

"one long patrol unraveling from his memory, a line of green disappearing into a vastness of green. A yearning." He has tried often enough to find them that the hill people of the Golden Triangle call him *Kon Ahn Harm Kon Die*: "The One Who Carries the Dead." And though his previous attempts have led him to conclude grudgingly that "the missing were just another illusion" of the war, he agrees to make one more expedition into the jungle because "in his heart he wanted the missing to be there; he searched because he wanted to find, not just for the money" Weyland, Mundy and the filmmakers are offering.

To explain how that search unfolds and what it finally reveals would be to ruin the suspense of a wonderfully suspenseful mystery tale, but I'll say this much; I can't recall ever before encountering so many twists and turns and counterturns in 215 pages. Karlin is a deft storyteller and a master of brevity, wasting no words yet creating vivid characters and luminous images. Here is his introduction to Bangkok: "The rest of the world in fifty years: permanent gridlock, the sidewalks thick with people grinning as if caught in a joke they could do nothing about." This is Aye Than, a.k.a. Sadong, a.k.a. Kitty: "A hole in the earth for secrets." Here's Fat Al explaining why Mundy and Weyland have come to Loman's bar:

We'll be an expeditionary force. That's why you want us vets, right? We've been to the edge and the edge is us. You can take the boy off the edge, but you can't take the edge out of the boy. There it is. It don't mean nothin'. That's why we love it so. We can use double negatives. We can do anything we want. Then we go back to the World.

This is the first encounter between Mundy and Taksin:

Taksin reached out and seized his face between her hands. She pushed hard on both sides of Mundy's face, bringing her own face closer, staring as if a sickness of her own death had been given eyes into which she could stare. Mundy's eyes darted back and forth, as if trying to look for a way out of his head.

Karlin writes both emphatically and knowledgeably about other peoples and other cultures. Of his three previous novels, *Crossover* and *The Extras* are both set in the Middle East and neither has an American character in it; *Lost Armies* is set in Elliott Mundy's tidewater Maryland congressional district, but contains a number of Vietnamese characters both major and minor. *Us* moves fluidly from Bangkok to Rangoon to tribal villages where what is Thailand and what is Burma become lost in what is merely "mountains. Mountains doan care. Got teak, got elephants, got tigers." Mountains where nats live, prankster spirits of animism predating Buddha and found in one form or another all over Southeast Asia, mischief makers who "do much harm to the order of the world unless appeased with money, food, and the respect of belief."

This particular quality of Karlin's writing—his ability to see through the eyes of people not only different from himself, but culturally removed from us—reminds me very much of Robert Olen Butler. Indeed, until recently, when Butler won a Pulitzer Prize for his seventh book, *a Good Scent from a Strange Mountain*, the two men shared the bittersweet distinction of being the most undeservedly underappreciated writers to emerge from the Vietnam War (Karlin having served as an enlisted Marine in a helicopter squadron).

Now Karlin holds that dubious honor alone. *Free Fire Zones*, a short story collection Karlin co-edited in 1973, and in which his first published stories appeared, was utterly lost in the national hysteria of silence that enveloped this country before the Vietnam War was even over. His three novels prior to *US* all received favorable but limited reviews, low sales in hardback, and no offers for paperback editions. It appears as though *Us* is headed for the same fate.

This is a great shame because Karlin is a fine writer and because *Us* is an informed and unusual exploration of that most nettlesome of legacies from that most nettlesome of American wars. *Us* weaves history, geography, and humanity into a seamless narrative that is relentlessly compelling, frequently startling, and quietly profound. Loman's assertion notwithstanding, Karlin skillfully reminds us that there are indeed facts concerning America's MIAs—what did or didn't happen to them, and why their ghosts have achieved a kind of immortality—that are both disturbing and dangerous, and he tells a heck of a good story in the process.

❖ ❖ ❖

The War That Won't Go Away

[Originally given as a talk at the Austrian Association of American Studies 20th Annual International Conference, University of Klagenfurt, Austria, November 13, 1993.]

In his second inaugural address, delivered only days before the signing of the 1973 Paris Agreements, President Richard Nixon declared that the historic moment was approaching when "America's longest and most difficult war comes to an end." On the day of the signing, he added, "We today have concluded an agreement to end the war and bring peace with honor to Vietnam and Southeast Asia."

Nixon's pronouncements turned out to be a bit premature. Indeed, the war proved to be more durable than Nixon himself: eight months after he ceased to be president, his successor told the American people that the evacuation of the last Americans from Vietnam "closes a chapter in the American experience," insisting that the Vietnam War "is finished—as far as America is concerned."

In the aftermath of the fall of Saigon, however, came the first wave of so-called Vietnamese "boat people" to America's shores, the capture and bungled rescue of the U.S. freighter *Mayaguez*, books like *Born on the Fourth of July* and movies like *Taxi Driver*, all of which served to remind Americans that the Vietnam War was still very much unfinished.

Thus, 21 months after Gerald Ford's too hasty pronouncements, yet another president felt compelled to explain, as he offered a limited pardon to Vietnam War resisters, "I think it's time to get the Vietnam War over with.... The whole thing's over."

Alas, Jimmy Carter's amnesty only reminded Americans just how unfinished the war remained, and the acrimonious debate between those who felt amnesty should be extended to military deserters and those who felt neither draft resisters nor deserters should be given any quarter at all was rapidly followed by the first public revelations about Agent Orange, a second wave of boat people, and the horrors of the Pol Pot regime, each an ample demonstration that Carter had been as overly optimistic about the end of the Vietnam War as his predecessors had been.

One might think it was high time for a bit of reality, but reality had never been actor Ronald Reagan's strong suit, so even before he became president, the former pitchman for Lucky Strike cigarettes declared that it was high time to admit that "in truth, ours was a noble cause" in Vietnam. Nevertheless, throughout his presidency, he was constantly forced to insist that his policies in Central America would not lead to "another Vietnam," and in fact he was driven to great—and often illegal—lengths in order to keep that pledge. Though Reagan would probably have loved to send the Marines storming into Managua, the war in Vietnam was alive and well enough in the hearts and minds of enough Americans that he was forced to rely on a mercenary army and the likes of Oliver North, the Sultan of Brunei and the Ayatollah Khomeini to carry out his wish to destroy Nicaragua's revolution and stymie El Salvador's.

Meanwhile, in a series of concerted efforts to shake off what had long since become known as "Vietnam Syndrome" and re-establish the legitimacy of global U.S. military intervention, Reagan sent the Marines to Lebanon, invaded Grenada, and attacked Libya, all of which he was able to do at virtually no political cost and indeed with the applause of large numbers of Americans. Perhaps the war in Vietnam was finally coming to a conclusion after all.

Nevertheless, when George Herbert Walker Bush invaded Panama, he was very careful to insist that he was only arresting a fugitive drug dealer, he launched his invasion on the least newsworthy day of the year in order to minimize media attention and public reaction, and he made certain, as Reagan had done in Grenada, that the American people saw only what he wanted them to see.

These little exploits of Reagan and Bush, however, were finally petty affairs which convinced no one that the war in Vietnam could be safely forgotten. Thus, more than fifteen years after the last U.S. helicopter lifted off the roof of the U.S. embassy in Saigon, Bush still felt constrained to reassure the American people that the looming war in the Persian Gulf would not be "another Vietnam." This time, he insisted, American soldiers would not be forced to fight "with one hand tied behind their backs." His assertion belied the reality of U.S. firepower in Vietnam, but it effectively tapped into by then deeply rooted beliefs about why the U.S. lost in Vietnam.

Indeed, if Bush did not deliberately provoke Saddam Hussein into invading Kuwait, he clearly recognized what he thought was a golden opportunity, once Saddam did attack, to eradicate forever from the hearts and minds of the American people the seemingly endless war in Vietnam. And when the brief slaughter was over, he very publicly told a group of Desert Storm veterans, "You know, you all not only helped liberate Kuwait; you helped this country liberate itself from old ghosts and doubts." Just in case anyone might fail to understand what those old ghosts and doubts were, he added, "Let this new spirit give proper recognition to the Vietnam veterans. Their time has come."

Of course, Vietnam veterans had been told our time had come when Jimmy Carter declared "Honor Vietnam Veterans Day" in 1979, and again when the Vietnam Veterans Memorial was dedicated in 1982, and again when New York and Chicago and other major cities hosted Welcome Home parades for Vietnam veterans in 1985. But never mind that; this time, it really did look as if, in the words of one contemporary news commentary, "On February 27th [1991], the war ended. The Vietnam War, that is."

In the 22 years since the Tet Offensive of 1968, large numbers of Americans, including significant elements of the military and civilian leadership, had come to believe that the U.S. lost the war in Vietnam not because our intervention was insupportable and our objectives unachievable, but because meddling politicians had refused to let the military fight to win, a liberal press had turned the American people against the war, and a treasonous antiwar movement had undermined the morale of the troops.

Bush would not allow such "mistakes" to be made this time. From the day the Iraqis invaded Kuwait until the day Bush called a halt to the U.S. assault, the military was given everything it asked for. The meddling politicians were dispensed with in a pseudo-debate months after Bush had already determined to go to war in any case, with only a few honorable exceptions the media docilely acquiesced to a level of censorship and sham reportage that made restrictions on World War Two journalists look lax, and a government-sponsored "Support Our Troops" campaign skillfully tapped into lingering societal guilt over the fate of Vietnam veterans in order to insure that any attempt to organize anti-Gulf War resistance would be drowned in a sea of yellow ribbons.

Thus, by early March 1991, it did indeed look like the Vietnam War was finally, finally over. Unfortunately for Bush, the flame of sweet victory was not enough to light his way to another term as president. His defeat must have been especially bitter, coming as it did at the hands of a man who had taken some pains both to avoid and to protest the U.S. war in Vietnam.

Undoubtedly that defeat had much to do with the sorry state of the U.S. economy, but it is also true that as Americans watched the destruction of Iraqi Kurds and Shiites at the hands of the man Bush had so recently claimed to have defeated, as the details of our own lopsided massacre belatedly began to emerge, as they came to learn that our Patriot missiles had actually caused more friendly casualties than the Scud missiles they were supposed to defend against, that Iraqi soldiers hadn't actually torn Kuwaiti babies from their incubators, and that our so-called smart bombs were neither all that smart nor all that widely deployed, many Americans quietly came to the uncomfortable realization that perhaps the Gulf War had not buried as many ghosts and doubts as Bush and they themselves had wanted to believe.

Indeed, before the tickertape and confetti had been swept up behind the last of the Desert Storm victory parades, the Vietnam War was back on the front pages and in the 6 o'clock news, as unresolved and disturbing as ever, this time in the form of photographs purporting to be aging American servicemen still held prisoner in Southeast Asia. It mattered not one whit that the evidence quickly turned out to be fraudulent. Once again the very public debate made it clear that the Vietnam War was alive and well and living in America.

Likewise, from Bob Kerrey's New Hampshire primary swipes at Bill Clinton to George Bush's televised questioning of Clinton's patriotism, the Vietnam War ran like a deep ocean current through the 1992 campaign season. While Al Gore may have much to recommend him on his own merits, I doubt that he would have been Clinton's choice for vice president were he not a U.S. army veteran of the Vietnam War. And anyone who saw the vice presidential debate could not have avoided the conclusion that Ross Perot chose James Stockdale as his running mate only because Stockdale also was a Vietnam veteran and a former prisoner of war to boot.

But as if to demonstrate that election or no election, his victory in Desert Storm had nevertheless freed the U.S. from the straitjacket of "Vietnam Syndrome," in the time between his election defeat and his departure from office, the liberator of Kuwait invaded Somalia. I am tempted to suggest, now that the folly of U.S. military intervention in Somalia has become clear, that Bush's decision was a perverse and deliberate attempt to stick a thorn deep into Clinton's side, but it must be said that I often see brilliant conspiracies where there is only arrogance, hubris and stupidity.

In any case, though it appeared at the time as if the Somalia operation was going to be as easy and lopsided as Desert Storm had been, Clinton inherited a more obvious disaster in the form of Bosnia, and Desert Storm notwithstanding, the parameters of the domestic debate about how the U.S. should respond in and to Bosnia have been very much framed by the late and still flourishing war in Vietnam. Moreover, as the situation in Somalia has deteriorated, comparisons with Vietnam have become equally explicit. On Cable News Network not long ago, I heard a U.S. Representative from Connecticut say, "I'm beginning to think [Somalia] is like the situation in Vietnam."

Thus the American War in Vietnam goes on and on, an open sore on the body politic, a powerful and evocative talisman whose meaning is as multifarious and incomprehensible as the tongues that emerged from the rubble of the Tower of Babel.

Why should this be so? Let me briefly suggest a few of many reasons. For one thing, the United States lost. Americans are not accustomed to losing wars. We didn't actually do all that well in the War of 1812, roughly half of us lost the Civil War, and the Korean War didn't come out as a resounding victory either, but Americans are a people largely oblivious to history, our own or anyone else's. The vast majority of Americans take it as an article of faith that we've never lost a war, and thus the end result of the Vietnam War came as a very rude shock, to say the least.

Most Americans also believe that we are a selflessly good and caring people, a nation of altruists acting for the benefit of others, the downtrodden and the oppressed, often at great cost to ourselves. The United States and its military would never stoop to morally insupportable deeds. Nor would our government willfully lie to us, deceive us, or betray our trust. For many Americans, it remains another tenet of faith that we have, regardless of its flaws, the most perfect form of government the world has ever seen.

Thus, what happened in Vietnam shook our sense of self, both as individuals and as a nation, more deeply and profoundly than any other event in this century. Only the Great Depression posed something like that same challenge to America's self-image, but the ghosts and doubters of that era were buried, or at least glossed over, by the great and unifying crusade of the Second World War, and by the boomtime prosperity that the war and its aftermath brought to Americans.

But because the American war in Vietnam ended as it did, slowly and painfully petering out over the seven years between January 31, 1968, and April 30, 1975, our failures many and manifest, the divisions among us open and raw, and no uplifting and unifying experience coming after to calm and distract and reassure us, nothing like a national consensus on the meaning and lessons of the American war in Vietnam has ever emerged. Attempts to forge such a consensus have repeatedly failed just as surely as the attempts at closure by a long succession of presidents. For each voice that says, 'The meaning of the war is thus and so," there are other voices saying, "No, it is this or that other thing instead."

Let me give just one recent example: Senate passage of a nonbinding resolution urging the lifting of the economic embargo against Vietnam.

The resolution was co-sponsored by Senators John McCain and John Kerry, one a former prisoner of war and a Republican, the other a former member of Vietnam Veterans Against the War and a Democrat. One might think that the alliance of two such disparate men symbolically indicates that Americans are finally ready to end the Vietnam War, but no sooner was the resolution passed than it was condemned by spokespeople for both Vietnam Veterans of America and the American Legion.

The battle lines were drawn even before U.S. troop strength in Vietnam reached its peak, and the bitterness of the struggle for the meaning of the war is hard and unforgiving. So long as such divisive and strongly held feelings remain, the American War in Vietnam will continue, and I believe such divisive and strongly held feelings will remain so long as those who survived those years have breath enough to argue. For better or worse, Americans will put the Vietnam War behind us only when the last surviving member of the Vietnam generation is shoveled into the ground.

❖ ❖ ❖

I Could Not Help My Friend

It's not every day that somebody comes up with something new to say about a poem that's been around for 2700 years. Indeed, more has been written about Homer's *Iliad* than any other work of literature except the bible, so you'd think that what's to say has already been said. What makes great literature great, however, is its ability to speak not only to its own age, but to succeeding ages as well. Jonathan Shay believes the *Iliad* speaks to our own age in ways more contemporary than anyone could have imagined even a few years ago, and his *Achilles in Vietnam: Combat Trauma and the Undoing of Character* (Atheneum, 1994) offers an unusual perspective both on the ancient epic and on a disturbingly contemporary problem.

Shay first began to consider the *Iliad* in the context of the American war in Vietnam while he was working as a psychiatrist in a Boston-based counseling program for Vietnam veterans suffering from severe post-traumatic stress disorder. In his introduction, he explains that he was struck by the similarities between his patients' war experiences and those of Homer's Achilles. Moreover, he says, "Homer has seen things that we in psychiatry and psychology have more or less missed."

Briefly, Shay's reading of the *Iliad* is as follows:

Agamemnon, Achilles' commander, betrays "what's right" by wrongfully seizing his prize of honor; indignant rage shrinks Achilles' social and moral horizon until he cares about no one but a small group of combat-proven comrades; his closest friend in that circle, his second-in-command and foster brother, Patroklos, dies in battle; profound grief and suicidal longing take hold of Achilles; he feels that he is already dead; he is tortured by guilt and the conviction that he should have died rather than his friend; he renounces all desire to return home alive; he goes berserk and commits atrocities against the living and the dead.

This is also, Shay suggests, the story of many combat veterans, including those he has worked with, and he offers the stories of those veterans alongside that of Homer's Achilles. His essential contention is that "catastrophic war experiences not only cause lifelong disabling psychiatric symptoms, but can *ruin* good character." Further, he argues, the two most frequent circumstances which trigger chronic PTSD are a betrayal by someone in authority over him of a soldier's sense of "what's right" (*themis*) as defined by the soldier's culture, and a state of berserk rage following the death of a comrade during which a soldier loses all sense of self-restraint.

Shay's purpose is not merely to point out interesting similarities between the Trojan War and the Vietnam War, but to "protect [our] soldiers with every strength we have, and honor and care for them when inevitably they are injured by their service." To that end, he also discusses differences between the Greek army in Asia Minor and the U.S. military in Southeast Asia, frequently suggesting that the U.S. military could benefit by emulating many of the Greeks' customs and practices. (I use the term "Greek" here, as does Shay, to mean those forces arrayed against King Priam and the city of Troy, forces variously referred to by Homer as Achaeans, Danaans, and Argives.)

He argues, for instance, that the near-instantaneous removal of U.S. corpses from Vietnam battlefields, together with the absence of opportunities to grieve, denied surviving comrades the opportunity to come to terms with the loss of their friends. He also writes that dehumanizing the enemy, reducing them to "gooks," "slopes," "dinks" and the like, caused young soldiers to seriously underestimate their Viet Cong opponents, often resulting in disastrous physical and psychological consequences. He demonstrates, in contrast, that Achilles and his peers frequently engaged in open and prolonged displays of grief, and almost never denigrated their opponents.

He suggests a number of changes in U.S. policies that, in his estimation, would reduce the incidence of PTSD among future soldiers, among them better unit cohesion through reliance on unit rather than individual rotation, recognition of the value of grieving, discouragement of berserking (which he says was frequently mistaken by commanders in Vietnam to be the mark of a good soldier rather than one who was out of control), elimination of intentional injustice as a motivational technique, respect for the humanity of the enemy, and acknowledgement by the military of psychological casualties.

The comparisons he makes between Troy and Vietnam aren't perfect, as Shay recognizes. Achilles and the other named soldiers in the *Iliad* are the equivalent of senior officers, while the veterans Shay works with are enlisted men or very junior officers, men Odysseus describes as "common soldiers ... weak sisters, counting for nothing in battle or in council." There are vast cultural differences: for Achilles, for instance, betrayal of what's right means taking away from him a young woman he himself has recently taken from a town he has sacked, killing her husband and her three brothers in the process. And war itself has changed: imagine, if you can, Lyndon Johnson, Richard Nixon, William Westmoreland and Creighton Abrams among the first rank of fighters, going toe-to-toe with Vo Nguyen Giap and Pham Van Dong.

Still, Shay's comparison is compelling, and he makes a good case for the universality of combat trauma. "I could not help my friend in his extremity," Achilles laments, "He needed me to shield him or to parry the death stroke." And here is one of Shay's vets: "If I was there, he wouldn't be dead.... When he needed me, I wasn't there." Says Achilles, "For me there's no return to my own country." Says another Vietnam vet: "I didn't see myself going home. No ... nope ... no, I didn't."

So complex and ambitious a book, however, is bound to be flawed, and the closer one looks, the more disturbing those flaws become. Let me turn first to the *Iliad*.

Agamemnon does violate "what's right" in Book I by taking Achilles' prize of honor (Briseis) from him, and Achilles does go berserk after he learns in Book 18 that Patroklos has been killed. In between, however, in Book 9, Agamemnon recognizes the injustice he has committed against Achilles and tries to make up for it, offering to return Briseis (whom he swears he has not touched or slept with) along with seven new tripods, ten gold bars, twenty cauldrons, twelve thoroughbred horses, and seven additional women. Moreover, what Agamemnon offers Achilles if Troy falls to the Greeks takes Homer another thirty lines to enumerate. Odysseus, Ajax and Phoinix deliver Agamemnon's apology to Achilles, and add to it their own pleas for Achilles to accept Agamemnon's offer.

But Achilles refuses. One must ask, then, has Achilles' social and moral horizon shrunk because of Agamemnon's betrayal of what's right, or because he is simply, as Diomedes says, deep into his own "vanity and pride"? Is it perhaps Achilles himself, as Ajax points out to him, who betrays what's right by refusing to accept Agamemnon's abject and generous apology? Indeed, Richmond Lattimore, in the introduction to his 1951 translation of the *Iliad*, calls the poem "the story of a great man who through a fault in an otherwise noble character ... brings disaster upon himself[.]"

Shay might rightly respond that Lattimore and other scholars of the classics haven't considered the *Iliad* in the context of PTSD, which wasn't even identified as such until the later 1970s. But Shay is obligated to explain the events of Book 9 in the context of his analysis, for if Achilles' behavior is the result of internal flaws in his character rather than the external forces Shay has identified, at best the extrapolations from Achilles to Shay's patients lose much of their force, and at worst one might conclude that the veterans' problems, like Achilles', are also the result of their own flawed characters. Yet Shay neither explains nor even mentions Agamemnon's apology or Achilles' refusal to accept it.

A second major problem with Shay's analysis of the *Iliad* is contained in Shay's Chapter 7, "What Homer Left Out." Earlier in the book, Shay praises Greeks and Trojans alike for "honoring the enemy," for refusing to dehumanize each other, and he praises Homer for being so acute an observer and for refusing to take sides in the war he describes, instead portraying both Trojan and Greek as honorable and worthy. Even as Agamemnon prepares to put Troy "to fire and sword," he calls the city "holy Ilion" and describes its king as a "good lance."

But in Chapter 7, Shay explains that:

> the bard's need to stay in the good graces of hundreds of Ionian nobles who, through intermarriage, traced ancestry to *both* sides of the Trojan War may account for the astounding absence of villains

in the *Iliad*. This he says just after he has told us:

> [d]eprivation cannot be shown in the *Iliad*, because this would stigmatize the ancestor as poor, reflecting dishonor. This also rules out death by fragging [being killed by one's own men], disease, or friendly fire.

We also learn in this chapter that:

> Homer censors the suffering of the wounded.... Homer shows us only part of the suffering of civilians.... [Agonies falling] upon women after defeat are either passed over in complete silence or minimized.... Homer is silent on [the] hardship [of famine].... Terror is notably absent from Homer's picture of civilians.

How are we to know when Homer is seeing things that we "have more or less missed," and when he is merely pandering to the egos and biases of his patrons? If Shay's failure to explain the events of Book 9 of the *Iliad* leaves a gaping hole in his argument, his astute and articulate explanation of "What Homer Left Out" raises fundamental questions about the veracity of the poet he is relying upon to carry his argument.

One further point on the *Iliad*: toward the end of *Achilles in Vietnam*, Shay argues that "the *Iliad*'s prevailing message on what is of value in life is not Achilles' *kleos aphthiton*, 'unfailing glory,' but rather the social attachments of the domestic world at peace." As evidence he offers a collage of excerpts totaling 28 lines, yet Agamemnon expended more lines than that just to explain all the goodies Achilles would get if he helped in the destruction of Troy and the killing or enslaving of every inhabitant of the city. In a poem that is 15,693 lines long, where Homer's glowing description of the armor made for Achilles by Hephaistos takes up 129 lines, and expressions like "the test that brings men honor" are regularly used to describe combat, Shay's argument that the prevailing message is the value of the social attachments of the domestic world at peace is not convincing.

Let me turn now to the other half of Shay's equation: the Vietnam War and its veterans. To begin with, Shay is all too willing to take has patients' words at face value. As a therapist and healer, he may well be obligated to refrain from second-guessing or judging these men. But as an author who is offering a vision of Vietnam veterans and their world, he is obligated to do exactly that. For instance, one veteran describes himself as "just a typical American boy," but he also says of his childhood:

> I didn't just go to church Sundays. It was every day of the week. I'd come home from school and go right down to the church and spend an hour in the church.

No boy I knew when I was growing up, to my knowledge no boy I have ever met since, went to church for an hour every day after school, willingly or unwillingly, yet this man describes himself as "just a typical American boy ... nothing unique." What else in his testimony is inaccurate? We have no way of knowing, and thus it all becomes suspect.

In another case, Shay describes a patient who:

> was the first to enter a civilian hospital in Hue after the North Vietnamese retreated from the Tet offensive. The North Vietnamese had systematically hacked from the patients' bodies any limbs they had found bandaged with American bandages or hooked up to American I.V.s.

This account is highly suspect, to say the least. I fought in Hue during the Tet Offensive, and I neither witnessed nor heard any report of such an incident. Moreover, I have studied this battle and its aftermath at great length over the years since, and I have never encountered such a story in any source, historical or literary, written or oral, until now. What are we to think about the veteran who has told Shay this story, or about the author who reproduces it without question?

This brings up a related problem: Shay repeatedly writes, "My impression is that...," "the prevailing impression I have been given is...," and similar phrases. In most instances where such a phrase appears—as in his "impression" that the majority of U.S. soldiers in World War Two went overseas, fought, and returned home with the same unit with which they had trained—the information could have been verified, yet Shay does not offer verification, only his "impression." Who gave him that impression? How accurate is it? Why did he not verify it?

Likewise, he uses phrases such as "Everyone knows that...," and "no one questions...," which any good composition teacher will circle in red pen every time they appear. Is Shay, a doctor of philosophy and a doctor of psychiatry, a highly educated and obviously brilliant man, really susceptible to such fundamental errors of argumentation, or is he trying to pull the wool over our eyes? We don't know, but once again, doubts are raised.

Those doubts are deepened as the book progresses and we begin to realize that we are hearing the same few voices over and over again, and even the same words. Though Shay says some 250,000 to 300,000 Vietnam veterans are suffering from full-blown PTSD, and though he speaks of the "many" Vietnam veterans he has worked with, those actually quoted in his book are very few. The testimony of the "typical American boy," for instance, appears three different times in three different contexts, providing "evidence" for a different point each time. If so many veterans are suffering from PTSD, and he has worked with so many of them, why does he have to rely on so few of them to support his arguments? There may well be a good explanation, but Shay offers none.

Let me turn to a problem of a different sort. Shay pays lip service to the notion that veterans of other American wars have also had severe difficulties we now understand to have been PTSD, writing in his introduction that Achilles' story is "also the story of many combat veterans, both from Vietnam and from other long wars." But the very title of the book carries an implicit suggestion that Vietnam veterans have had far more difficulty with PTSD than other generations of American soldiers, and at other places he makes the suggestion something more than implicit. At one point he writes:

> I am often asked why Vietnam apparently caused such a high rate of long-lasting psychological injuries compared to World War II. We have no data for the Second World War ... but I always begin my answer to the question

by focusing on the fact that most World War II soldiers trained together, went overseas together, fought together, had R&R together, and came home together. The typical Vietnam soldier went over alone, ... went on R&R alone, and came home alone.... He had no chance to "debrief," to talk about what had happened[.]

Though he acknowledges in passing that no data exist to support the question's premise, he proceeds to answer the question at length instead of challenging its premise.

A few pages later, he writes:

In World War II, ... that the military services ... evacuated [psychiatric casualties] may have been a major factor that reduced the rate of lifelong psychological injuries from that war.

If there are no statistics, how can he know there has been a reduced rate of lifelong psychological injuries from that war? And reduced in comparison to what? The context makes clear that the comparison is to the Vietnam War, and Vietnam veterans as a group come out on the short end of it. This was the prevailing perception through much of the 1970s, the image of the troubled and broken Vietnam veteran who had failed to handle the rigors of war with the grace and strength of his father's generation, and while sources as diverse as MacKinlay Kantor's 1945 *Glory for Me* and Paul Fussell's *Wartime* suggest the emptiness of the perception, and Steve Bentley's January 1991 essay in the *VVA Veteran*, "A Short History of PTSD: From Thermopylae to Hue," explicitly refutes it, here it is again, in 1994, and coming from someone who ought to know better.

Finally, I want to raise one more objection. Shay's book is subtitled *Combat Trauma and the Undoing of Character*, and he constantly uses the phrase "combat veteran," but he never defines what a "combat veteran" is. Certainly a rifleman who participated in the battle of the Ia Drang Valley, or a mortarman who withstood the siege of Khe Sanh, is a combat veteran, but what about the artilleryman on a firebase that came under ground assault once in the six months he spent there? What about the truck driver whose convoy received occasional sniper fire while driving between Saigon and Bien Hoa? How about the pay clerk at the huge base at Da Nang who took to the bunkers when the base received enemy rocket fire, though no rocket ever landed within a thousand meters of him?

Moreover, can a soldier who is not a "combat veteran" suffer from PTSD? Can a "combat veteran" who didn't have a commander betray "what's right" or lose a special friend or go berserk suffer from PTSD? Most people reading Shay's book would probably conclude that the answer to all these questions is "no." Yet Patience H.C. Mason, in her 1989 book

Recovering from the War, especially "Part One. Vietnam: What It Was," makes a compelling case otherwise, and I am inclined to agree with her.

There are a number of smaller matters I find irritating as well, such as his assertion that black and white soldiers were at risk from each other during the war, though racial tensions did not become a serious problem until after the assassination of Dr. Martin Luther King, Jr., midway through the war, and his misuse of the term REMF (rear echelon motherfucker), which did not include, contrary to Shay's definition, "higher officers and civilian political authorities," all of which raise doubts about the depth of knowledge Shay brings to the war about which he is writing.

For all my reservations, though, I find *Achilles in Vietnam* a book worth serious consideration. That is precisely why I have spent so much time explaining the problems I have with it, rather than dismissing it out of hand. Shay's ideas are thought-provoking and frequently insightful. It was indeed strange and disconcerting in Vietnam that the body of one's friend could be gone almost before it got cold, and one was often left with nothing but the eerie feeling that perhaps one's friend had never really been there at all. And I remember being required to attend a memorial service in the Philippines for two officers who had died in a training accident and thinking with great bitterness that no one had held such a service for the many enlisted friends of mine who had died in battle in Vietnam the year before.

Shay's comparison, too, of Homer's *Iliad* with the story of David and Goliath in the Old Testament's I Samuel 17 is illuminating to say the least, as is his explanation of the differing ramifications and consequences of monotheism and polytheism. He is caustic in exposing the pornographic male fantasy that lies behind Homer's depiction of Briseis, and his equation of Zeus with high politicians and generals who see and present themselves as "deeply caring and compassionate" but whose actions suggest otherwise is wickedly delightful.

Indeed, there is much in Shay's book to admire, and I wish Shay had noticed and tried to correct at least the more obvious problems in order not to detract from the book's strengths. The biggest problem of all, however, the problem that lies at both the heart of the book and the heart of Shay's work, is probably beyond solution.

Twice Shay acknowledges that the only sure way of avoiding "the undoing of character" (i.e. PTSD) is to put an end to war. Rightly observing that an end to war may be a long time in coming, however, and wishing to minimize the numbers of future veterans who end up like the sad and broken men with whom he's been working, his immediate desire is to foster and support "measures to prevent as much psychological injury as possible." To that end, he offers his suggestions for mitigating the worst effects of war on those who fight.

But wishing does not make it so. Perhaps some of his suggestions might help, but I doubt it. The last time we see Achilles in the *Iliad*, he is peacefully sleeping next to Briseis, "lovely in her youth," but Achilles may well avoid "lifelong disabling psychiatric symptoms" not because he prepared Patroklos' body for cremation with his own hands, or because he did not believe in a righteous God whose very conception defined Achilles' self-worth, or because his Myrmidon company trained and fought and went on R&R together, but simply because he is killed in battle soon after the *Iliad* ends.

Sad as it is, Shay and the rest of us must recognize that perhaps sending young men (and now women) off to war is all the "betrayal of what's right" that's needed to ensure that some of those soldiers will come home permanently damaged in their souls. As unusual and interesting as *Achilles in Vietnam* is, finally it is likely to be more useful to those who study and teach the classics than to those who try to prevent and heal the wounds of war.

❖ ❖ ❖

This Is All We Wanted

Most Americans have always defined the Vietnam War as something that happened to us. Consider, for instance, the Vietnam Veterans Memorial, a sober reflection upon our 58,000 dead that avoids any acknowledgement of some three million dead Asians. Or the manner in which we use the phrase "the Vietnam War," ignoring the fact that in this century alone, the Vietnamese have fought "Vietnam Wars" against the French, the Japanese, the French again, the Americans, the Khmer Rouge, and the Chinese. In fact, most Americans, when referring to the war, say only "Vietnam," as if Vietnam itself were a war instead of a country.

Not surprisingly, our national self-absorption is mirrored in the literature that has come out of what more accurately might be called the American War in Indochina (since the war engulfed Cambodia and Laos as well as Vietnam). While any number of books deal with American experiences in Vietnam, very few offer much insight into the people who were both our allies and our enemies. Two that do are Lady Borton's 1984 *Sensing the Enemy*, and her new book *After Sorrow: An American Among the Vietnamese* (Viking, 1995).

Borton first went to Vietnam in 1969, spending two years training Vietnamese to make artificial limbs for civilian amputees at the Quaker

Lady Borton, currently living in Hanoi and representing American Friends Service Committee, addressing the opening of a campaign to support families affected by Agent Orange, March 2001. (Photograph provided by Lady Borton)

Service Rehabilitation Center in Quang Ngai. Then in 1980, she worked as a health administrator in Pulau Bidong, a Malaysian refugee center for Vietnamese "boat people," out of which came *Sensing the Enemy*. But as Borton explains, the boat people made her wonder about "the huge majority of Vietnamese who remained behind, struggling to rebuild their war-ravaged country…. I felt compelled to know those who had chosen to stay."

After Sorrow is the result of that compulsion. Between 1987 and 1993, Borton lived in and shared the life of three peasant communities in Vietnam. She is the first American granted such access by the Vietnamese government since the end of the war, and because of her fluency in Vietnamese and a selfless ability to listen, Borton also gained access to the experiences and feelings of the people among whom she lived. "We have never told these stories," one woman reveals. "Not to each other. Not to anyone."

"When insects ate most of our harvest," Senior Uncle tells Borton of life in French colonial times, "the landlord took whatever was left, and then the landlord took back his land, and he would take your house, and if you had a pretty daughter, he took her. If you still couldn't pay, he beat you! Do you hear me? The landlord beat my grandfather to death!"

"I'll tell you about the time I first learned about 'dead,'" Second Harvest recalls. "My maternal grandfather … and his friend had just celebrated

Tet when the Foreign Legion entered Ban Long.... I came back from working for the rich landlord to find the two elders lying on the earthen floor. Grandfather had bullet holes through his hands, bullet holes through his eyes. That was 1948. I was ten."

In 1954, with the French defeat at Dien Bien Phu, the Vietnamese thought they'd achieved independence. Instead, Autumn explains, "the Americans brought [Ngo Dinh] Diem here to be prime minister.... Diem had been in the United States for four years before! How could he be a Vietnamese leader?" Recalling life under Diem, Second Harvest adds, "The prisons, the beatings, [the executions], that's why we organized [the 1960 Uprising]." And after the American soldiers arrived, Fourth Spring Blossom tells Borton, "Two Americans held cigarette lighters against our house.... They burned our rice, too.... After Agent Orange, we had no fish, and we had nothing to drink."

Finally Borton asks Second Harvest if she is a Communist. "'None of us you've spent time with in Ban Long are members of the Communist Party.... Don't you understand?' Second Harvest says, gesturing toward the creek and the house with its ladder of light lying on the fresh water urns under the thatch eaves. 'This is all we wanted.'"

These are not the stories of generals and diplomats and statesmen, but of the nameless, faceless peasants we interrogated, defoliated, relocated, bombed, shot, burned, bent, folded, stapled, spindled and mutilated, all the while imagining that we could either win their hearts and minds or break their will, and Borton presents these stories, and the people who tell them, with a graceful eloquence that would touch the heart of a stone.

Indeed, *After Sorrow* is filled with a humanity it seems impossible that American policymakers ever actually considered, and one can hardly avoid the conclusion that the outcome of the war was never in doubt, but only its duration. Reading Borton's descriptions of the economic and political changes that have swept Vietnam since the mid–1980s, however, it is equally hard to avoid the conclusion that the belated arrival of the consumer age may well achieve what U.S. military might could not.

❖ ❖ ❖

Freedom Is
Cigarettes and Beer

During retired Admiral James Stockdale's 1992 campaign for vice president, running mate H. Ross Perot, the media, and Stockdale himself regularly reminded voters that he had been a prisoner of war in Vietnam. Likewise, Senators John McCain and Jeremiah Denton rarely appear in the news without explicit mention that they, too, were Vietnam POWs. And Everett Alvarez, Jr., a Vietnam POW for eight and a half years, not long ago was featured in a full-page nationwide advertisement for Philip Morris Industries, Inc., commemorating the 200th anniversary of the Bill of Rights.

To be a Vietnam POW is a badge of honor. Almost by definition, to be a Vietnam POW has come to mean being a hero. Well before the last of the Vietnam POWs were even captured, let alone released, the Vietnam POWs had become the best-known group of POWs in U.S. history. After Operation Homecoming in early 1973, when the majority of Vietnam POWs returned to the U.S. amidst much fanfare and hoopla, they also became the most celebrated group of POWs in U.S. history. And while those who didn't return—the missing in action—have commanded more frequent and more strident attention in the years since, those who did return have entered into the fabric of American culture as perhaps the only easily recognizable and readily accepted heroes of an otherwise failed war.

The impact of the Vietnam POWs has been remarkable, even astounding, especially when one considers just how few POWs there were. The numbers vary depending on who and how one counts, but out of some three million Americans who served in Vietnam, there were certainly fewer than 800 Americans held captive by the Viet Cong and the North Vietnamese throughout the entire American war. Compare this with over 130,000 U.S. POWs in World War Two and over 7,000 POWs from the Korean War, yet POWs from those wars never received the sustained attention and overt adulation heaped upon the Vietnam POWs, or the political capital and material reward accruing to the Vietnam POWs.

Why should this be so? U.S. Army major Elliott Gruner thinks this question is important, and so do I, but you won't find out by reading University of Hawaii English professor Craig Howes' *Voices of the Vietnam POWs: Witnesses to Their Fight* (Oxford, 1993). Indeed, as you read this book, you will be hardpressed to remember that most of this attention, together with its attendant benefits, has fallen not to "the Vietnam POWs" as a whole, but largely to a select group of Vietnam POWs, the so-called "hardliners" or "diehards," those men who were captured prior to 1969, who were imprisoned in and around Hanoi, who refused to cooperate with their captors in any way except when tortured into doing so, and whose stories have collectively become legend. The rest of the POWs, by far the majority, have mostly been deleted from history—certainly they have been deleted from popular memory—as though their captivity never happened.

Howes makes clear that a handful of highly intelligent, highly trained, largely white career military officer/pilots "shared in captivity the desire and time necessary to get their story straight," and even while in captivity prepared what would become "the group history, the official story" of U.S. captivity in Vietnam. He also describes how this "official story" has become "secular scripture" through what he calls "mainstream memoirs" written by various hardliners and through *P.O.W.: A Definitive History of the American Prisoner-of-War Experience in Vietnam, 1964-1973*, commissioned by *Reader's Digest* and published in 1976.

Howes points out, for instance, that even the dedication to *P.O.W.* "reproduces the official story's assumptions from top to bottom.... The Hanoi POWs are first, on top, and named; the civilians get mentioned in passing; and a mass of anonymous enlisted men brings up the rear.... By carefully selecting, excluding, proportioning, and orchestrating their materials, the senior officers ... wrote ... an official defense of the POWs' performance."

But even as Howes acknowledges that "the official story" does not tell either the whole story or the real story of most Vietnam POWs, his own book proceeds to reproduce this distortion so exactly as to make one wonder if he is being disingenuous or merely naive. The chapter titled "The Story's Other Sides," for instance, takes up only 33 pages of this 256-page book, and 11 of those pages are devoted to discredited former enlisted Marine Robert Garwood, the only Vietnam POW ever court-martialed for his actions while in captivity, leaving just 22 pages for the hundreds of POWs who survived the jungle prisons of the Viet Cong in South Vietnam, or who were civilians, or who were women, or who were enlisted rather than officers, or who cooperated with their captors, or who were imprisoned in Hanoi but took an approach to their captivity to one degree or another less doctrinaire, less "hardline," than the relative few who have since shaped "the official story."

Compounding the distortion is Howes' frequent use of phrases such as "the POWs," "many POWs," or "the Hanoi POWs" when he is often talking only about the hardliners. Indeed, the book's very title suggests an inclusiveness that the text simply does not deliver. While there is a veneer of balance to the book, it does not hold up under examination.

Howes tells us, for instance, that while "the Hanoi POWs strongly believed they had followed [the Code of Conduct article requiring that the military chain of command be observed and obeyed in captivity], and survived because of it, ... one group of prisoners survived without any hierarchy at all." We are, however, subsequently given only a single sentence, comprising four and a half lines of text, by way of explaining who survived without any hierarchy and how they did it. Meanwhile, Howes quotes hardliner after hardliner giving testimony to the all-important saving grace of the chain of command. Elsewhere, while acknowledging American mistreatment of Viet Cong and North Vietnamese POWs, he does so in one sentence of less than five lines. Directly thereafter come 17 pages describing in vivid detail the "appalling crimes against U.S. POWs" committed by the North Vietnamese.

Even the veneer of balance falls away during Howes' discussion of antiwar POW George Smith's decidedly non-mainstream memoir, *P.O.W.: Two Years with the Vietcong*. He does not even give Smith's memoir a title until the last paragraph of his six-page discussion, instead identifying it only as a book published by Ramparts Press, and adding that "a writer for *Ramparts*, Donald Duncan, was [Smith's] 'editor'; and the *Ramparts* staff compiled the notes[.]" Howes tells us disparagingly that "Duncan sounds like a pro-Indian Cotton Mather," but he does not tell us—does he really not know?—that before Duncan became a writer for *Ramparts*, he had been a U.S. Army Green Beret master sergeant who had served 18 months of combat duty in Vietnam, facts which lend considerably more credibility to Duncan's assertions that "Vietnam was a racist war" and "American propaganda dehumanized all Vietnamese" than to Howes' assertions that Duncan is "paranoid and polemical" and Smith's story is "self-consciously revisionist."

Nowhere in his discussion of the "mainstream memoirs" does Howes resort to such loaded language, and all of this is packed into the first paragraph of Howes' discussion of Smith's memoir, thoroughly undercutting any appearance of fairness Howes subsequently offers. Indeed, wherever he touches upon "voices" that do not share the viewpoint of "the official story," wittingly or unwittingly he reinforces the marginalization of such voices.

By the time we get to the last chapter of Howes' book, "Keeping the Faith—James Bond Stockdale," it has become very hard to imagine that the impressions Howes creates are unwitting. He calls Stockdale "a philosopher warrior." Soon thereafter, he begins to refer to Stockdale as "Jim," and to Mrs. Stockdale as "Sybil," intimacies that are neither explained nor afforded to any other person in the book. Indeed, there is a quality to Howes' chapter on the Stockdales that can only be described as fawning.

What Howes is trying to accomplish with his book never becomes clear, as though one is watching a movie filmed with the camera's lens not quite in focus. He occasionally refers to early American captivity stories from the New England frontier, but these references are neither frequent enough nor developed enough to provide any useful insights into the Vietnam narratives he discusses or to give any sense of historical context or continuity. The third section of the book is titled "One Man's View," but two of the three chapters contained therein, including the chapter titled "A Prophet Returns to His People," discuss multiple memoirs. At best the book seems little more than a synopsis of the "mainstream memoirs" of captivity in Vietnam, offered with virtually no analysis or criticism or attempt to explain why these particular memoirs have become "mainstream" while the experiences of the vast majority of Vietnam POWs, even those who have published memoirs, have been relegated to the margins of cultural memory.

Far more interesting, lively, and informative is Gruner's *Prisoners of Culture: Representing the Vietnam POW* (Rutgers, 1993), a concise book packed full of powerful observations and provocative insights. Gruner relies upon virtually the same sources as Howes, but his reading of those sources is at once more critical and more thoughtful, and he effectively brings to bear on his discussion a whole range of additional materials such as films and earlier captivity narratives, providing both a historical context and a richness of intellectual engagement that is lacking in Howes' book.

Consider, for instance, Howes' observation that "the lack of attention paid to the 31 servicemen and 3 civilians who 'escaped from or evaded' captivity" is "puzzling.... The best explanation for this neglect is probably a simple accident of history." For Gruner, this in not puzzling at all, and is certainly no accident: "The most prominent POW figures ... were those authorized by the American President and sold by the American media. The most prominent POW figures, the authentic POWs, were those who were freed by the efforts of Henry Kissinger at the Paris peace talks. Others, those who escaped or were otherwise released, did not have the qualities of fame accorded those who were repatriated as part of Operation Homecoming.... In hindsight, the POW almost had to play a passive-victim role to be an authorized hero."

Likewise, Gruner convincingly explains what Howes does not: why some POW memoirs became "mainstream" while others languish in obscurity. Put simply, those narratives which conform to a pre-existing mythology of American innocence and goodness pitted against the forces of darkness and evil become mainstream; those narratives which confirm America's religious, cultural, political, material and even sexual superiority over the captors become mainstream; those narratives in which the POW insists he is a better man for his experience become mainstream; those narratives that provide uplifting closure and validation of the POW experience without raising questions about how and why the authors became POWs become mainstream.

All other stories, along with their authors, disappear from the cultural landscape. "Popular POW texts," Gruner writes (what Howes calls "mainstream memoirs"), "reject equally possible and valid accounts of captivity.

Monika Schwinn, George Smith, James Daly, Dieter Dengler, and John Dramesi do not get government jobs, advertising contracts, and television spots. Their texts slip from the cultural venue and fail to adhere to the surfaces of mass media particularly because they deny the privileged authority many of the other texts claim." POWs who deny privileged authority by "shrinking from describing their experience as some highway to heaven, furnace for natural selection, or scheme of self-improvement" doom themselves to obscurity. Conversely, "everybody who tells the right kind of story will be a 'good soldier.' Everyone who finds some form of redemption, some politically validating truth, becomes a 'good soldier.'"

But as Gruner himself makes clear, he is less interested in the actual experiences of Vietnam POWs while in captivity than he is with what has become of them and their stories since, from whence derives the title of his book. He argues that even those POWs whose stories have become what Howes calls "mainstream," those POWs who were able to exercise so much apparent control over "the official story," have become pawns of larger cultural, political and economic interests:

> The POWs' fame took on a life of its own; the POW image was flattened to a decal. The real "heroes," the ones Americans paid the most to see, the ones who became rich and famous, were the ones who embodied what Americans needed to see rather than what was; the ones who fed their audience imaginary resolutions that created the optical illusion of a just, honest war.... The Vietnam POW had become a prisoner of America's expectations and needs.... The press, the spin doctors in the White House, and the producers in Hollywood would have it their way.

Instructive is the case of Everett Alvarez and the Philip Morris ad ostensibly celebrating the Bill of Rights. The ad shows Alvarez in civilian clothing, and carries the headline, "You'll never know how sweet freedom can be unless you've lost it for 8½ years." Further down in the text, talking about his return to freedom, Alvarez adds, "Everything I touched felt good. Everything I ate tasted good. Everything smelled so good." Gruner points out that among the products sold by Philip Morris, the largest profit-producer—tobacco—is not even mentioned in the ad, yet "freedom apparently has the sensual qualities of the cigarettes and beer Philip Morris wants to peddle. A more accurate caption to this ad therefore might be 'Freedom is cigarettes and beer.'"

But that's not all. Gruner observes that in wearing

> the costume and facial mask of power in this country ... [Alvarez] is the emblem of the recovered Vietnam veteran, ... an emblem for Americans who not only have put the war behind them but also have learned and profited

from their wartime experience. His image is an implicit refutation of the negative effects of the Vietnam War and accompanying post-traumatic stress disorder. His appearance is an antidote for American anxiety in the aftermath of the Vietnam War.... Alvarez's icon value ... allows him to appear at the national level in media publications framed by deceptive claims. Philip Morris has appropriated Alvarez and the POW story from Vietnam to spread its message of 'freedom.' Of course, this concern for freedom is not so much a philanthropic gesture as an appeal for public support to thwart the increasing restrictions on cigarette smoking in America.... At least implicitly, bans on the use of cigarettes equate with imprisonment by the North Vietnamese.

Page after page, Gruner offers this kind of cogent analysis, boring through the surface of things, challenging assumptions, forcing one to look and look again. And he is up front about what he wishes his book to do, which is to answer the question: "Have we taken lived experiences and learned from them, or are we more interested in entertaining ourselves with myths?" At the end of the book, referring back to one POW's description of North Vietnamese efforts to exploit their captives as "the best orchestrated propaganda show this century has beheld," Gruner bluntly concludes: "There was more than one 'orchestrated propaganda show' featuring the Vietnam POW, and the 'best' one opened and continues to appear right here in America."

But Gruner's purpose is not merely to debunk. Toward the end of the book he tells the story of how his own daughter sometimes "plays Cowboys and Indians. She often plays the captive. She enjoys the thrill of the role.... But such imaginative identifications are ultimately destructive. It is no fun being a captive.... After all is said and done, how do I tell my daughter it's no good playing captive?

"Those who read POW stories should know what is at stake and how the stories are produced," he continues. "We should make more of the overall story known before the next human being marches into captivity armed with the Code of Conduct and a myth. Ultimately, I would like us to think about why we have prisoners at all." Gruner goes a long way toward forcing one to ponder that question. Howes avoids it entirely. Therein lie the relative merits of the two books.

❖ ❖ ❖

A Letter from Robert Redford

I got a letter from Robert Redford last week. He wanted me to contribute to the Natural Resources Defense Council to help save America's

National Parks. A worthy cause no doubt, but I couldn't help noticing the irony of a multi-multi-millionaire asking for money from a guy who makes less than $20,000 in a good year.

Usually my junk mail goes straight from the mail slot to the waste basket without passing go or collecting $200. But recently I got curious and decided to see what I was missing, so I saved it all for a week. At the end of the week, it took me over three hours just to sort and cursorily peruse the pile that had accumulated.

Catalogs were by far the most numerous item. I must confess up front that I own several *L.L. Bean* shirts, which is probably where all those other catalog companies got my name and address, but God forgive the slowness of my brain, I just can't comprehend a logic that says if I buy a flannel shirt, I must surely want a $120 set of scrimshaw dominoes from the *Museum of Fine Arts, Boston*. Consider the following, if you will:

Williams & Sonoma, a Catalog for Cooks, offers two and a quarter pounds of Stilton cheese for $46, and for another $22 you can buy an "heirloom quality" silver-plated Stilton cheese scoop. *Levenger, Tools for Serious Readers*, sells a Mandarin Yellow Duofold Fountain Pen for just $679. What that has to do with serious reading, I don't know.

Nor do I know what major league baseball has to do with children's music, but *Music for Little People* offers a three-video set called "Play Ball the Major League Way" from which, for $47.85, your little person can "learn the important fundamentals from the pros."

And that's not all. In *Wireless, A Catalog for Fans and Friends of Public Radio*, you can get four cans of Dale's Wild Meats (rattlesnake, alligator, elk, and buffalo—"all legally obtained," we are assured) for $29.50, but in *Signals, A Catalog for Fans and Friends of Public Television*, you can't get Dale's Wild Meats at any price. Who decided, I wonder, that people who listen to public radio enjoy wild meat while people who watch public television do not?

Meanwhile, if you're looking for bargains, *Brainstorm* sells a giant gumball machine with 3,400 gumballs for $995. And if that doesn't tempt you, how about the $1,800 globe from *Rand McNally Compass*? I'll bet Christopher Columbus would have jumped at the chance to own one of those.

One catalog I usually *don't* throw away until I've studied it thoroughly is *Victoria's Secret*.

This time, however, I had to wade through 46 pages of outerwear before I got to the one—this is the truth—the *one* model in the entire catalog sporting a bra and matching panties. What's so secret about bib overalls, that's what I'd like to know.

But catalogs weren't the only things I got. William F. Keenan, vice president of NatWest Bank, is eager to give me a Gold MasterCard with no annual fee and a $10,000 credit line, and all I have to do is fill out the Applicant Information Card. Wait till he sees my annual income. He won't be so eager to give me a Gold Card then.

Of course, I may be able to change my financial prospects if I take Laurence J. Pino up on *his* offer. He sent me two complimentary tickets to his International Factoring Institute workshop, where he'll teach me how to earn $3,000, $4,000, even $5,000 a week! Nowhere in his four-page letter does he explain why he wants to be so kind to me, but he did include a coupon for a free continental breakfast before the workshop. What a guy.

So is Kenneth Feld, producer of Walt Disney's World on Ice, who wants me to know that "a night of sensational magic awaits the Ehrhart family!" And speaking of family, Mark S. McAndrew, president of the Globe Life and Accident Insurance Company wants to know if I would like to give my grandchildren "the advantage of a $5,000 life insurance policy for $1." Never mind that my only child is just nine years old. When it comes to life insurance, too much is never enough.

On the other hand, too much is more than enough when it comes to junk mail. My one week's collection weighed in at eleven pounds. Over the course of a year, my letter carrier has to haul 572 pounds of mail I don't want. There are twelve other households on my block. That means he's annually toting 7,436 pounds of junk mail up and down my block. That's nearly four tons.

Now imagine how many blocks there are in Philadelphia, where I live. And how many households there are in a nation of 270 million people. It makes my lower back hurt just to think about it. And how many trees does it take to supply all that paper? And how many acres of landfill to dispose of it all?

Maybe Robert Redford should consider calling me next time. Then again, maybe not: he'd probably call just when I'm sitting down to dinner.

Shaking Hands with Abe Lincoln

Recently, while visiting Detroit, I managed to get two tickets to a Redwings hockey game. They cost me the proverbial arm and a leg, but it would be worth it to see Steve Yserman play. I hadn't been to a hockey game in years.

I did not know, until my friend Mike tried to pick me up at the YMCA where I was staying, that the game happened to be the same night President Clinton was making an appearance in Detroit. When Mike finally arrived—late—he explained that he'd had to drive well out of his way because many of the streets were blocked off.

We assumed the president must be speaking at the Fox Theater, only a few blocks from the Y, because we could see the theater encircled by city buses, as if they were a wagon train defending itself against hostile attack. Farther out from the buses stood numerous police cars, police barricades, and finally police on foot.

After much delay, we got past the detours and ensuing congestion only to find an even worse situation as we neared Joe Louis Arena, adjacent to Cobo Convention Center. As we sat in traffic going nowhere, Mike said to a nearby police officer, "I thought the president was at the Fox." The cop laughed. "That's only his motorcade," he replied. By the time we got to the game, we had missed half the first period.

The next morning, as I did most mornings during my stay in Detroit, I went jogging along the Detroit River. A Coast Guard launch was slowly patrolling near Renaissance Center, and I wondered what it was looking for. Then I saw a dozen motorcycle cops, and farther up police cars blocking off several streets. I realized that the president must have spent the night in the center's hotel, but when I asked the motorcycle cops what was

up, they just glared at me as if I were an Iraqi spy seeking information I might use to do the president harm. Moments later, the Coast Guard intercepted a small outboard motorboat with two middle-aged fishermen aboard and sent it back upriver. Maybe they thought its occupants were my accomplices.

I understand that we live in a dangerous world. I have seen one U.S. president killed and another wounded. But it makes me sad that in the name of presidential security, ordinary law-abiding Americans just trying to go about the business of their lives are routinely treated as threats to the president.

This has nothing to do with partisan politics. When George Bush was president, he once gave a speech at the high school football field in Seaford, Delaware. Friends of mine who live in Seaford said that advance secret service personnel warned people living within sight of the field not to open their windows during the president's speech, lest they get shot by government sharpshooters protecting the president from would-be assassins.

Yes, we live in a dangerous world. Jill Messick was raped and murdered in a hotel room in Los Angeles. Sam Rotenberg was robbed and pistol-whipped in his own front yard in Philadelphia. Debbie Johnson has undergone three operations to reconstruct her jaw after getting beaten by thugs who apparently wanted nothing except to beat her. Where were the advance teams to keep Jill and Sam and Debbie safe from danger? Where are the barricades of buses and the phalanxes of police to keep my wife and child safe from danger?

I know we can't return to the days when just about anyone could walk into the White House and shake hands with Abe Lincoln (who was, after all, shot by an assassin). But is it really necessary to close off half of downtown Detroit, disrupting the lives of thousands upon thousands of people, to keep the president safe? Is it really necessary to hold at bay anyone and everyone who can't afford $10,000 to dine with the president at Cobo Center? It strains the credible to believe that any president so insulated and isolated from everything from street crime to traffic jams can have the foggiest notion of the hopes and fears, sorrows and joys of the tens of millions of ordinary people our presidents like to claim they represent.

❖ ❖ ❖

The Summer I Learned to Dance

I thought we were going to make it until I saw the car coming up Park Avenue from Ninth Street. Down at the bottom of the hill, Park Avenue takes a ninety-degree turn to the left, and we were going to reach the turn just about the same time that other car reached it.

"There's a car coming," I said.

If we cut the turn tight to hold the road, we would hit the other car head-on. If we stayed in our lane to avoid a collision, we were going too fast to make the turn. There appeared to be no solution. In one of those terrible moments of revelation that come only rarely in a lifetime, I suddenly understood what all those dead poets I had to read in English class were trying to tell me. In about two seconds, I could be as dead as they were.

My grandfather died, but I'd been so young I could barely remember his funeral. Old Mrs. Crouthamel dropped dead right in the middle of church one Sunday morning, but the angels had come for her—she'd even said so just before she keeled over—and who can argue with angels? My cat had died, and we buried it in the back yard by the garage. Death was supposed to happen to old people and pets. It wasn't supposed to happen to me.

All sorts of things were happening that weren't supposed to happen. When an accident happens, time is supposed to slow down, but it didn't. I saw that car coming, had just about enough time to realize we were in big trouble, and then I had blood all over me and Ray's body slumped over my right shoulder. I never saw the other car go by. I never saw the tree stump we hit. I never felt the impact or heard the crunch.

It was a Friday afternoon only a week after school had let out for the summer, and we were just out cruising. Cruising was what you did if you had any style at all. It meant you didn't have to ride your bicycle like a kid, or ask your parents to take you, or explain where you were going or why. You could go any place you pleased any time you wanted to for any reason or no reason at all. A car was everything. Even if it wasn't yours.

This one belonged to Rich Sharp. It was a 1949 Chevy, one of those humpbacked rolling turtles the size of a tank. The paint was gone, the tires were bald, and Rich always had to park it on a hill because the starter wasn't too dependable, but so what? Rich was driving and I was riding shotgun, my feet up on the dashboard, smoking cigarettes and flicking the ashes out the open window.

Two months earlier, I had wanted to go to a dance one Saturday night at St. Isadore's Church in Quakertown, but my mother had said, "I don't see why you have to go all the way to Quakertown to find something to do."

"It's only seven miles, Mom," I said. "For crying out loud, they've got priests and nuns for chaperones."

"There's plenty to do in Perkasie," she said.

But there was nothing to do in Perkasie, a town of fewer than five thousand souls, and that included the cemeteries. A town with no traffic lights and only one cop car. Even the nearest movie theater was three miles away in Sellersville. I was fifteen years old—sixteen in another four months—and I wanted to dance. Martha and the Vandellas were calling out around the world, "There'll be dancing in the streets," but no one was dancing in the streets of Perkasie.

That Saturday night, I had told my mother I was going over to Jeff Apple's house to mess around, but I didn't go to Jeff's. Instead I hitchhiked to the dance at St. Isadore's. There I met a girl from Quakertown named Andrea Jenkins, and when we danced a slow dance together, it made me feel as if the freedom I desired was mine for the taking, if only I were bold enough to take it. Later Rich Sharp offered to give me a lift home, and I eagerly accepted because it was really cool to be pals with someone who had his own car. He dropped me a block from my house, so that my parents wouldn't see me getting out of a car, and they were never the wiser for the finest night I had ever lived.

That was easy, I thought, and I had done it again the next Saturday night, only I didn't have to hitchhike because Rich was waiting for me up on Seventh Street by Benner's grocery store. I was no longer just a kid with a bicycle. A car was everything, even if it wasn't yours.

Rich and I both worked in the bathhouse at the borough swimming pool. We had to give people wire baskets for their clothes, then the bathers would change and give the baskets back to us to keep while they went swimming. It wasn't much of a job, but it paid eighty-five cents an hour, and we got to mess around with the girls who came to the pool. Debbie Hendricks and Lynn Godshall were only thirteen, and they acted like it, but they had the bodies of sixteen-year-olds. Cheryl Wynn was a peach. It gave us something to think about.

The day of the accident, Rich and I had the afternoon off, so we jumped into Rich's car and cruised over to pick up Ray Thomas and George Edwards. We went by the Dairy Queen, but there were only some kids with bicycles hanging around, so we drove up to the Farmers' Market in Quakertown. It was a good place to go if you didn't have much money. You could walk around and look at the hog maws and skinned rabbits, and maybe there'd be some girls to look at, too, if you got lucky. But there weren't any girls that afternoon, and you can only look at hog maws and skinned rabbits for so long, so after a while we left.

Coming out of the parking lot, Rich put his foot on the brake pedal and it went right to the floor. He pumped it several more times, but nothing happened except that we rolled right out onto the road into the path of a pink '56 Ford. The Ford expected us to stop, and when we didn't, the Ford had to swerve into the opposite lane to avoid broadsiding us. The driver laid on the horn and so did Rich. He shook his fist at us as he disappeared down the road, and we shook ours back at him. There was a service station about half a mile behind us, but we only had fifty-seven cents between the four of us.

"No point in going there," said George.

"I bet Ricky Mills would fix it for us," said Rich. Mills, who dated George's cousin, was a mechanic at his father's Texaco Station.

"Drive back to Perkasie?" said Ray.

"Sure," I said. "Just go slow. We can make it."

The first six miles were easy, a country two-lane road with a few shallow hills and no stop lights and not much traffic. We made it to the top of the ridge overlooking town with no problem. Then we started down the long hill into town.

"Downshift," I said as we started to pick up speed.

"I did," said Rich.

"Jam it into first," I said.

Rich tried, but the gearbox only howled like a meat grinder chewing on ten-penny nails. Those old cars didn't have synchronized gears. You had to be at a dead stop to get it into first. The engine drag in second gear slowed us down some, but not much. By the time we ran the stop sign at Ridge Road, we were doing about 35 miles an hour.

It was a blind intersection until you were almost on top of it. Rich was riding the horn, and we were all hollering out the windows as we shot through the intersection just ahead of two cars approaching from opposite directions on Ridge Road. I got a good look at the face of the woman driving the car on my side. Her eyes were as big as saucers and her lower jaw was somewhere down below the dashboard. I waved to her as we flashed by.

We were gaining rapidly on a car that had just turned off the ridge onto Park Avenue. There was a blind curve to the right coming up fast. Rich was still all over the horn, and we were screaming to beat the band, but the car in front of us wouldn't speed up or pull over, so we had to pass it or ram it. Rich moved out to pass, crowding the other car as close as he could, but we were still out in the wrong lane all the way around the curve. As we came up even with the driver, I could have leaned out and patted the man on his bald spot, but instead I hollered, "Move over, mister, we don't have any brakes!" Then I grinned and waved.

We hit the steepest part of the hill with that ninety-degree turn waiting at the bottom. That's when I saw the car coming up from Ninth Street. It was a station wagon. Even in second gear, we were doing 40 or 45 by now, cranking about seven thousand rpm's, the sheer weight of the car dragging us down the hill, the engine screaming louder than we were, begging for mercy.

And then I was sitting there covered with blood and Ray was draped over my shoulder like one of those skinless rabbits. The windshield in front of me had a big hole in it. I didn't know why. I couldn't tell where the blood was coming from. I didn't feel any pain. I lifted Ray's head. When I let go, it dropped. I looked at Rich. The steering wheel was broken, and Rich was bleeding from his chin and chest. "Let's get out of here," I said. I tried to open my door, but it wouldn't budge, so I followed Rich out the driver's door with George right behind me.

I crossed the road and headed for the nearest house. An old woman came out just as I reached the porch, took one look at me and screamed. Then a younger man came out, took one look at me and disappeared back inside. I put a hand to my throat and came away with a handful of blood. *That's mine*, I thought, but I didn't feel any pain.

A couple of cars had stopped by now, and somebody pushed me down onto the porch steps. I couldn't understand what everyone was so excited about. The man who had run back inside the house came out with a dish rag or something, and somebody put it against my neck and told me to hold it there.

The house didn't have a telephone, so people started running from house to house, trying to find somebody home in a house that did. They looked like actors in a bad foreign film on late-night television, their gestures overdone, their words disconnected from their lips. Rich sat down next to me, holding a cloth to his chin. The cut on his chest was just a scrape. George was walking around talking to people. He didn't appear to be hurt.

"Is Ray dead?" Rich asked.

"He looked dead to me," I said.

"I'll go see," said George.

"What if he's dead?" I said.

Rich looked at me as if he didn't understand what I was saying. The cloth I was holding had become saturated with blood and the blood dripped through my fingers as I held it. After a while, George came back. "I think Ray's alive," he said.

"I thought he was dead," I said.

"I think my car's totaled," said Rich.

"We almost made it," I said. From where we were sitting, you could practically see Mills's Texaco. I still didn't feel any pain. I didn't feel much of anything except a dull throbbing in my neck and a kind of giddy lightheadedness that was not at all unpleasant. It reminded me of how I felt when I was dancing with Andrea.

Judy Harrison's car came down the hill and stopped. "Oh, my God, what happened?" said Judy as she and Pam Magee ran over to where Rich and I were sitting.

"I totaled my car," said Rich.

"I think Ray's dead," I said.

"I don't think so," said George.

"I hope not," I said.

"What are you doing here?" said Rich.

"We were just out cruising," said Judy, who had a blue Ford Falcon.

The girls sat down on either side of us, and Judy took my bloody right hand and held it in hers, stroking it gently as if it were something rare and precious. She was a year ahead of me in school. She dated seniors, and even college guys, and she had never paid more attention to me than you would pay to your kid brother or a cousin you only see on holidays. I was beginning to like the idea of being in an accident.

After a while, Chief Nase drove up with his lights flashing and his siren wailing. Right behind him came the ambulance, also with lights flashing and siren wailing. Ralph Daggett, one of the ambulance crew, ran over to me, took the bloody rag away from my neck, and whistled. Then he took a large wad of gauze and jammed it hard against the wound.

As if someone had turned on a very bright light and shined it directly into my eyes, my head suddenly filled with pain. Blinding, excruciating pain. Then he started wrapping me in gauze, wrenching my head this way and that way and this way again, as if he were wrestling with it.

"Hey, goddamn it!" I shouted. "What the fuck are you doing?"

"Your father would be ashamed if he heard you talking like that," said Mr. Daggett.

"Get away from me!" I hollered. My head felt like the clapper of a very large bell. Mr. Daggett shook his head slowly, as if a great sadness had descended upon him.

Ray had been knocked unconscious. They put him on a stretcher and loaded him into the ambulance. Then Rich and I walked over and climbed in with Ray. When George tried to climb in with us, the ambulance crew told him to go away. It took us several minutes to convince them that George had been in the accident, too. Then we waved goodbye to the girls and off we went.

Perkasie didn't have a hospital either, so the ambulance took us to the emergency room at Grand View Hospital in Sellersville. The doctors and nurses looked George over and told him to go home. They stitched up Rich's chin and released him, too. Ray had a huge lump on his head, so they admitted him for observation.

I got the worst of it. The car had been going fast enough to throw me into the windshield when it hit the tree stump, but not fast enough to throw me out. My head had punched a hole through the glass to my shoulders, then I had fallen back into the seat, shredding the underside of my jaw on the jagged glass. It took Dr. Wynn, Cheryl's dad, five and a half hours and sixty-two stitches to clean out all the glass and sew me back together, but the blood had come mostly from shallow cuts, and none of the cuts had done any real damage. "You were lucky," Dr. Wynn said. "If your jugular vein had been severed, you would have bled to death in minutes."

But I had not bled to death in minutes. When I woke up the next morning, I was in the intensive care unit. A few hours later, they moved me onto a regular ward. My parents were waiting for me.

"I thought you were working yesterday afternoon," my mother said, one eyebrow raised.

"They changed the schedule," I said. "Rich was giving me a lift home, but he had to get something at the Farmers' Market, so I went with him."

"You went to Quakertown?" she said.

"For crying out loud, Mom, it's only seven miles."

I spent the rest of the day entertaining a steady stream of friends. I went home the day after that, and a week later I was diving head-first off the three-meter board at the pool. The following week the stitches came out, leaving me with an ugly knot of bright red scars.

And beautiful scars they were, too. The next time I went to St. Isadore's, Andrea asked if she could touch them. She reached out her hand and gently rubbed her fingertips over them, as if they might begin to bleed if she touched too hard. "You could have been killed," she whispered. Then she kissed me on the mouth, her lips lingering against mine just a moment longer than they needed to, her breath sweet and inviting.

"I know," I said. But in one of those beautiful moments of revelation that come only rarely in a lifetime, I suddenly understood that all those dead poets were wrong after all. My scars were the proof. I had danced with death and lived to tell about it, and now I was dancing with Andrea Jenkins. I knew I could do whatever I pleased. I knew I would live forever.

❖ ❖ ❖

Tugboats on the Delaware

Imagine your car parallel-parked on a major thoroughfare. Think of someplace familiar. You've been to a movie or visiting friends, but when you return to your car, you discover that two other cars have parked really close to your front and rear bumpers, and you realize with a groan that you're going to have one heck of a time getting your car out. "Thanks a lot," you mutter under your breath, the thoughts in your heart considerably darker than the words on your lips.

You think you've got a problem, but it isn't as simple as that because now you need to imagine that your car weighs fifty thousand tons and is 680 feet long. Did I tell you that the road surface itself is moving, like those moving walkways at the airport? Well, it is, so all three cars are tied to fire hydrants and telephone poles to keep them from being carried away. And the lines are all crisscrossed, so you have to be careful not to get fouled in the other cars' lines.

Oh, and you have to consider wind and tide, since a miscalculation of either could result in having your external rearview mirror torn off, or maybe getting the whole side of your car stove in. And it's nighttime, so visibility isn't the greatest. And you can't actually get into your car and drive it; someone you can't see is sitting inside the car giving you directions by radio while you try to move the car with a small lawn tractor.

"Good luck, pal," you're thinking, "and more power to ya." But this is exactly the kind of problem the crew of the tugboat *Teresa McAllister* handles routinely. This time, the problem comes in the form of a ship named *Agia Sofia*, docked at Camden's Beckett Street Terminal: parallel-parked on the Delaware River, you might want to think of it, the bow of the ship pointed upriver, with two other ships docked fore and aft; three big ships, all in a line, with *Agia Sofia* in the middle. *Teresa*'s crew must pluck *Agia Sofia* out of the line and send it on its way without disturbing the other two ships.

Michelle Musto, *Teresa*'s mate, brings the tugboat up under *Agia Sofia*'s port bow. From the wheelhouse, she can look almost directly across at the ship's deck crew, but down on the tugboat's main deck, deckhand Mike Gavin must tilt his head nearly straight back to see the men leaning over the ship's railing high above him. Mostly what he sees is the ship's hull, a dingy black wall of steel liberally streaked with rusty red, towering over him and appearing to lean toward the tug as if it were about to fall on him.

Given that it's two o'clock in the morning, Gavin wouldn't even be able to see that much were it not for the powerful lamp mounted at the front edge of *Teresa*'s wheelhouse roof. It illuminates the forward main deck, allowing Musto and Gavin to see what they need to see, like a small circle of daylight carved out of the surrounding darkness. The sound of water rhythmically slapping steel reverberates above the noise of the tug's idling diesel engine.

Teresa's captain, Bob Foltz, and the docking pilot up on the ship's bridge (that someone you can't see, sitting in your car giving directions by radio) have decided to attach a single line from the tug's main bit to the ship's port bow. There are bits all around the main deck of the tug: shoulder bits, double bits, quarter bits, stern bits, all of them used for securing lines. The main bit is a fat steeel "H" bolted upright to the deck forward of the wheelhouse.

The big 8" lines are too heavy to throw, so Gavin tosses a heaving line up to the ship, the throwing end given heft by a "monkey fist," a round rope knot about the size of a grapefruit but two or three times as heavy. As the ship's deckhands haul the heaving line up, Gavin attaches a heavier line by a series of loose half-hitches, then finally attaches an 8" line, securing the other end to the tug's main bit with a Baltimore hitch followed by three figure-eights, finishing with a single turn around one of the H's uprights, a gesture that signals to Musto up in the wheelhouse, "I'm done; you can pull now."

Once the tug has the ship firmly in its grip, the ship's mooring lines are cast off from the dock. Then Musto puts *Teresa*'s engine in reverse and begins to pull. As the strain on the rope increases, the knot on the main bit begins to "sing"—a sound not unlike Jimi Hendrix playing "The Star-Spangled Banner" at Woodstock—and Gavin scoots around to the side of the wheelhouse just to be safe: lines don't usually break, but when one does, it behaves like a giant rubber band stretched until it snaps, and it will maim or kill anyone it hits.

At first nothing happens. There is only that strange singing, and the heavy rumble of the tugboat's engine straining against thousands of tons of inert steel, and the washboard thumping of the tug's propellor struggling for purchase, and the boiling water churned up by the prop and encircling the tug like a white wreath.

Slowly, however, ever so slowly, the ship's bow begins to pull away from the dock. Finally, as *Agia Sofia*'s bow swings clear of the ship ahead of it, the ship's own engine joins in. This will ease some of *Teresa*'s strain while keeping the ship's stern from slamming into the dock as its bow swings out into the river, but *Teresa* continues to haul the ship's bow counterclockwise, like a small terrier tugging on the ear of a mastiff, because the ship must be rotated a full 180 degrees before it is ready to proceed down-river under its own power.

With the more experienced Captain Foltz quietly coaching, the young mate makes the whole maneuver look about as difficult as pulling your wallet out of your pocket. A graduate of Fort Schuyler, the New York State Maritime Academy, Musto is 27. She holds an unrestricted third mate's license, and got her first ship out of Bahrain during the Gulf War, a voyage that included mines in the Persian Gulf, machete-wielding pirates in the Philippines, a blown engine in the South China Sea, and two months in a Singapore drydock. She was most recently working barges before coming to McAllister Towing of Philadelphia.

Though her license entitles her to sail as mate or even captain of a tug-boat, Musto is quick to say that she still needs a lot more experience with tugs, and she couldn't be luckier than to come under the tutelage of Bob Foltz. Now 63, Foltz quit school at 17 to go to sea, and except for two years as an army combat engineer at the end of the Korean War, he's been sailing ever since. Starting as an ordinary seaman and working his way up to captain, he's worked aboard everything from tankers to pig iron barges to harbor tugs. And if the multiple tattoos on his hands and forearms make him look vaguely like an aging biker, in fact he is a gentle and soft-spoken man, unflappable, possessing good humor in abundance and the patience of a master teacher.

The actual maneuvering of *Agia Sofia* takes about 45 minutes, but *Teresa* is out nearly two hours because the tug has also had to cross the river to pick up the docking pilot on the Philadelphia side and bring him back across to the ship, then pick him up again once the ship is under way (if you want a little thrill, try climbing down a rope ladder at night from the deck of a moving ship to the deck of a moving tug) and return him to the Philly side before recrossing once again to Camden's Two Broadway Terminal, where McAllister keeps its tugs.

By the time *Teresa* ties up and shuts down, it's 3:15 a.m., but by 3:20, all four crew members—the fourth is engineer Joe Molino—are in their cabins and headed for Dreamland. In the tugboat business, you learn to sleep when the opportunity presents itself. *Teresa* will be going out again in less than three hours.

Nestled up close to *Teresa* are *Eric McAllister, James McAllister,* and *Suzanne McAllister* (a rarely used spare tug), in the stillness of the night looking for all the world like a scene out of a children's storybook or a litter of sleeping kittens. No one is awake except the night watchman, sitting in the small office of a barge permanently tied to the pier that serves as McAllister's dockside maintenance and storage facility.

Tied to the same pier is a small Liberian tanker, *Justine,* while the Bahamian freighter *Nyanza,* unloading cocoa beans, is docked at One Broadway, just across the slip from the McAllister tugs. *Moshulu,* a four-masted square-rigger converted into a restaurant and currently under repair, is docked out at the end of One Broadway.

If you stand on *Teresa*'s boat deck, the moving lights of the Philadelphia Electric Company Building, the blue twin peaks of Liberty Place, two of City Hall's yellow clock faces, the red FS of the Philadelphia Savings Fund Society Building, the white lights of the U.S. Customs Building, and the Pennsylvania side of the Benjamin Franklin Bridge all appear through the black skeleton of *Moshulu*'s bare masts and spars, and for a ghostly moment or two you can almost imagine what the riverfront must have looked like a hundred years ago.

The tugboat *Teresa McAllister* approaching its berth at Two Broadway Terminal, Camden, New Jersey, 1996. (Photograph by Randle Bye)

But let's not go back that far. Let's just go back to a cold rainy April morning too shapelessly gray to tell if the sun is up yet or not. Then, as now, tugs and crews are silent, though you can hear a steady stream of water splashing into the slipway from a small opening high up on *Nyanza's* hull, as if someone has left a spigot on, and the dull throb of machinery coming from somewhere deep within the freighter's bowels.

Seabag over one shoulder, duffel bag in hand, I stagger clumsily from pier to barge to the deck of *Teresa*. From an open hatchway on the starboard side, I can look up the two short, steep flights of stairs leading to the wheelhouse. "Permission to come aboard," I call tentatively. The second time I call, a head pokes out of a cabin at the landing halfway up to the wheelhouse. The head belongs to Bob Foltz, who introduces himself, then shows me to a cabin on the main deck port side directly below the wheelhouse. He explains that *Teresa* has just returned from a job up at Tioga Terminal across from Petty Island, tells me there's coffee in the galley, then goes back to bed.

The cabin is just wide enough for a double bunk bed with space to stand and walk to one side of it, and just long enough for the beds and two wall lockers. Two drawers are built in below the bottom bunk bed. The room has an overhead light, and each bed has a reading light attached to the wall or bulkhead. On the opposite bulkhead are two portholes, and below them a radiator. Because the tug's superstructure tapers toward the bow, so does the cabin, and because the main deck sweeps upward as it approaches the tug's high prow, the floor of the cabin sweeps upward, too, though the bunks are level. It's the kind of cozy, oddball niche little kids go nuts over, and it's all mine. At least for a few days.

In the same year Michelle Musto was born, I spent a summer as a deckhand aboard a small Irish coastal freighter carrying general cargo between Dublin and Liverpool. I loved that ship, and I loved that life, and four years later, when I finished college, I went sailing again, this time aboard an American oil tanker off the West Coast. I loved that ship, too, though I was not destined to spend my life as a seaman. Eventually I moved on to other things, but I have never forgotten the sheer joy of a life spent on moving water, and I have never seen a ship or a tug or even a barge in all the years since that hasn't wrenched from my heart a wistful sigh.

So there's no need to tell you that when the opportunity to spend a few days aboard *Teresa* arose, nobody had to ask me twice. I roll out my sleeping bag on the lower bunk, put a few things in one of the lockers, then set out in search of the galley, which turns out to be back toward the stern, separated from the wheelhouse and crew's quarters by the engineroom.

It's hard to avoid the engineroom on a tugboat, but more on that anon. Meanwhile, in the galley, there is thick black coffee in a glass carafe, a deep stainless steel double sink with cabinets above and below, and an industrial-strength stainless steel combination freezer and double-door refrigerator. A table with a bench built into one wall and three stools bolted to the floor resembles a breakfast nook, complete with several rumpled sections of yesterday's newspaper, a half-eaten bag of potato chips, and a loaf of raisin bread. One of the two doors opens onto the starboard main deck, the other into—take a guess—the engineroom. A television sits on a shelf high up the side of the refrigerator, but the beating heart of the galley is a squat iron stove fueled by diesel oil and almost never turned off.

Back in the old days, which for tugboat crews on the Delaware River means prior to the 1987 strike the crews ultimately lost, each crew included a cook (along with an oiler and a permanent mate), but these days crew members get $10-a-day food allowance, and must provide and cook their own meals. For lunch on the day I came aboard, Foltz ate a dish of cottage cheese and peaches, Gavin cooked up a hamburger, and Molino reheated leftover lasagna Musto had made a few days earlier.

But the galley is much more than a floating kitchen. When *Teresa* is not out on the river working, the galley serves as social hall, family room, and waiting lounge all rolled into one. At all hours of the day or night, you are likely to find someone in the galley—sometimes as many as four or five people, if *Eric* and *James* are both at dockside, too—drinking coffee, eating a snack, reading the paper, talking, teasing, just hanging out. Passing time. The picture on *Teresa*'s television goes black every few minutes, so someone has to get up and turn the set off, then turn it on again, the process repeated over and over again with hardly a word of complaint, as though televisions always behave in this manner.

A little before nine a.m., Molino, the engineer, enters the galley through the engineroom door, looking as if he's just gotten out of bed, which he has. His hair tousled and with several days' worth of stubble on his chin, he pours a cup of coffee and sits down heavily. Moments later, Gavin comes in through the other door, looking as wide awake as Molino, and pours himself a cup of coffee. He gets about two swallows down before Foltz comes in and says, "Start 'er up, Joe."

A tugboat is really just a floating engine girdled with huge rubber fenders made from old truck tires. The engineroom of *Teresa* occupies the entire midship from the bilges up through the main deck to the smokestack poking up above the boatdeck behind the wheelhouse. When you step through the door from the galley, you can either use a catwalk made of metal grating to go forward to the crew's quarters and wheelhouse, or go down a steep flight of metal stairs to reach the belly of the engineroom. Surrounded by various generators, pumps, gizmos and all manner of pipes and valves and whatnot, the engine itself—think of your car's engine block without all the paraphernalia attached to it—is about the size of my Subaru Legacy station wagon, not quite so wide but longer and taller.

Forty years ago, when the engine was new, Molino says it could produce 2400 horsepower, but now he's lucky to coax 2100 out of it. Brooklyn born and raised, Molino, 48, has been sailing for 22 years, working his way up from engine wiper (basically a seagoing janitor) to engineer. His first ship was a sludge boat hauling sewage. As he goes through the startup sequence—moving from engine block to pre-lube valves to main bus (the main electrical panel) to DC generator to alarm panel, back to the main bus, to the AC generator, back again to the main bus, all the while throwing levers and flipping switches—he appears to be dancing with his machinery, a measured waltz amid a rising din that culminates in starting the diesel itself, whereupon verbal communication becomes no longer possible.

As soon as the engine is running, Gavin disconnects the power cable that provides electricity from dock to tug when the tug's engine is shut down, then casts off. Gavin, 42, used to work on a fishing boat out of Cape May, catching mackerel in winter, squid in summer, until a cannery in Alaska bought the boat out from under him. He went from fishing to unemployment to another tugboat company and finally to McAllister. Holding an ablebodied seaman's rating, he can throw a line over a dockside bollard as easily as a cowpoke roping a steer, and he can pop it off again with a snap of his arm.

As soon as the lines are clear, Foltz backs the tug out of the slip, then turns upriver. *Teresa*'s job this morning is to undock the Panamanian fruit carrier *Kyma* from Tioga Terminal, then dock it again at Holt Terminal just below the Walt Whitman Bridge. *Teresa* carries a crew of three today. A mate comes aboard only when the work schedule requires an extra hand, so Musto is working aboard *Eric*.

Hard rain has given way to soggy mist carried by a raw wind, and the tops of the taller buildings on the Philly side of the river drift in and out of the clouds. On its way upriver, the tug passes working docks where ships and barges and tugs are tied, abandoned docks that are little more than rotting pilings with trees and bushes growing out of what used to be concrete, and still other docks converted into condominiums. Seen from below, the Franklin Bridge, astoundingly graceful from any angle, gives the illusion of a gargantuan mooring line in the absence of which New Jersey might well slide off the edge of the continent and drift out into the Atlantic Ocean.

While the galley is where it's at when *Teresa* is docked, the wheelhouse assumes that function when the tug is under way. It is much like a cupola, high up and with large windows all around for 360-degree visibility. The windows facing forward open by dropping the glass straight down. The next day, Molino will demonstrate convincingly the usefulness of having windows that open. When a ship's deckhand drops *Teresa*'s line in the water instead of onto the tug's deck (if you think an 8" line is hard to handle, try handling one when it's waterlogged), Molino opens a window and lets fly a series of colorful oaths calling into question the thoughtless crewman's parentage and mental capacity.

Not surprisingly, there's a wheel in the wheelhouse, but neither Foltz nor Musto uses it, Foltz explaining that it's less responsive than the steering handles mounted on either side of it. These handles, positioned so you can steer from either side of the wheelhouse, are reminiscent of a sailboat's tiller, but unlike a tiller (push right, turn left), they work like the wheel (push right, turn right). There is also a throttle on either side just forward of the steering handles: push the throttle to go forward, pull it back for reverse, and the harder you push or pull, the more power you get.

Wheelhouse furniture consists of a built-in map table and two old padded stools like you'd find in George's American Cafe, one of Gavin's favorite hangouts. Two radios hang from the ceiling, along with a depth finder. A sign above the back window reads: "Perfectly Confused." Even with the engine working hard, the wheelhouse is quiet enough to carry on a conversation in a normal tone of voice.

Teresa is back home at Broadway Terminal by 11:30 A.M., with no other jobs scheduled until 8 P.M. The men eat lunch, then Foltz goes to the bank, Molino works on the tug's heating system, and Gavin tops off the fresh water tanks, then cleans the wheelhouse windows. At four o'clock, Foltz, who lives in Clarksboro, New Jersey, and Gavin, who lives in Southwest Philly, go home for a few hours. Molino, who lives farther way in Tuckerton, New Jersey, remains aboard.

Over the next 36 hours, *Teresa* docks one ship, undocks four others, and has one job cancelled before the tug arrives on station. In that same stretch, the tug is idle for periods ranging from one to seven hours. During the longer breaks, Foltz goes home four times, and Gavin three, while Molino and Musto (who rejoins *Teresa* in the midst of these comings and goings) manage to make a run to the grocery store.

Ships come and go at all hours of the day and night, so if you like regular hours and a predictable routine, you don't work on tugboats. For those who do, just to make it more interesting, it's a rare ship that arrives or leaves on schedule. *Pacific Star* goes out two hours early, catching Foltz and Gavin at home, and the two men have to hurry back to work. *Ellen Knutsen*, scheduled to leave at 11 P.M., reschedules for 4 A.M., then keeps *Teresa* waiting another three hours once the tug arrives, so instead of getting a few extra hours of sleep, Foltz, Molino, and Gavin get to watch the sun come up behind the Betsy Ross Bridge. ("You gotta be patient in this business," Foltz says, exercising admirable restraint.) Later in the day, *Teresa*'s crew spends an hour and a half watching *Kyma* unload boxes of fruit with a single deck crane, four pallets to the load, two forklifts scurrying furiously back and forth between ship and dockside warehouse like busy ants storing up for the winter.

Each docking and undocking is different, but in every instance the tugboat's job is the same: to provide the power and agility big ships lack in close quarters at slow speeds. Well, almost every instance.

At sunrise of my third day aboard *Teresa*, the tug goes out to meet a rare visitor to Philadelphia, the cruise liner *Kazakhstan II*, 550 feet long, painted brilliant white, with eight decks above the water line, looking positively regal as it steams under the Walt Whitman Bridge. With *Teresa* running alongside, we can see dozens of ship's attendants, men and women, dressed in black tuxedoes with white shirts and red bow ties—this is at 6:45 in the morning, mind you—and as we approach Penn's Landing, passengers, all of whom seem to be senior citizens, begin to appear on the upper decks so far above us we wonder why they don't all have nosebleeds.

The converted Black Sea ferry comes up almost under the Ben Franklin Bridge, lazily turns counterclockwise until it's parallel to and just below Penn's Landing, then reverses its main engine, engages its bow thrusters, and slowly pushes itself backward and sideways right up to dockside. *Teresa* never does put a line over to *Kazakhstan II*, or rub its grubby black working class fenders up against the liner's pristine hull. Granted that docking at Penn's Landing isn't quite like putting *Nyanza* into the slip at One Broadway, it's still an impressive performance by a ship that's almost two football fields long and taller than the old Lit Brothers Department Store Building just up Market Street beyond the Liberty Bell.

Back at Two Broadway, there is no work today for *Eric*, a mixed blessing for the crew: it's a day off, but also a day without pay, the rule being "no work, no pay." *Teresa* and *James* are scheduled to go to Delaware City— nearly four hours each way—to undock the Indian supertanker *Kishore*. *Teresa*, slower than *James*, sets out at 10 o'clock. Before we reach the mouth of the Schuylkill River, Gavin is asleep, and Foltz, too, soon goes below. Molino remains in the wheelhose, keeping Musto company.

After two unseasonably harsh days with the wind whipping the river into whitecaps, this day is gorgeous—clear and bright with temperatures in the 60s—and the river is full of traffic: a red and black barge moves upriver, pushed by the tug *Morton Bouchard, Jr.;* *Teresa* overtakes the barge *Phoenix*, towed by *Miss Yvette* out of Houma, Louisiana; a pretty little red, blue, and white Dutch tanker, *Hoendiep*, comes upriver.

Though it looks small next to the ships it handles, *Teresa* is 92 feet long and draws 14 feet of water. Running wide open, the tug pushes a white wall of roiling water in front of it and leaves deep swells fanning out from its stern. So powerful is it that every time it passes or overtakes a barge and tug, Musto must slow down for fear that *Teresa*'s wake will snap the lines holding barge and tug together.

Teresa passes under the Commodore Barry Bridge, soon coming upon two small launches headed upriver with something in tow. A helicopter circles overhead, and the launches are soon joined by a small Corps of Engineers tug. Musto and Molino take turns with a pair of binoculars.

"It's a harbor seal," says Molino.

"A harbor seal?" Musto replies. "It's as big as the boat!"

"Maybe it died of obesity," Molino says with a wink. (It turns out to be a dead fin whale that makes the front page of the next day's *Philadelphia Inquirer*.)

By the time *Teresa* passes under the twin spans of the Delaware Memorial Bridge, *James* is closing from astern. The tugs arrive together at the entrance to the Chesapeake & Delaware Canal, just below Pea Patch Island, then turn up Bulkhead Shoal Channel to Delaware City, where *Kishore* is waiting. The tanker is a behemoth: 900 feet long, drawing 60 feet when fully loaded. Since the Delaware River channel is only 40 feet deep, the tanker has had to offload part of its cargo to barges before entering Delaware Bay to discharge the rest directly at dockside. Now the ship is empty and ready to leave.

Gavin is out on deck by now; Musto is still at the helm. The docking pilot puts *James* on the tanker's starboard stern. *Teresa* will start out on the tanker's starboard bow, then switch around to the port bow. Musto brings the tug right up under the ship's massive bulk, which literally blocks out the sun, leaving the tug, including the wheelhouse, completely in shadow. The ship's starboard anchor, angry rust red and as big as a Winnebago, hangs out threateningly over *Teresa*'s forward main deck where Gavin works. Foltz comes up to the wheelhouse and casually asks Musto why she's positioned the tug so far forward.

"The pilot wants me on the stem," she replies.

"Don't listen to him," Foltz replies, laughing. "You're the captain of this ship." But then he goes on to explain that she only needs to be up near the stem—the very front of the bow—once she switches the tug over to the port side.

"I've never done this before," says Musto.

"Well, now's your chance," says Foltz. He grins, then adds, "No one's perfect. That's why they have White-Out for the dispatchers. You're gonna make mistakes. The important thing is to learn from them. You're doing damn good."

Once the tanker's mooring lines are clear, *James* must keep *Kishore*'s stern away from the dock while Musto maneuvers *Teresa* between the tanker's bow and a barge docked just upriver, then between the ship's port bow and the dock, a little tugboat ballet. Gavin has not put a line up to the tanker's deck; the tug will simply push against the tanker's hull with it's bow fender. "Okay, open it up," the pilot radios once the tug is in place.

Once again, nothing seems to happen for a few moments except a lot of sound and fury, but at last the tanker's bow begins to move away from the dock. While *Teresa* pushes, *James* pulls until the tanker is far enough off the dock, then *James*, too, comes in close and begins to push, the two tugs rotating the ship 180 degrees in the narrow channel as if it were the arrow on *Wheel of Fortune*'s game board.

"Okay, go have your lunch now," Foltz tells Musto once *Kishore* is moving under its own power. "You've done all the work."

"I felt like I was going to hit everything," Musto replies.

"But you didn't hit anything," says Foltz. "You're projecting. Don't worry about it until you hit it. Close doesn't count in this business. You take it too seriously. Life's a comic strip."

"When you see me in my lifejacket with my wallet in a plastic bag," adds Molino, "then you get worried."

After Musto goes below, Foltz says, "She worries too much. She's a good boat handler."

By the time *Teresa* takes the docking pilot off *Kishore* and returns him to the dock, *James* is long gone. Musto and Gavin are both sleeping. Foltz sits on his barstool, leaning against the wall, one hand resting on the starboard steering handle as casually as if he were tooling down the interstate in the family sedan. Molino lounges comfortably at one end of the map table, using an old sofa cushion for padding. The two men, with 66 years of experience between them, quietly watch the river sliding by beneath them on its way to the sea.

Late in the afternoon, with *Teresa* still well downriver, the dispatcher radios that there's no work scheduled for the next day: all three boats will be laid off; all three crews will get no pay. Foltz and Molino take the news stoically; you can't work tugboats if you can't roll with the punches. For the crew of *Teresa*, there will be other days and other ships to handle.

For me, there will not. When we tie up tonight, I'll pack the seabag I haven't used in 24 years and will probably never use again, and I'll return home to my wife and daughter. I'll be happy to see them again, for I have missed them very much, which is why, perhaps, I was never destined for a life on the water. But tonight I will dream the smell of diesel fuel, and the piping hoot of *Teresa*'s whistle, and the heft of an 8" line. And tomorrow I'll wake up remembering that what for most of us is the stuff of dreams, for some uncommon few is the way things are.

❖ ❖ ❖

"*What Grace Is Found in So Much Loss?*"

"It would not be unreasonable to assume," I wrote in a 1987 essay called "Soldier-Poets of the Vietnam War" (*Virginia Quarterly Review*, v.63, #2), "that by this time whoever among Vietnam's veterans was going to surface as a poet would by now have done so…. But the appearance in 1984 of D. F. Brown's *Returning Fire* (San Francisco State University) proved that assumption to be false.

"Best of all," I added, "poets like Bruce Weigl and John Balaban are still young and still producing. One hopes for the same from Brown, Gerald McCarthy and others. A poem of Walter McDonald's recently appeared in the *Atlantic*. And other poets may yet emerge. Vietnam veteran Yusef Komunyakaa has published excellent poems in recent years in magazines and anthologies…. Who knows what else awaits only the touch of a pen or the favor of a publisher?"

The essay was a survey of the remarkable body of poetry written by American veterans of the war, the size and quality of which then already exceeded that produced in the wake of any previous American war. Have the poets I wrote about continued to produce? And have other poets emerged? The answer to both questions is yes.

Here is what the poets I discussed have accomplished since I wrote that essay: John Balaban has published a children's novel, a memoir, and another collection of poems, *Words for My Daughter* (Copper Canyon, 1991), which was a National Poetry Series winner; Horace Coleman has published *In the Grass* (Viet Nam Generation & Burning Cities, 1995); Yusef Komunyakaa has published seven collections of poetry, including *Neon Vernacular* (Wesleyan, 1993), which earned him a 1994 Pulitzer Prize; Gerald McCarthy has published *Shoetown* (Cloverdale Library, 1992); Walt McDonald has published eight additional collections of poetry, including *The Flying Dutchman* (Ohio State, 1987), winner of the Elliston Prize, and *After the Noise of Saigon* (Massachusetts, 1988), winner of the Juniper Prize; Bruce Weigl has published *Song of Napalm* (Atlantic, 1988) and *What Saves Us* (Triquarterly, 1992), as well as co-translating *Poems from Captured Documents* (Massachusetts, 1994) with Thanh T. Nguyen.

A number of other soldier-poets have also published first books since I wrote that essay, including R. L. Barth, George Evans, Jon Forrest Glade, David Huddle, Steve Mason, Leroy V. Quintana, Larry Rottmann, Bill Shields, and Lamont Steptoe. Of particular significance was the publication of *Visions of War, Dreams of Peace* (Warner, 1991), an anthology of poetry by women Vietnam veterans, few of whom had ever been published before, edited by two former army nurses, Lynda Van Devanter and Joan Furey. For the first time, the voices of women—some 15,000 of whom served in Vietnam with the U.S. military, the Red Cross, the USO, American Friends Service Committee and other organizations—joined the chorus of Vietnam War poets, filling a conspicuous void.

All of the poets I've thus far mentioned are discussed in Vince Gotera's *Radical Visions: Poetry by Vietnam Veterans* (Georgia, 1994), but within 18 months of the publication of Gotera's landmark study, four still newer collections of poetry appeared, each of them by Vietnam veterans in their mid–40s to early 50s yet only now publishing first books.

Doug Anderson, a navy corpsman attached to the Marines in Vietnam, contributes to the body of Vietnam War poetry *The Moon Reflected Fire* (Alice James, 1994), which earned him the Kate Tufts Prize for a first book of poetry (he had previously published a chapbook, *Bamboo Bridge*, Amherst Writers & Artists, 1991).

The Moon Reflected Fire begins with a sequence of poems set in Vietnam during the war. In the first poem, "Night Ambush," while lying in wait, listening to the unsuspecting villagers—"children and old people"—Anderson considers what he has become:

> Things live in my hair. I do not bathe.
> I have thrown away my underwear.
> I have forgotten the why of everything.

The unresolved tension of the poem's conclusion—"A black snake slides off the paddy dike / into the water and makes the moon shiver"—sets up the poems which follow.

In "Two Boys," a machine gunner uses "three / children dawdling to school along a paddy dike" for target practice. In "Free Fire Zone," an eighteen-year-old Marine "who thinks / Christ is about to rain death on commies / kicks the family altar to pieces in an old mud hut." In "Infantry Assault," an entire village (perhaps the one in "Night Ambush"?) is destroyed in one long sentence fragment spanning twenty lines and four stanzas (the fragment is a device Anderson is fond of, using it here and elsewhere to good effect).

The consequences of such actions are everywhere. In "Bamboo Bridge," Anderson's patrol comes upon a young woman bathing in a stream who "turns and sees us there, / sinks into the water, eyes full of hate." The same hatred stiffens the courage of two Viet Cong snipers in "Judgement" who pin down Anderson's unit, taunting them:

> *We will die to hold you here*
> *while the others slip away toward the mountains.*
> *What will you die for?*

—and the recklessness of the old woman in "Mamasan" who "stands in front of the lead tank / [and] breaks the tank's searchlight with her hoe." The final poem in the opening sequence, "North to Tam Ky, 1967," suggests both how Anderson survived and what it cost him:

> I had inside of me in those days a circuit breaker between head
> and heart that shut out everything but the clarity of fear.
>   * * * * *
>   I flipped the switch and went cold,
> the same whose wires I tinker with these twenty-three years after,
> a filament flickering in the heart and then the blaze of light.

The middle two sections of the book offer a historical and literary context for Anderson's Vietnam War poems. Part Two, "Los Desastres de la Guerra," is a ten-part poem set during the Spanish Civil War. Part Three consists of poems based on Homer's *Iliad* and *Odyssey* in which Anderson repeatedly holds up for scrutiny the difference between legend and truth, myth and reality. The final poem in this sequence, however, "Erebus," deals not with Homer's place of darkness, but with Anderson's. In a dream, he finds himself among the dead he thought he'd left behind:

> *What took you so long, Doc,* they say.
> They ask where you've been and you can't tell them.
> Over twenty years since you got lost coming home,
> and now you're back, ... but this time
> naked and without a weapon.

It is this vulnerability, the sense of being "naked and without a weapon," which gives the final section of the book so much power. "Used to be I'd get a bottle," he writes in "Blues":

> and drink until the lights went out
> but now I carry pain around everywhere I go
> because I'm afraid
> I might put it down somewhere and lose it.

In "The Wall," he writes, "We who fought there never imagined we would return to such a world, / to such a monument, numb, we did not yet imagine that for us the war / had just begun." In "Yes," he describes how Corporal T

> pushed the old man into a bunker,
> rolled a grenade in after him
> and I said *No,*
> four seconds before the mortal crunch.

Reflecting upon the incident years later, Anderson concludes:

> ... that sound, *No,*
> echoes even now in me,
> a resonance from which so many yesses come,
> and I've grown to love the part of me that spoke it.

But there can be no final resolution, no clean way to make it all come out okay in the end. In "Mugging, Brooklyn, 1981," he writes: "How my life is known by glints that promise knowledge / and how with every truth the darkness seems to double."

Kevin Bowen's poems are quieter, less apparently anguished than Anderson's. In *Playing Basketball with the Viet Cong* (Curbstone, 1994), one glimpses only occasionally the war itself, as in "Body Count: The Dead at Tay Ninh," where he writes of "bodies so close together lies came easy. / They slept; they weren't really dead. / They'd wake up when the war was over," or in "Incoming":

> Don't let them kid you—
> The mind ... moves of its own accord,
> even hears the slight
> bump the mortars make
> as they kiss the tubes goodbye.
> Then the furious rain,
> a fist driving home a message:
> "Boy, you don't belong here."

But even "Incoming," beginning in the *then*, slides into the *now*, concluding:

> This is why you'll see them sometimes,
> in malls, men and women off in corners:
> the ways they stare through the windows in silence.

Most of these poems deal not with the war, but with the war's multiplicity of consequences. A former 1st Air Cavalry trooper, Bowen has spent the past decade as director of the William Joiner Center for the Study of War and Social Consequences at the University of Massachusetts at Boston, working with American and Vietnamese veterans in both the U.S. and Vietnam.

In "Reunion," dedicated to Vietnamese painter Le Tri Dung, Bowen describes the first meeting in forty years between a former North Vietnamese soldier and his aunt who left Vietnam and settled in Louisiana: "All night, like figures in his paintings, / they reach for sun and moon on wings, / ride above a plain of sorrow." In the title poem, he plays basketball in his Dorchester driveway with filmmaker Nguyen Quang Sang. To Bowen's amazement, the former Viet Cong guerrilla sinks ten baskets in a row. "It's a gift," Sang tells him, "good for bringing gunships down."

Bowen's Vietnamese are neither faceless enemies nor inscrutable allies nor helpless victims, but people who are, and always were, not much different from us. In "River Music," he describes a postwar evening in Vietnam in the company of friends:

We drink rice liquor, toast
ten reasons men fall
in love on a river.
The old men smile into their instruments.
A woman sings, such beauty
even the moon might die
on her shoulder.

And if in Vietnam today,

bombs still explode,
rip arms and eyes from farmers.
Fish never returned.
Each year more topsoil washes off.
Spring, the forests lose more cover,

as he writes in "Graves at Quang Tri," nevertheless "the full moon on the hill / returns belief, and nights the young go dancing."

The young don't go dancing in the poetry of David Connolly, who is the poetic equivalent of a punch in the solar plexus. So visceral and immediate are the poems in *Lost in America* (Viet Nam Generation & Burning Cities, 1994), they will take your breath away. Consider "Food for Thought, 3:00 A.M.," quoted in its entirety:

They moved in unison
like dancers in a ballet,
the spider, twenty inches from my rifle,
the VC, twenty feet farther out, in line,
each slowly sliding a leg forward.
I let the man take one more step
so as not to kill the bug.

Or these lines from "Thoughts on a Monsoon Morning":

I hate every fucking one of you
who make dollars from our deaths.
I hate every fucking one of you
for my friends' dying breaths.
I hate every fucking one of you
banker or corporation head.
I hate every fucking one of you
for so many, so young and dead.

Connolly, who fought as an infantryman with the 11th Armored Cavalry Regiment, is peerless at bringing to life the ruthless drudgery of battle. In "The Chicken-man," he describes how a friend died "blowing snot and bloody bubbles, / eyes wide and full of fear, / fingers digging at the clay." In "Tet, Plus Twenty Four," one of six extraordinary prose poems in the collection, he beckons: "See, around that corner, in neat lines along the street, there are beautiful trees in full bloom and American soldiers, dead for days, in full bloat." Even the humor is ruthless, as if, D. F. Brown once wrote, "something warped it out of place." Something did. Here is "No Lie, GI," again in its entirety:

Poet and Vietnam veteran David V. Connolly at home in South Boston circa 1997. Connolly served in Vietnam with the 11th Armored Cavalry Regiment. (Photograph by Anne Ehrhart)

We had a deal, he and I, of no bullshit between us.
If one of us got wounded,
the other wouldn't lie.
So when he got hit
and he asked me,
"How's my leg?"
I looked him straight in the eye
and told him, "It's fine."
It looked fine to me,
laying over there,
looked as good as new.

Connolly, like Bowen, has arranged his poems in one continuous but nonchronological sequence, moving back and forth between *then* and *now*. Because the center of gravity in Connolly's collection is located closer to the war itself, however, the effect of the resulting juxtaposition is more pronounced, reflecting the ways memory weaves the war in and out of Connolly's life. In "Psych Evaluation," a young graduate student

is asking me why I'm smiling.
His eyes can't see my Brothers
on either side of him
giving him the finger,
blowing kisses at this punk
and his clipboard full of questions.

In "After Hearing Hueys and a Hunter in the Woods," he suffers a flashback while walking with his two young daughters. In "The Lost Piece," he says, "I still stand / with my back / to the wall." And in "The Little Man," he wakes up from a recurring nightmare "screaming, gagging," his wife trying to comfort him:

"Dave, it's OK."
But you see it will never be OK. That [VC] will make his run in my head as I helplessly watch and neither time nor her tears will make him stop. It is not my fault I couldn't stop him. I know that. I've always known that. But now she thinks it's her fault because she can't.

What animates Connolly is the desire to teach others—especially young people—what he has learned, so that another generation might not have to learn the same lessons all over again. He is under no illusions, however, about his prospects for success. "Don't believe a word I say," he writes in "Don't Go to War Stories":

Don't even listen.
I was nineteen once
and I knew it all.
Say, "Frig him"
over your shoulder
and go off
to kill other children.
Do it and die,
or drag home
what's left of you
and try to deal with it.

Dale Ritterbusch, too, places the lessons of the war at the heart of his writing, even titling his book *Lessons Learned* (Viet Nam Generation & Burning Cities, 1995), but his expectations are, if anything, even lower than Connolly's. In "Geography Lesson," he decries "the silence of the world/in response to inarticulate horrors." Speaking to dead comrades in "Friends," he laments, "All that death for nothing but a few stories," then adds incredulously:

      there are those who wish they'd
joined you—seen the gunship downed,
the fuelship blown up on the pad,
body parts strung out like ornaments,
who wish they'd gone and gotten a few themselves—

           * * * * *

Friends, a fool's rain falls
and falls upon your sinking graves.

Not surprisingly, these poets return often to the dead, and Ritterbusch is no exception, condemning the callous squandering of so many lives. In "Shoulders," he recalls a pre-war conversation with a fellow officer in which the two men talked not of women's breasts or legs, but of their shoulders, then goes on to say that

      some nights when I lie with my wife,
I curl my hands around her shoulders and pull tight—
and see your hands, your heart and lung all shot away,
and somewhere, shoulders, shivering.

In "When It's Late," he imagines the wife, son, and daughter another dead friend never got to have. But it is not only his own dead he mourns.

Officer Candidate Dale Ritterbusch, U.S. Army, Fort Benning, Georgia, 1967. (Photograph provided by Dale Ritterbusch).

In "Winning Hearts and Minds," he writes of a woman who "has lost one son to the VC, another / to an air strike," and who tries to flee, an infant in her arms, from the Marines who are burning her house down, but instead "falls / against the hard luck of Vietnam," a country he describes in "On the Gulf of Siam" as "a land much loved by war."

Ritterbusch, an army lieutenant and liaison officer based in Thailand, coordinated a program for the aerial mining of the Ho Chi Minh Trail. But in "Search and Destroy" and other poems, he writes as convincingly of the ground war in Vietnam as if he had been an enlisted rifleman:

> So we threw in another grenade and one of the
> dinks brought down his arms, maybe he started
> to sneeze with all that crap running out of his face,
> maybe he had a weapon concealed, I didn't know,
> so I greased him. Wasn't much else I could do.
> A sudden move like that.

After his discharge, Ritterbusch comes back to a world to which he no longer belongs. "I don't recognize the family portrait / hanging on the wall," he writes, again in "Geography Lesson," describing his own front yard as a "land I cannot recognize as home." Returning to college, in "Back in the World," he has to borrow some notes from a professor:

> I was ... responsible for
> my men, their lives, and megabucks worth of equipment and
> such, and here he kept asking me if I'd bring
> that chickenshit paper back to him.
>   * * * * *
>
>   "Yeah, right." I knew then
> I'd never make it.

The predominant feelings one gets from these poems are bitterness, disillusionment, and betrayal, but there are poems in this collection (and not a few of them) whose tenderness startles all the more for being found in the midst of harsher emotions. In "At the Crash Site of a B-52: January 1994," he writes of a Vietnamese mother whose young son died beneath the wreckage of an American bomber, and of the American recovery team that comes looking, years later, for evidence of the plane's crew:

> They find a major's insignia.
>   * * * * *
>
> They dig deeper, screen more bone.
>   * * * * *

Poet and Vietnam veteran Dale Ritterbusch visiting the Citadel in Hue City, Vietnam, 2000. With him is his guide, Hoa. (Photograph provided by Dale Ritterbusch)

> She recognizes the bones of her son
> the way she imagines the major's
> mother would recognize hers, if she let go,
> … if she'd only learn
> that war is not something you come back from
> whether you are killed or not, that resurrection
> is only a story for the gods—that a candle,
> the perfume of burning incense, a flower
> growing from the garden of this blackened earth
> brings more than a lasting peace, more
> than a mother can hope for.

And in "Taps," when his daughter hears taps being played in a war movie on television and, having heard the tune only around a Brownie Scout campfire, asks, "How do *they* know that song?" Ritterbusch silently prays

> to all the gods who ever
> interfered in the lives, the wars, of men
> never to have her know that music
> other than around the fire toasting marshmellows.

I concluded "Soldier-Poets of the Vietnam War" by saying, "One would like to think that the soul of the nation might somehow be cleansed [by poetry], but that is hardly likely. More realistically, one hopes that in writing these poems, the poets might at least have begun to cleanse their own souls of the torment that was and is [the Vietnam War]."

Since I wrote those words, American soldiers have invaded Panama, Iraq, Somalia, and Haiti (and as I write this, are poised to enter Bosnia); the most popular public figure in the United States is a Vietnam veteran named Colin Powell; and a president who actively avoided service in Vietnam has extended economic and diplomatic recognition to Vietnam. For the nation as a whole, the Vietnam War has become only a bizarre assortment of myths and misrepresentations and lies rapidly disappearing into the fog of history.

But at least for those who fought the war, the ugly truth of it simply will not go away, as Anderson, Bowen, Connolly, and Ritterbusch vividly demonstrate. Revisiting old battlefields in "Nui Ba Den: Black Virgin Mountain," Bowen wonders, "What grace is found / in so much loss?" These poems are the answer to his question. These poems are the grace that's found in so much loss. And if governments and nations remain impervious to the grace of poetry, I'll still pick poetry every time.

❖ ❖ ❖

On Inflammatory Rhetoric

Twelve years ago, while my wife and I were house-hunting in Philadelphia, our car broke down. When we casually told the tow truck driver that we were looking for a house, he replied, "Oh, this is a good neighborhood. You won't find any niggers living here." We never looked at another house in that neighborhood. Instead we bought one in the integrated neighborhood where we've lived ever since.

No thoughtful person would ever suggest that racism has been eliminated from the American landscape. The racist attitude of that tow truck driver was so deeply ingrained he simply assumed that if we were white, we must surely think like he did. But I find that man's attitude no more disturbing than the attitude embodied in the concluding statement of a press release, recently issued by the Pennsylvania Office of Democratic Legislative Information, concerning the African American Reparation Study

Commission Act. The sentence read: "America continues to allow the disease of racism to continue without seriously attempting a cure."

While slavery was legal between 1619 and 1865, it is also a fact that all through those years significant numbers of Americans—black and white—refused to accept or tolerate slavery, sometimes at considerable personal sacrifice. And while the benefits of emancipation were largely nullified by multiple and nefarious means both legal and illegal over the course of the following century, again significant numbers of Americans—black and white—refused to accept or tolerate Jim Crow, sometimes at considerable personal sacrifice.

In my own lifetime, we have witnessed the removal of every single legal manifestation of racism in American society from transportation to education to employment to sports and recreation. If the Supreme Court's decision in *Brown v. Board of Education*, the Civil Rights Act of 1964, the Voting Rights Act of 1965, to mention only a few landmark events of the past fifty years, are not serious attempts to cure racism in America, I'd like to know from what dictionary the Pennsylvania Office of Democratic Legislative Information takes its definition of the word "serious."

A great many people are still racist, of course, and I am not for a moment suggesting that removing the legal manifestations of racism is the same as removing its actual manifestations. But when people get caught being racist these days, as often as not they have hell to pay for it, as the recent outcry over the "Texaco Tapes" once again made clear. You can still be a racist in America, but it's getting harder all the time.

Meanwhile, one might do well to consider that while the father of my Marine Corps buddy John Harris fought in a segregated military, Harris himself did not, and Harris's son is a lieutenant of Marines. And if it is true that Martin Luther King, Jr., was murdered by a white man, it is also true that I cannot hear Dr. King's "I Have a Dream" speech without my eyes welling up with tears at the beauty of his words and the profound sadness of his loss.

Indeed, though you can still find all too many people like that tow truck driver my wife and I met, right in our own neighborhood you will also find good and caring people—black and white—who are trying very hard and with much success to live their belief in racial equality and social justice, sometimes still at considerable personal sacrifice.

I'm not convinced that we need a special commission "to determine," in the words of Pennsylvania state representative John Myers, "whether slavery in fact does have a lingering impact on descendants of Africans and African Americans," since the answer to that question already seems pretty obvious. I am convinced, however, that we do need an atmosphere of openness and cooperation that will foster continuing progress toward the complete elimination of racism in America. And I am equally convinced that the Pennsylvania Office of Democratic Legislative Information does not cultivate such an atmosphere by making factually indefensible and divisively inflammatory assertions.

❖ ❖ ❖

A Modest Proposal

I was watching a National Football League playoff game last December when an advertisement came on that left me absolutely flabbergasted. It was a beer commercial, but instead of beer bottles wearing football helmets or Clydesdales pulling a sleigh down a snowy country lane, U.S. soldiers in Germany were sending holiday greetings to their families and friends before deploying to Bosnia.

Now that's taking commercialism too far, I thought. Since only a handful of the 20,000 U.S. soldiers headed for Bosnia got the chance to say hello to Mom and Dad, this was clearly a cynical attempt by Corporate America to hustle beer under the guise of providing a public service to our brave men and women in uniform.

But the more I've thought about that ad, especially in light of the apparently endless and certainly shameless posturing by Congress and the President over balancing the federal budget, the more I've come to believe that good old American commercialism hasn't gone far enough.

Advertising, it seems to me, is the means by which we can balance the budget and eliminate the deficit without cutting a single program the loss of which might result in the failure of an incumbent member of Congress to gain reelection. The government can underwrite the entire cost of the Defense Department through corporate advertising, thus reducing federal expenditures by billions and billions of dollars at one fell swoop.

Consider, for instance, that beer ad. Do you think Michael Jordan pushes Nike sneakers for free? Charles Barkley peddles Right Guard because it changed his life? Why shouldn't those soldiers get paid by Miller Brewing Company, thus relieving U.S. taxpayers of at least that much of the burden of their salaries? And why shouldn't Miller pay the army a fee for the use of those soldiers? After all, they're supposed to be working for you and me, not for some brewery.

But that's only the beginning. Except for rank insignia, name tags, and a few other odds and ends, soldiers' uniforms are mostly free of adornments. The rest of the uniform is space to be rented to the highest bidder. Picture the Apple logo on every soldier's helmet, a Marlboro patch on the left shoulder of the dress uniform, maybe a Calvin Klein jeans ad on the back of the field jacket.

Or advertisers could specialize. Navy uniforms could sport ads for Evinrude and Mercruiser; United Airlines and USAir could advertise on Air Force uniforms. Champion could sponsor mechanized units, requiring their members to wear spark plug patches over the right breast pocket. Viacom could acquire exclusive rights to the Signal Corps, Bechtel Construction to the Corps of Engineers.

And don't forget all that hardware. That's ad space, too. Think about those racing cars at Indianapolis Motor Speedway. Why not Abrams tanks and Bradley Fighting Vehicles festooned with ads for Valvoline, Texaco, and the Pep Boys? Or F-16s with Dow Chemical painted on the underside of the wing next to the napalm bombs. National Rifle Association decals on the stocks of M-60 machine guns and M-79 grenade launchers.

An old saying has it that an army travels on its stomach, so those ready-to-eat meals soldiers carry into combat could carry ads for Betty Crocker, Nabisco, and Frito-Lay. Mess halls back in the more secure rear areas could be managed by Pizza Hut, Burger King, and McDonald's. What a difference those golden arches might have made in Mogadishu a few years back.

Much as Corporate America has commandeered the post-season college football bowls, we could have the Revlon First Marine Division, the L'Eggs 101st Airborne Division, the Boeing 37th Bomber Wing, and the FedEx Seventh Fleet. Regional and local companies, too small to afford a whole division or carrier group, could sponsor smaller units like Filene's Basement Regimental Landing Team, the Blue Diner Battalion, the Shelly & Festermacher Hardware Store Rifle Company, and Ralph's Sandwich Shop Platoon.

Really big spenders, on the other hand, could purchase the rights to entire deployments, police actions, and wars. Consider the Chrysler NATO Implementation Force (U.S. contingent), the Chiquita Banana Haitian Occupation, or the Wells Fargo Bank Bosnia American Zone. Broadcasters and journalists would be obligated to state the full name each time it comes up, much as sportscasters have to say the Core States Spectrum or the USF&G Sugar Bowl.

In the unfortunate event that some of our brave soldiers fall in battle or otherwise come to a sad end, we could even sell advertising space on those government-issue plain aluminum caskets: "With Deepest Sympathy, The Prudential."

Tasteless, you say? Is it any more tasteless than using Bosnian-bound soldiers to sell beer? Especially when you consider that Bosnia is a predominantly Muslim country, and Muslims don't drink alcohol, and our government doesn't want to be insensitive to the host culture, so those soldiers in the beer ads won't even be allowed to drink beer the entire time they're on deployment. American soldiers far from home and in harm's way, and they're not even allowed a beer once in a while after a hard day of peacekeeping? That's not only tasteless, it's cruel and unusual punishment, and that's a violation of our Constitution.

But it's also business, and what's good for General Motors is good for America, so don't tell me about tasteless. This is a plan that can save Medicare, Head Start, AmeriCorps, aid to education, the entire Commerce Department, Newt Gingrich and Bill Clinton while balancing the budget and eliminating the deficit: "Old Milwaukee and the Green Berets. It doesn't get any better than this!"

❖ ❖ ❖

Indecent Techno-assault

Over the past five years, the pressure to get on the Information Superhighway has been building mercilessly. I have not been eager to tackle the Worldwide Web because I have enough trouble dealing with my computer as it is. Every time I turn it on, it says, "You are one sorry techno-dummy." As if I needed to be reminded, but there it is: a mistake I made the first time I plugged it in, and I can never undo it because only at Step Four did the manual I'd been religiously following tell me, "Back on Step Three, you had one chance to do it right, and you didn't. Too bad. Now your computer will taunt you for the rest of its life."

I came within an eyelash of ending its life right then and there. It's no state secret that I'm very much more handy with a 16-pound sledgehammer than I am with a Macintosh Performa and I very much enjoy smashing things that make me angry. But it had taken me ten and a half years to amass the money needed to replace my breathtakingly, heartbreakingly antiquated Apple IIe, and after a terrible internal struggle that went on for many tense minutes, a kind of wisdom had prevailed.

Learning to use my new computer was about like trying to saddle break a zebra—I mean, they *look* like horses, don't they? It shouldn't be this hard—but eventually I managed to master it well enough to begin producing manuscripts of poems, essays, and articles neatly printed on my astoundingly slow but barely affordable laser printer. Only then did I discover what has remained ever after yet another almost daily reminder of just how techno-incompetent a fellow with two college degrees can be.

In my profession—writing—technology has become so advanced that editors don't want you to send them manuscripts anymore. They want—indeed, demand—that work be submitted on computer diskettes, so all they have to do is pop the diskettes into their own computers and produce camera-ready copy without the need for typists, typesetters, or layout people. (Ever wonder where all those homeless street bums came from?) Meanwhile, the editors themselves collect fat paychecks for doing next to nothing.

It's a great racket if you can get into it, but the first time I sent a diskette to an editor, she popped it into her machine and it came out gibberish. The same thing happened when I sent another diskette to another editor. It happened a third time, and a fourth time, and finally a techno-nerd I know asked me a few questions and discovered that I had somehow managed to purchase an Apple computer with something called BeagleWorks installed on the hard drive, a combination apparently no electronic translator on earth can decipher.

So every time an editor tells me to send it on diskette, I have to say, "You won't be able to read it." And invariably the editor says, "I can read anything. Send it." And three or four days later, I'll get a telephone call that begins, "What the hell kind of techno-jerk are you, anyway?" And I think about my sledgehammer.

So I haven't been too keen to launch myself into cyberspace. But when even my travel agent asked me for a fax number, and greeted the news that I didn't have one with a palpably contemptuous silence, I knew I could hide from techno-progress no longer. I had a second telephone line installed, bought a fax machine, and called an internet provider.

I don't need to tell you that none of this stuff is cheap, and I haven't the stamina to tell you the adventures I had installing the internet software except to say that along the way I managed to disconnect most of my neighbors from the local power grid while plugging my television directly into the video security system at the Central Bank in Addis Ababa, but eventually I got it up and running well enough to discover that I need a faster modem if I want to get on the Internet in under three hours, and I need to triple my computer's memory if I want to stay on the Internet longer than three minutes at a time.

I'm told all this techno-gadgetry will increase my earning power. Right now I could use a little earning power because I'm stymied until I can figure out how to pay for a new modem and more of those RAM things. The bank tells me there's no such thing as a third mortgage, and even Phil Rizzuto at the Money Store won't go near a guy with a word processing program run by the Beagle Boys. But a nice young couple from Schenectady who can't have children of their own because his techno-weenie shortcircuited in an electrical storm is very interested in my first-born child.

If you meet me in cyberspace, you'll know I closed the deal.

❖ ❖ ❖

Military Intelligence

One Friday morning in March 1997, I found myself sitting at the kitchen table of a house in West Point, New York, while a U.S. Army colonel—in uniform, a silver eagle gleaming on either shoulder—stood at the stove cooking scrambled eggs and bacon for my breakfast. It was at once perfectly normal and perfectly strange, and I couldn't help thinking to myself, "My, my, haven't you come a long way."

You must understand that when I was an 18-year-old Marine in Vietnam, my battalion commander was only a lieutenant colonel, and he was God. You had to go all the way to regimental headquarters to find a full colonel, and I don't recall ever actually speaking to one. Now I had one making breakfast for me. You must also understand that ever since I got out of the Marines, I have been a vocal and persistent critic of the American war in Vietnam in particular and of the U.S. government in general.

So you wouldn't really expect to find me hanging around colonels' kitchens, but the story gets even stranger because I'm at West Point to speak to a group of U.S. Military Academy cadets who have been reading my poetry in Colonel Joseph T. Cox's English class. Later that morning, a cadet will ask me what I think the U.S. should have done differently in Vietnam. I will reply that the United States government had only one choice to make, and that was on September 2nd, 1945, the day Ho Chi Minh declared Vietnam an independent country. I will tell the cadets that we made the wrong decision in refusing to recognize Vietnam's independence from France, and from that day forth, all other choices we made regarding Vietnam were not only wrong but irrelevant to the final outcome of the war. The only question left to be settled was how much destruction and misery and death the French and then the Americans would inflict upon the Vietnamese before the Vietnamese got their independence.

I spent three days at the Military Academy, speaking in a half-dozen classes and giving a poetry reading for the English Department faculty, and more than once I noticed heads nodding in agreement, especially among the officers—even at times when I wouldn't have expected it.

If you had told me just ten years ago that I would be reading poetry at West Point, I'd have asked you what you'd been drinking, and could I have some? I would certainly not have included members of the U.S. military among those interested in what I have to say.

But in December 1993, at Notre Dame University at a conference on the war, I met Joe Cox, Lt. Col. Thomas G. Bowie, Jr., and Maj. Elliott Gruner. It is a rare and wonderful thing for me to meet someone who has actually read and likes my work. These three had and did, and the fact that they were active duty military officers certainly got my attention.

Cox gave a paper titled "American War Myths and Vietnam Veteran Narratives," and Bowie gave one called "Reconciling Vietnam: Tim O'Brien's Narrative Journey," and for all the world they sounded just like

Colonel Joseph T. Cox with the author at the U.S. Military Academy, West Point, New York, 1997, where Cox was then teaching in the English Department. Cox retired in 1998 after 30 years of service and is now headmaster of the Haverford School in Haverford, Pennsylvania. (Photograph by David F. Brown)

a couple of scholarly college professors. I soon discovered that whatever else each man is—Cox is a paratrooper and a ranger, Bowie's a B-52 navigator, Gruner's field is Special Forces—each is also a Doctor of Philosophy and a college professor.

My encounter with these men was a kind of epiphany for me. It is my opinion that the officer corps of the U.S. military was decimated by the Vietnam War. Large numbers of thoughtful and competent officers were driven out of the military for objecting to U.S. policies in Vietnam, or quit in disgust, leaving behind those who either supported the war or were willing to hold their tongues in the interest of their careers. (As an army major in Vietnam, for instance, Colin Powell wrote an official report dismissing rumors of a massacre at My Lai and other atrocities, concluding that "relations between [American] soldiers and the Vietnamese people were excellent." Powell's assessment, which can only be explained as blockheadedly incompetent or calculatedly dissembling, would have gone unchallenged had it not been for the courage of a young soldier named Ron Ridenhour and the tenacity of an investigative reporter named Seymour Hersch.)

Two things I had not taken into consideration, however, until that conference at Notre Dame: first, at least some good officers did stay in, men like Joe Cox, who earned two Bronze Stars in Vietnam; second, an entire generation of younger people like Tom Bowie and Elliott Gruner had entered the military after the end of the Vietnam War. These men considered the war something to be examined, pondered, and learned from. For someone whose main contact with the military in the previous 25 years had been watching Stormin' Norman Schwarzkopf dressed in his spotlessly clean desert camouflage fighting uniform boldly addressing television cameras 300 miles from the fighting, these men were something to think about.

Shortly after the conference, Cox sent me some poems he'd written. Along with a couple that dealt with war themes (none about his own experiences) were a love poem, an elegy for Geronimo, an imagined meeting between Walt Whitman and Emily Dickinson, and a reverie about his father as a young man. They were beautiful and well-wrought poems.

Gruner, meanwhile, sent me a copy of his just-published book, *Prisoners of Culture: Representing the Vietnam POW*, a book so insightfully iconoclastic that I literally had to keep looking at the blurb on the back cover to remind myself it had really been written by an active duty army major.

Also within weeks of the conference, I got a letter from Bowie asking if I might submit some of my poetry to *War, Literature, and the Arts*, a journal of the humanities published by the Air Force Academy English Department. Back in 1985, during my first postwar visit to Vietnam, I met the editors of the Vietnamese army literary journal, and I remember thinking, "Imagine the U.S. Army publishing a literary journal." Which I could not—but here it was. Okay, this was the air force, not the army, and it wasn't started until 1988, but close enough.

The next year, Bowie and the journal's managing editor, Donald Anderson, asked me if I would come to Colorado to the academy for four days in the winter of 1996 when Bowie would be teaching my book *Passing Time: Memoir of a Vietnam Veteran Against the War.* I accepted the invitation.

This, remember, was a year before my visit to West Point, and I was not at all accustomed to hanging around with field grade officers. People kept introducing themselves as Jack Shuttleworth and Rich Lemp and Jim Meredith, and I'd look at those silver eagles and silver and gold oak leaves, and I'd think of my battalion commander who was God, and for a day and a half I'd smile and nod and say, "Pleased to meet you." They clearly didn't want me to call them "colonel" or "lieutenant colonel" or "major," but for the life of me I just couldn't get "Jack" or "Rich" or "Jim" out of my mouth. You don't call God by his first name.

Finally, however, during a four-mile run with Shuttleworth, Gruner (who was on interservice loan to the air force) and Bowie, it finally began to sink in at gut level that I wasn't a Marine lance corporal anymore.

"You're a writer," I thought, "And these guys think you're a good writer, God bless 'em, and most of them are younger than you are anyway. So why don't you just relax and have some fun?" Thereafter, it was "Jack" and "Elliott" and "Tom," and I had lieutenant colonels opening doors for me and majors fetching sodas for me, and I didn't even deign to talk to captains or lieutenants unless I was feeling especially benevolent.

Donald Anderson, editor of *War, Literature, and the Arts.* Though Anderson, formerly a lieutenant colonel, retired from the U.S. Air Force in the mid–1990s, he still teaches in the English Department at the Air Force Academy in Colorado. (Photograph provided by Donald Anderson)

I didn't actually get that carried away, not overtly at least, but I did enjoy myself and the company in which I found myself, and once again I learned things that gave me pause. Donald Anderson, for instance, "joined the air force to avoid the draft—*the army tour of Vietnam*—my choices ruled by the distant battle," as he explains in the introduction to *Aftermath*, his anthology of post-Vietnam War fiction.

Anderson recently retired as a lieutenant colonel after 22 years, but remains on the academy's English Department faculty. He is an accomplished fiction writer, receiving a National Endowment for the Arts fellowship in 1996. "*Aftermath* and 'Twenty Ways to Look at Fire' [a short story of his] are antiwar," he told me. "Of course they are! All good art about war falls into that category. I can't imagine a pro-war novel or story."

Of today's cadets, Anderson says, "Sometimes people think the kids I teach go home at night and polish shell casings, but that's not true." Indeed, I've discovered that the responses I get from cadets aren't much different from those I get on any college campus: some students think I'm a Commie creep, some listen with focused intensity, some have their minds on Thursday's physics exam or Friday night's date. The primary attractions of the service academies are a good education free and the prospect of a career upon graduation. While the cadets wear uniforms and salute almost anything that moves, on balance they're neither more nor less ideologically motivated than any other group of college kids.

Still, teaching *Passing Time* to future military officers? After all, the book presents a very unflattering portrait of the country we live in and the government we live under. I asked Bowie about that, to which he replied, "If these kids don't think about these issues now, they never will think about them until it's too late."

"I don't mind paying taxes for *his* salary," I thought.

Meanwhile, *Busted: A Vietnam Veteran in Nixon's America*, published in 1995, was having a tough time. *Publisher's Weekly* dismissed it. The *Washington Post* said it contained nothing new. The *Philadelphia Inquirer* excoriated it. Among the few good reviews it received were one in the *Nation* (no big surprise, I suppose, given that magazine's general bias), but also one in the *Marine Corps Gazette* (which is, as its masthead states, "The Professional Journal of the U.S. Marines," and which was, at least to me, a big surprise indeed). The *Gazette* ran not just a book review, but a three-page essay dealing with all three of my Vietnam War-related memoirs, written by Edward F. Palm, a retired Marine Corps major who'd served as an enlisted man in Vietnam.

The following year, 1997, I went to West Point, which brings me back to where this essay began. A few weeks before I arrived at the Point, I had received an invitation from a major general to attend the 43rd Annual National Security Seminar at the U.S. Army War College at Carlisle

Barracks, Pennsylvania, in June. "Now this is getting too bizarre," I thought. "What am I doing wrong that all these military types are suddenly taking so much interest in me?" But when I told Cox about the invitation, his response was, "Oh, no, you should go. You're exactly the kind of person these people should be hearing from."

"These people" are lieutenant colonels who spend a year at the war college on their way to becoming colonels. Not all of them will become generals, but you don't become a general without passing through the War College. Civilians attend the seminar at the end of the year-long curriculum to provide the uniformed officers with civilian perspectives and to reconnect them with the people for whom they ultimately work—or at least that was the rationale provided in the invitation. In practice, it seemed mostly an opportunity for the army to score public relations points. One might less charitably call the week a "Dog & Pony Show." Among other things, we were serenaded by the 82nd Airborne Division chorus, presented with glossy color photographs of our seminar groups, and awarded certificates at least as impressive-looking as the one it took me four years at Swarthmore College to earn.

To be sure, the dozen or so officers in my seminar group were bright and educated people, but they were not, for the most part, interested in teaching 19th century American literature or writing scholarly articles about Edmund Blunden. One officer described to me with almost childlike glee the effect of American depleted uranium artillery rounds on the occupants of Iraqi tanks. Another suggested we might take a lesson from the Saudis and cut off the hands of thieves.

Most disturbing was the general reaction to one speaker who argued that the high homicide rate among young black men should be treated as a public health problem. Of the men who spoke up, the clear consensus seemed to be that this is a family values problem that must be solved by parents teaching their children character. Their ideas were far removed from the reality of life in contemporary urban America, and when I tried to explain the fact of crime even in my middle class neighborhood, their reaction was, "Why don't you move?!" As if my moving would solve the problem, end of discussion. And I could not help thinking, "What America do these guys imagine they're defending?"

Even in Carlisle, however, there were pleasant surprises and certainly much to learn. One member of our seminar group, the only woman and the only African-American, privately thanked me for my comments about urban America. It also turns out that the war college library has nine of my books, and Lt. Col. Tim Lynch had taken the trouble to read three of them before I arrived, sharing them with his wife and 14-year-old son David as well. So when Lynch asked me to have dinner with them one evening instead of taking the tour of the Gettysburg battlefield, I readily agreed. After dinner, Dave got out some of his poetry, and the two of us spent a good hour huddled together over the dining room table talking poems. When Lynch drove me back to the hotel that night, he tried to thank me for the time I'd taken with his son, but the pleasure was mine.

So what next? Poetry at the Citadel? Who knows? I do know that ten years ago I would not have been able to spend an evening drinking beer at the Carlisle American Legion Post with a group of army officers who see the world very differently than I do, let alone enjoy myself in the process. And if one of those officers has a fondness for artillery shells that I can't share, there were other things I could share, and much in him to admire and appreciate. (For one thing, he makes home-brewed beer, which he calls Gunzelbrau, and it is very, very good.)

What's changed? Why now when not before? I was very young when I joined the Marines, 17, and I went to Vietnam eagerly and with the highest of ideals. What I experienced there permanently bent my life like a tree forever after denied the freedom to grow straight, and in the next few years, as I pored over documents from the *Pentagon Papers* to *Bury My Heart at Wounded Knee*, the confusion and hurt I had brought home with me deepened into bitterness and rage.

The author *(bottom row, second from left)* at the U.S. Army War College National Security Seminar, Carlisle Barracks, Pennsylvania, 1997. Also Lieutenant Colonel Tim Lynch *(top row, fifth from left)*. (Photograph provided by W.D. Ehrhart)

Two things became fixtures of my life. The first was a permanent distrust of my government, an unrestorable loss of faith in the system and the institutions that had placed me and my generation so needlessly and cynically in harm's way. The second was a passionate desire to salvage something worthwhile from the disaster that had befallen me, my country, and most of all the people of Indochina. I did not ever again want to find myself so horribly on the wrong side of humanity. I wanted my writing to make a positive difference in the world.

Maybe it has and maybe it hasn't. It certainly hasn't made the difference I'd hoped for, and the world doesn't seem much improved for my efforts, or anyone else's either. We mostly just keep muddling along, trading Vietnam and Biafra for Bosnia and Rwanda, and I often feel as though I'm the last member of my generation to realize that the Age of Aquarius passed us right by without even stopping to say hello.

But that same sense of resignation, of profound weariness, has also made it possible for me to look at other perspectives and other points of view without feeling as if I must make people see what I see or risk failure on a cosmic scale. Call it giving up, call it mellowing, call it maturity—I don't know. I do know that I'm just as weary of those I've come to call the "Professional Peace Crowd" as I am of those who want to settle every dispute by force of arms, and I've also noticed that as often as not, lately, it's the military trying to put the brakes on a civilian establishment righteously demanding, "Send the Marines!"

Indeed, I am coming to realize that the uniformed services are just about the only segment of American society that has actually turned around, stared the Vietnam War right in the face, and tried to come to grips with it. I don't agree with all the conclusions the military has come to—in fact, I don't think I agree with most of them—but I respect their efforts to learn something useful. Certainly our political institutions have never dealt with that war in any constructive way, and it's not likely they ever will. Most of the media haven't done any better, and our educational institutions, especially at the secondary level, have dealt with the war abysmally or not at all.

Rightly or wrongly, I still distrust my government, and I will never again willingly put my life into the hands of those with the legal right to dispose of it as they see fit, expecting that they will act in the best interests of the people (which, after all, includes me). And so there is a point at which I will eventually have to disagree fundamentally with men like Tom Bowie and Joe Cox and Tim Lynch because however much common ground we find between us, they are finally willing to entrust their lives to that government and I am not.

Nevertheless, these soldiers have broadened my horizons and taught me that good people are priceless, no matter where you find them. This essay came into being because the editor of my college alumni magazine wrote to me, "It's surprising to me that one of the military academies would have such a publication [as *War, Literature, and the Arts*]—and that they would feature an anti-war poet such as you in it." Let me close by quoting Donald Anderson, the editor of *War, Literature, and the Arts*:

"Some people think it a bit strange for a military academy to be behind a journal of the humanities, but to us it makes perfect sense. Soldiers, more than anyone, need to know what they're capable of destroying. Even though soldiers take an oath to defend the constitution, I point out to my students that what they're defending, too, is a culture that values the individual, a culture that provides the occasion for people to read and write books, to wear t-shirts or affix bumper stickers that make criticisms about our government, and that this is a miraculous aberration in the long haul of history. I tell them they're defending libraries."

I still wish we lived in a world that had no armies at all, but if we're going to have them, that's the kind of guy I want in mine.

❖ ❖ ❖

Soldier-Poets of the Korean War

I

On June 25, 1950, North Korean troops crossed the 38th parallel, the demarcation line between Kim Il Sung's Communist North Korea and the non-Communist South (Republic of Korea, or ROK) established by the Allied victors at the end of World War Two. It was a full-scale assault, the object of which was the reunification of the Korean peninsula by force of arms. Whether the attack was provoked or not is a matter of debate; certainly U.S.-backed autocrat Syngman Rhee had made no secret of his desire to conquer the north by military force. In any case, the attack caught both South Koreans and Americans completely off-guard and disastrously unprepared. The North Korean army reached and took Seoul, Rhee's capital, in just a few days, and by September, subjected to defeat after defeat, US/ROK forces were holding on by their fingernails to a tiny perimeter around the southernmost port city of Pusan.

But the North Koreans had exhausted themselves and could not penetrate what came to be known as the Pusan Perimeter, and soon the sheer weight and volume of American industrial might, combined with the rapid mobilization of draftees and reservists (many of the reservists veterans of World War Two) allowed US/ROK forces to drive the North Koreans out of South Korea. But they did not stop at that. By November, US/ROK forces held most of North Korea as well, and were approaching the Yalu River, the boundary between North Korea and the newly Communist China, in spite of Chinese warnings to keep away.

The warnings went unheeded, however, and as the harsh Korean winter was beginning to settle in, tens and scores of thousands of Chinese "volunteers" smashed into the approaching US/ROK forces, sending them for a second time in six months into headlong retreat that did not stop until Seoul had been lost again. But by then Communist supply lines were once more stretched thin and US/ROK forces, with shorter supply lines and vast amounts of materiel, were able to push the Communist armies out of Seoul and back to the 38th parallel where the fighting had begun almost a year earlier. Along this line, for another two years and more while truce negotiations dragged on and on and on, a war of attrition was waged, rivaling in ferocity and futility if not in size the trench warfare along the Western Front during the Great War.

By the time the truce was finally signed in the summer of 1953, somewhere over a million Americans had fought in Korea (along with combatants from sixteen other United Nations countries, though other U.N. forces ranged from modest to token and were negligible compared to U.S. forces; the war was always, in reality, primarily an American war. One should also remember that while the war was American-led and directed, South Korea contributed even more soldiers, and South Korean military and civilian losses were horrendous). Peak American strength reached 440,000 in the spring of 1953. Thirty-seven thousand Americans died there, and 103,000 were wounded. By way of comparison, the Korean War lasted twice as long as American engagement in the Great War and only seven months less than American engagement in World War Two. Relative to the duration of the Vietnam War (which was approximately three times longer than the Korean War), the Korean War produced proportionately comparable numbers of wounded and disproportionately higher numbers killed in action. To call what took place in Korea a "police action" or a "conflict" was and is to play semantic games at the expense of reality. It was a war.

II

One fact of war is that wars produce literature. From Homer's *Iliad* to Whitman's *Drum Taps* to O'Brien's *The Things They Carried*, war and literature are each a subset of the other. And as soldiers have increasingly become more literate, the 20th century has seen a marked increase in the body of literature written by soldiers and veterans themselves. No longer does war await a Homer or a Tennyson or a Kipling to be translated into literature, but rather the Siegfried Sassoons and James Joneses and Robert Olen Butlers speak for themselves, making use of creative imagination to be sure, but fueling it with the raw stuff of lived experience.

Since my own encounter with war as a young Marine in Vietnam thirty years ago, I have invested a good deal of time and energy in writing my own war poems and editing and publishing the poetry of other Vietnam War veterans. My knowledge of war poetry in general, however, has expanded only slowly over the years, much like the ripples on a pond when a stone is thrown into it. Early on in my life as poet and veteran, I discovered the vast body of poetry to have come out of the British trenches of the Western Front during the Great War, but as recently as a decade ago, I wrote in an essay called "Soldier-Poets of the Vietnam War" (*Virginia Quarterly Review*, v.63, #2, Spring 1987) that little poetry had come from American veterans of World War Two and almost nothing from Korean War veterans.

With respect to World War Two, the assertion is, alas, both ill-informed and embarrassing. Though there is no American poet whose reputation is significantly bound up in his experiences in that war—as are a Sassoon, a Wilfred Owen, or an Isaac Rosenberg from the Great War, or to a lesser extent a John Balaban, a Yusef Komunyakaa, or a Dale Ritterbusch from the Vietnam War—a significant number of accomplished poets of the World War Two generation served in the war and wrote good poetry based on their experiences. A short list of the most prominent includes Hayden Carruth, John Ciardi, James Dickey, Alan Dugan, Richard Eberhart, Anthony Hecht, Richard Hugo, Randall Jarrell, Thomas McGrath, William Meredith, Howard Nemerov, Louis Simpson, and W. D. Snodgrass.

III

About the Korean War, however, I had not hitherto come upon any particular reason to revise my observation that it did not produce any significant body of poetry. There are, it turns out, a number of novels and memoirs to come out of the Korean War; some of them—such as William Styron's *The Long March* and Martin Russ's *The Last Parallel*—are quite good, though none has earned the readership or durability of books like Norman Mailer's *The Naked and the Dead* or Philip Caputo's *A Rumor of War*. U.S. Military Academy English professor Colonel Rick Kerin, in a

1994 unpublished doctoral dissertation from the University of Pennsylvania called "The Korean War and American Memory," asserts that at least 25 combatants later wrote novels about their experiences. But he concludes that there "is apparently but one collection of Korean War verse, Rolando Hinojosa's 1978 *Korean Love Songs: From Klail City Death Trip*." For the most part, he writes, "verse inspired by the Korean War experience seems to be limited to the doggerel of contemporaneous figures writing for service journals or sincere but unpolished tributes written by veterans."

Implicitly bolstering Kerin's conclusion are a number of anthologies of modern war poetry, including Paul Fussell's 1991 *The Norton Book of Modern War*, which includes no Korean War poets, and Carolyn Forshe's 1993 *Against Forgetting: Twentieth Century Poetry of Witness*, which includes only one Korean War veteran, Etheridge Knight, though none of Knight's four poems deals with the war. (Indeed, careful inspection of Knight's military records strongly suggests that he is not a Korean War veteran at all, though that is a subject for another essay.)

Over the years, I have often wondered why so very little poetry came out of the Korean War. Surely some few of those 1 to 1.2 million soldiers must have been or become poets of some minimal skill. Indeed, when Jan Barry and I were editing *Demilitarized Zones: Veterans After Vietnam* in the mid-seventies, the poet and Korean War veteran Reg Saner sent us a sharp, hard-edged little poem called "They Said," which we included because it applied as well to our war as to his. Was that really it?

I found that hard to believe, but never had much opportunity to pursue the question until Dr. Jon Roper, Head of the American Studies Department at the University of Wales in Swansea, United Kingdom, offered me the chance to investigate further through a departmental research fellowship. Roper's colleague Dr. Phil Melling immediately sent me a copy of *Korean Love Songs*, about which I shall have more to say shortly, but in the early going of my research, it looked as if Kerin's assessment would remain the final word.

Letters and Internet queries to scholars of literature, American studies, and history produced not a single lead. Additional queries to veterans groups and repositories of military documents unearthed only the kinds of eminently forgettable soldiers' doggerel and nursery rhyme veterans' drivel that Kerin graciously characterizes as "tributes." Title and subject searches of such vast holdings as the Library of Congress and the New York Public Library, as well as computer database searches, turned up next to nothing.

Even looking through Ethridge Knight's entire body of poetry turned up only one poem that even mentions the Korean War, "At a VA Hospital in the Middle of the United States of America: An Act in a Play," but the reference is generic and comes in the midst of stock references to the Great War, World War Two, and the Vietnam War. (This curious absence is inexplicable if Knight is a Korean War veteran wounded in combat, as he claimed to be, but makes much more sense if he never actually served in Korea. But again, now is not the time or place.)

Similarly, Korean War veteran William Meredith, who won the 1944 Yale Younger Poets Prize while on active duty as a navy carrier pilot during World War Two for a collection of poems heavily based on his wartime experiences, wrote only two poems over the course of his long career that make any reference at all to his later Korean War service, "The Old Ones" and "A Korean Woman Seated by a Wall," and in each case by inference only.

I did, however, eventually come upon a book called *The Hermit Kingdom: Poems of the Korean War* offering the first suggestion that there might be somewhat more than anyone had thus far been aware of. Edited by Paul M. Edwards of the Center for the Study of the Korean War, and published in 1995, it was out of print and dropped by its publisher in less than two years, and for the most part not surprisingly. Edwards's intentions are noble—to bring some attention to a much neglected war and the much neglected people who fought it—but with a few exceptions, the best poetry in the book is written by people who have only tenuous connections to the Korean War (a Vietnam War veteran, for instance; an Iowa Writers Workshop M.F.A. graduate with no military service; a former intelligence analyst who won't say for whom he analyzed intelligence, but will say that it was long after the Korean War era), and the rest of the poetry, by veterans and non-veterans alike, is amateur stuff that ranges from not very good to painfully bad.

In his introduction, Edwards himself acknowledges the anthology's weaknesses. But as I said, there are exceptions—James Magner, Jr., William Wantling and Keith Wilson—and for these I am grateful to Edwards and his anthology. Finally, to the list of Hinojosa, Saner, and these three, all serious poets who are Korean War veterans, I added William Childress after Georgina Murphy, Collection Development Librarian at Philadelphia's La Salle University, came upon his poem "Korea Bound, 1952" in a 1968 anthology called *America Forever New*, and brought it to my attention.

All in all, these six poets cannot be called a hidden wellspring of poetic response to the Korean War, and at this late date they are not likely to represent the tip of a poetic iceberg that awaits discovery. Kerin's general observation about the amount and quality of Korean War poetry remains more true than false. But the Korean War poems of these poets are worth considering, and together they constitute a small but important body of work that has thus far been almost entirely neglected.

IV

How to consider them, how to organize and structure such a discussion, is a bit problematic however. In "Soldier-Poets of the Vietnam War," I took a chronological approach, discussing books and poets as they appeared, year by year. But in this instance, only Hinojosa and Wilson have book-length works dealing wholly or largely with the Korean War. At the other extreme, Saner and Magner have only a handful of Korean War poems scattered over three decades of writing and publishing. I have chosen, therefore, simply to deal with these poets in alphabetical order.

William Childress grew up in a family of sharecroppers and migrant cotton pickers. He joined the army in 1951 at age 18 and was sent to Korea the following year, where he served as a demolitions expert and secret courier. After the war, he became a paratrooper and remained in the army until 1959. He subsequently earned a B.A. from Fresno State and an M.F.A. from the University of Iowa. Over the years, Childress has worked as a college teacher, juvenile counselor, writer-editor for the National Geographic Society, and speechwriter for Phillips Petroleum, but mostly he has earned his living as a freelance writer and photojournalist. From 1983 until 1997, he wrote a column called "Out of the Ozarks" for the *St. Louis Post-Dispatch*.

Childress's two books of poetry appeared within a year of each other—*Burning the Years* in 1971, *Lobo* in 1972—and his most active years as a poet came between 1960 and 1970. A 1986 reprint combining both books, *Burning the Years and Lobo: Poems 1962-1975*, includes fewer than a dozen poems not in either of the earlier two.

Childress takes his subject matter from a wide variety of sources: the natural world and its inhabitants, the agricultural west and southwest of his childhood, the unnatural worlds of urban poverty and button-down America, and the whimsy of his own imagination. But war occupies a significant percentage of the total body of his published work, and his Korean War poems are wedged in between World War Two (in the form of his long eight-part poem "Hiroshima") and the Vietnam War (in poems such as "The War lesson" and "Washington Peace March, 1969").

Indeed, while those who fought the Korean War were closer in age and temperament to the veterans of World War Two, the Vietnam War seems to have been a catalyst for most of these poets, releasing pent-up feelings that had perhaps been held in check by the personal and cultural stoicism bequeathed to them by their generational older brothers. While Childress, for example, did write several of his best Korean War poems prior to the vast American air and ground commitment in Vietnam ("The Soldiers" in 1961 and "Shellshock" in 1962), his poems become more pointed, more cynical, and more bitter as the sixties—and the Vietnam War—advance.

Private First Class William Childress, 11th Airborne, U.S. Army, Germany, 1957. (Photograph provided by William Childress)

And while Childress can say (in a June 1997 letter) with what sounds very much like pride, resentment, and envy all at once, "Korean veterans did not come home and start throwing tantrums like many Viet vets did. We simply faded back into civilian life—no monuments, and not even a dough-nut wagon to meet the [troop ship] I came home on," his poems suggest that the price of simply fading back into civilian life was very dear indeed.

It is difficult to consider Childress's poems in any particular sequence because Childress himself seems ambivalent about how he wants to present them. In the original *Burning the Years*, for instance, he places "For My First Son" directly after "Death of a General," but in the original *Lobo* he reverses their order and puts four other poems between them. More-over, some poems, like these two, appear in both books, while others appear in only one or the other. He adopts yet another configuration in the 1986 reissue of his poems. I have taken the liberty, therefore, of attempting to arrange and discuss them in a sort of thematic progression.

I begin with "Soldier's Leave," a sweet and melancholy poem written in ballad stanzas in which a soldier reflects upon the onset of autumn and the approach of winter. Nothing in the poem overtly suggests war except the title, but Childress interjects an ominous tone with the image of "a surgeon's knife on bone," and the ambiguity of the final two lines is unresolvable: will the soldier soon be gone only from the riverbank and this place where he is now, or will he be dead? Neither the soldier nor the reader knows.

In one of his finest poems, "Korea Bound, 1952," another 12-line poem but this time without stanza breaks and with a different rhyme scheme, Childress emphasizes the unwillingness of those who are being sent to fight. The soldiers on the troop ship are "braced" against the railing as they listen to the "shrill complaining of the waves." Ostensibly free men in a democracy, they are likened to Pharaoh's slaves, and the ship itself to Pharaoh's burial tomb. And in the poem's final irony, they sail past Alcatraz Island, then a maximum security federal prison, where the prisoners' "lack of freedom guarantees their lives."

As often as not, Childress uses both rhyme and meter, sometimes altering the pattern of the rhyme scheme within a given poem, or rhyming in some places but not in others, an admixture of free verse and fixed form that is oddly pleasing and reminds me of Gwendolyn Brooks. Occasionally he gets into trouble or forces a rhyme, but for the most part he handles form skillfully and is (excepting one poem by Wantling) the only one of these poets to work in anything other than free verse.

Poet, writer, and Korean War veteran William "Chilly" Childress. (Photograph provided by William Childress)

"Letter Home," however, is free verse, and in it he assumes the persona of a young American soldier, newly arrived and still able to see beyond himself and his own misery to the misery of "children with bellies swollen, / and O, the flowers / of their faces, petals all torn." Such empathy will not survive what is to come, however. In "The Soldiers," Childress reminds us that "lives narrow/around living's uncertain center" and "soldiers can't be soldiers and be / human." A well-constructed poem of six rhymed sestets, each line with nine syllables, it offers a cold, hard world where only the dead are resolute.

In "Shellshock," Childress moves from generic soldiers to a soldier with a name: MacFatridge. A poem about the cost of war on those who survive, it immediately suggests those men in John Huston's 1946 documentary *Let There Be Light*, which was filmed in the psychiatric ward of a military hospital—though that film was withheld from public release by the U.S. government until 1979, 17 years after Childress's poem first appeared in *Poetry*.

Childress's empathy for his fellow soldiers is matched and more than matched by his contempt for the generals who commanded them. Both "Combat Iambic" and "Death of a General" are scathingly unrelenting, reminiscent of Siegfried Sassoon at his angry best. And in "The Long March," a soldier pulls from a puddle

> the arm of someone's child.

> Not far away, the General
> camps with his press corps.
> Any victory will be his.
> For us there is only
> the long march to Viet Nam.

Here, suddenly, in the last line of a poem beginning "North from Pusan," Childress makes explicit what must have been a steadily rising horror among many Korean War veterans as the fifties became the sixties and the sixties became the Vietnam War. The "we" in the third line of the poem, and the "us" above, are not just the soldiers themselves, but the American people "dumbly follow[ing] / leaders whose careers / [hang] on victory."

"The War Lesson" deals entirely with the Vietnam War, but I include it in this discussion because Childress includes it in the midst of his Korean War poems in both *Burning the Years* and *Lobo*, because one doesn't realize it's not a Korean War poem until the second of the poem's two stanzas, and because if you replace "Khe Sanh" with "Chosin" and "Cong" with "Chink," it would be a Korean War poem, which I think is something more than mere coincidence.

"For My First Son," a bitter poem over which hangs an air of resigned helplessness, appears in several variants. I much prefer the earliest 1971 version which, in the penultimate stanza, after enumerating the "future of steel" toward which his son's "tiny fingers grope"—a flamethrower's blast, trenchfoot, worms, gangrene, shrapnel, empty eyes—Childress concludes:

        ... these are
the gifts of male birthdays,
the power and glory, and
the lies of leaders send them.

"Trying to Remember People I Never Really Knew" also deals with the
wreckage of war and the future that awaits male children, but this time,
after detailing the fates of three men he once knew, Childress refuses to say
if they have left sons behind or not. It is as if, if he does not acknowledge
that they had sons, he might somehow protect their sons from those who
would train them "as hunters of men" and from the "dark forests / where
leaden rains fall." It is only a gesture—this trying to shield sons from the
fate of their fathers—and Childress leaves little doubt that it is a useless gesture. For whatever he might have thought when he was still a boy with "fists
full of detonators and TNT" smiling "murderously / for the folks back
home," as he writes in "Burning the Years," war and the years have taught
him that "duty changes with each job, / and honor turns ashes soon enough."

V

Writing mostly in Spanish, Rolando Hinojosa is not well known
among English-speaking readers, but in the Spanish-speaking community
in the U.S., throughout Latin America, and even in Europe, he has been
widely published and widely read ever since winning the Premio Casa de
las Americas in 1976 with his second novel, *Klail City y sus alrededores*.
Although primarily a novelist and story writer, he is the author of *Korean
Love Songs*, the largest group of poems about the Korean War by a single
author. He is also the only one of the writers I've included in this discussion about whom there is a significant body of secondary literature, including the English-language *The Rolando Hinojosa Reader: Essays Historical and
Critical*, edited by Jose David Saldivar and published in 1985.

Hinojosa was born in south Texas to a Mexican-American father and
an Anglo-American mother. His Hispanic ancestors settled on the north
bank of the Rio Grande River in the 1740s; his Anglo grandfather arrived
from Illinois in the 1880s when Hinojosa's mother was a small child. The
tension and conflict between Hispanic and Anglo cultures, and the struggle of the Rio Grande Valley's Mexican-Americans to preserve and perpetuate their Chicano identity, lies at the heart of almost all of Hinojosa's
writing. Like William Faulkner and Yoknapatawpha County, Hinojosa has
created a fictional world—Klail City, Belken County, Texas—and peopled
it with a cast of characters who appear and reappear throughout his work
(including *Korean Love Songs*).

Sergeant Rolando Hinojosa, U.S. Army, Fort Buchanan, Puerto Rico, 1948. (Photograph provided by Rolando Hinojosa)

Hinojosa enlisted in the army out of high school in 1946, serving two years. He then began college, but was called back into the army in late 1949 and was doing occupation duty in Japan at the outbreak of the Korean War. He served in Korea as a tank crewman with a reconnaissance unit, sustaining two minor wounds. After his release from the army, he went on to earn a B.A. from the University of Texas, an M.A. from New Mexico Highland University, and a Ph.D. from the University of Illinois. In addition to his prolific writing, he has had a successful career as a university professor and administrator, and currently teaches at the University of Texas at Austin.

Published in 1978, *Korean Love Songs* differs from Hinojosa's other work in two significant ways: it is written in verse, and it is written in English. In Saldivar's *Reader*, Hinojosa explains: "I had originally tried to write about Korea in Spanish, but that experience wasn't lived in Spanish. Army life isn't conducted in Spanish, as you know. So, when I began writing *Korean Love Songs* in narrative prose and in English, it was easier. But it wasn't what I wanted either. Eventually, after reading many of the British World War I poets, I got the idea that maybe I should use poetry to render something as brutal as war."

As poetry, one has to point out, these poems leave something to be desired, and one wonders why Hinojosa didn't stick to narrative prose.

Indeed, all that differentiates these poems from prose is the fact of their layout on the page. The rhythms of the language are flat and prose-like. The delivery is expository and factual. Aside from death personified in one poem, there are no images, no metaphors, almost no poetic devices or techniques of any kind. Even the line breaks present no logic I can divine. If any body of poetry ever deserved to be called chopped-up prose masquerading as verse, this is it.

Or maybe I'm being too harsh. The fact is, taken as a whole, *Korean Love Songs* works, and rather well at that. Whatever deficiencies Hinojosa may manifest as a poet he more than makes up for as a storyteller. Though almost none of these poems could stand on the page by itself without the others clustered around to support it, together they become what amounts to a brief but rich novel-in-verse with the individual poems serving as little chapters.

The narrator of the sequence is Rafa Buenrostro—Rafe—a young artilleryman who figures prominently in many of Hinojosa's books, and as the sequence begins, his unit, the 219th Field Artillery Battalion, is still comfortably in Japan. But things turn deadly quickly. By the third poem, the battalion is inside the Pusan Perimeter, and the first casualties we encounter come not at the hands of the North Koreans, but from "Friendly Fire." In the poem by that name, the horror of "an abandoned arm ... looking for its partner" set against the matter-of-fact instructions to "raise those sights, Sergeant Kell, / The forward ob. says you're still short" is a warning of what's to come.

What comes, as the Americans slowly push northward, is death. In "A Sheaf of Percussion Fire," Rafe says, "...there was Death, / Out of breath, / Trying to keep count." And when the Chinese attack, the scale of death becomes almost incomprehensible. In "Rear Guard Action III," Rafe says, "My God, what a fire ... Three thousand rounds. / The breeches were black; the paint peeled.... Jesus, what a fire...." In "Possession for All Time," he adds:

> It's ugly.
> The division's out for blood ...
> ... It doesn't matter when Seoul is retaken:
> Now the mission is to kill;
> It's people we're after,
> Not land.

And kill they do. In "The January-May 1951 Slaughter," as the tide of battle turns yet another time, Rafe tells us:

> I'm sick. They didn't stop coming,
> And we didn't stop firing.

* * * * *

... They died in the city,
They died in the fields and in the hillsides.
They died everywhere.

In one of the most striking poems of the sequence, "Night Burial Details," Rafe watches as "the regimental dregs, / The deserters, the cut-and-runners, the awolers" are forced to retrieve the dead. All day long they work—and Rafe watches, enthralled. "Give it a rest," Frank Hatalski tells him, "You've been at the binocs all day." But Rafe only waves him off and goes on watching, unable to put down the binoculars. "From here they look like so many mail sacks," he says of the body bags loaded in the trucks. As the body detail labors on, Rafe cracks jokes. He's an old hand by now, a veteran, detached, not like the "rookies" who are "still shaken" by the carnage in front of their position.

But the cool detachment seems more like a mask than a true face. Only a few poems later, "Incoming" begins:

The radio guys are in pieces ... in pieces of meat and bone.
They've been blown up and down
Into small pieces ... Christ,
What am I doing here?

And as the sequence progresses, it becomes clear that no one is inured to the terrible stress of battle. In "Above All, the Waste," Lt. Phil Brodkey, "resourceful and kind, calm, precise," shoots himself to death. His replacement, in "Brodkey's Replacement," jumps into the latrine and refuses to come out. The company clerk, who in "Rear Guard Action I" watched as Chinese soldiers "walked right by. They waved. / Some of them waved at me," later in the sequence finds "a loaded carbine" and kills himself with it. And in "Jacob Mosqueda Wrestles with the Angels," when pieces of two of his companions end up on his sleeve, Mosqueda "screams and faints and soils his fatigues." Five times in the poem, Rafe tells us that "Mosqueda will forget," but it seems just as likely—to us, if not to Rafe—that Mosqueda will end up as "a bore, a bother, and a public nuisance."

It is not, of course, only the stress of battle that takes its toll, but the battle itself. The incoming round that so unnerves Mosqueda kills Hook Frazier and Joey Vielma, mortally wounds Hatalski, and wounds Rafe as well. "I read what driven steel could do to a body," Rafe says in "Fit for Duty":

But there was no account of the screaming fear,
And of the crying, or of the swearing, and the sniveling
        begging
For mercy and redemption and salvation and Jesus
        Christ Almighty Himself.

On medical leave in Japan, in "Nagoya Station," Rafe visits his hometown friend and army buddy Sonny Ruiz, who has earlier deserted and is "now a hundred and ten per cent Japanese." While Anglo-Chicano conflict is not the main focus of these poems—their being first and foremost about the Korean War—Hinojosa reminds us early on that Anglo prejudice and insensitivity are as real in Korea and the army as they are in south Texas. In "The Eighth Army at the Chongchon," trying to rally his troops to repel the Chinese onslaught, General Walton H. Walker tells them [and apparently he really said this]:

"We should not assume that (the)
Chinese Communists are committed in force.
After all, a lot of Mexicans live in Texas."

Later, when Walker is killed, in "Rest Due and Taken" Rafe says, "No grudges about the Mexican crack; / We don't have to prove anything to anyone here." But that doesn't ring entirely true, and toward the end of the sequence especially, it becomes clear that in the army, Mexican-Americans are often on no more equal terms than they are in the civilian world.

In Japan, however, this can have its advantages, among them the fact that to the Anglo-American military police, Sonny, dressed in a suit and tie, "looks Japanese" and so goes unsuspected and undetected even while the MPs demand to see the uniformed Rafe's leave papers. When Rafe asks Sonny about home, Sonny replies, "*This* is home, Rafe. Why should I go back?" To which Rafe has no reply: "He has me there. Why, indeed?"

Yet even if he can't explain why, for Rafe, as we learn in "Vale":

Poet, novelist, and Korean War veteran Rolando Hinojosa. (Photograph provided by Office of Public Affairs, University of Texas at Austin)

It's back to Klail,
And home. Home to Texas, our Texas,
That slice of hell, heaven,
Purgatory and land of our fathers.

It is significant that the sequence ends with these words. It is Hinojosa's way of tying *Korean Love Songs* into the larger universe of his work. That notwithstanding, however, these are finally poems about war, not about culture or ethnicity. One of the most bitter poems in the book, "A Matter of Supplies," begins:

It comes down to this: we're pieces of equipment
To be counted and signed for.
          On the occasion some of us break down,
And the parts which can't be salvaged
Are replaced with other GI parts, that's all.

War is an equal opportunity destroyer. "Gun barrels don't talk, and they won't listen," begins the penultimate poem, "This Is Where We Came In." In "Vale," the final poem, when Rafe tallies up all he has lost in Korea, though he mentions his Chicano friends first, he includes Hatalski and Frazier, "Boston John McCreedy from Quincy, Mass.," Phil Brodkey, Louis Dodge, and "others: Not friends, no, but just as dead." In "Up Before the Board," Rafe says:

As for every man's death lessening me,
John the Good was right on the button on that one:
Not counting the hundreds of unseen enemy
In the plains, vales, glens, hills, and mountain
          sides of this garden spot called Korea,
The violent deaths of Hatalski and Frazier,
          Brodkey and Joey Vielma and Charlie Villalon,
Have diminished not only me,
But my own sure to come death as well.

It seems beyond argument that Rafe is speaking not only for himself, but for Hinojosa as well.

VI

James Magner, Jr., is a much more reluctant Korean War poet than either Childress or Hinojosa. In the course of ten books and chapbooks over a span of 31 years, he has written fewer than a dozen poems that seem in any way related to the war. The chronological distribution of the poems, however, is interesting: three appear in his first book in 1965, one in 1968, two in 1973. Three subsequent books in 1976, 1978, and 1981 contain none, but another appears in a 1985 book. A 1992 book contains none, but his latest book, published in 1996, contains four. It is almost as if, throughout his life, he cannot make up his mind to confront the war or not. That ambivalence is inadvertently made apparent in a June 1997 letter of Magner's. At one point he writes, "How much shall you write about the horrific Knives of War that froze, wounded and killed so many of my brothers?" But on the next page he mentions his desire to publish "an elegy for *all* who have died in war, that they will not be lost but remembered in our hearts and souls."

After growing up in New York City, Long Island, and New Rochelle, Magner joined the army in 1948. He ended up in Korea during the first year of the war, that terrible year that saw the front move violently and swiftly from the 38th parallel south to Pusan, then north almost to the Yalu River, then south again to below Seoul, then north once more to where it all started. Magner, however, was not around to see the line stabilized again at the 38th parallel. While fighting as an infantry sergeant with Headquarters Company, 1st Battalion, 7th Regiment, 3rd Division, he was badly wounded by machine-gun fire in North Suwon in February 1951 and evacuated to a hospital in Japan.

His wounds were severe enough to preclude his ever returning to duty. Discharged from the army, he entered a Catholic monastery of the Passionist Order in Dunkirk, New York, where he remained for five years. Thereafter, Magner earned a B.A. in philosophy from Duquesne University, and M.A. and Ph.D. degrees in English from the University of Pittsburgh. In 1962, he began teaching in the English Department of John Carroll University in Cleveland, Ohio, where he has been ever since.

Though Magner never took the vows of a monk, and eventually left monastic life to return to the secular world, the body of his poetry overtly reflects his deeply religious concerns and his lifelong quest to bridge the gulf between human imperfection and divine perfection and to understand the mysteries and contradictions of creation. Even his language often has a Biblical feel to it—the tone, the diction, the choice of words—almost a kind of grandeur. And though his two most recent books reveal a marked change in certain elements of his style—he has moved, for instance, toward a more minimalist use of language—the air of questing, of straining to understand God's meaning and design, seems as strong as ever.

Magner's poems are not always completely successful. The language can sound pompous and stilted at times; the frequent references to God, Christ-God, Human-God and the like can be off-putting, especially for anyone who doesn't share Magner's religious bent. Indeed, I confess (an appropriate choice of words, perhaps, under the circumstances) that I almost did not include Magner here, feeling that his work just didn't come up to the level of the other Korean War poets I've chosen to discuss. Yet I kept coming back to it, I kept hearing it in my head, and finally I could not *not* include him. Whatever his weaknesses, there is a sweetness to these poems, a love for his fellow sufferers, a sense of innocent bewilderment, that touches the heart.

It is clear that Magner cannot bear the madness of the war, the unspeakable misery, the destruction of bodies and minds and hearts, without the hope and reality of divine grace and human redemption. Thus, in "Elegy for the Valiant Dead," Magner pleads "that those who've gone before / may be wrapped in the quilt of Thy arms of night." And in "Christ of Battle," he prays, "Christ-God carry me! / give hope in storm-mud and grave-bed."

Magner powerfully conveys the lonely anonymity of the battlefield. "The Man Without a Face" is "gutted, tangled—sprawled like a broken crab" on the barbed wire, "dead and alone in his body." We don't know if the dead man is Chinese or Korean or American, nor does Magner seem to care. That he is "one of those who fought" is all that matters. And the cold, bleak, unforgiving moonscape of Korea in winter could not be better rendered than in "Zero Minus One Minute":

> The dawn has come
> to sleepless night
> again
> and it is time for us to answer
> from the gray, crystal holes
> that seem to womb
> just northern night and nothingness.

It was this poem of Magner's, more than any other, that I kept coming back to, and this image in particular: "our bodies splinters / in bundled rags." The cold, the pain, the fear, the loneliness are palpable, as is a dogged perseverance in the face of every reason to give up and give in. And if, as Magner says, "the world doubts/that we exist," nevertheless, he insists:

> we are there
> and we shall creak
> our frozen bones
> upon that crystal mount
> that looms in silence
> and amaze the world.

Magner's need for God's mercy to give meaning and comfort to the "soldier-sinners" ("Christ of Battle") is matched by his insistence that those who fought and died be remembered. For Magner, to forget is to render utterly meaningless the suffering, the sorrow, the irreplaceable losses. "The Man Without a Face" may have no name nor even a nationality, but he is nevertheless "entombed in the heart of our mind." And in "Repository," Magner writes:

> Impossible to mind, impossible to heart
> that one so quick,
> who stepped so quick
> in pocket
> and rifled passes forty yards
> for alma mater and the infantry
> could die and be forgotten.

Magner struggles through four stanzas to remember the dead man's name, and when he finally succeeds in the fifth and final stanza, he shouts it over and over again "so someone will remember."

The four poems in Magner's most recent book are characterized by sparse language, matter-of-fact diction, and short often one-word lines. Take, for example, "The Prayer of the Former Infantryman," in which he writes: "One / Thing / I / know. / The / Ground / Is / My / Friend." Yet, however different they may be from his earlier poems, by their mere being they quietly testify to the fact that if the Korean War has never been overtly a major subject in Magner's poetry, it is never farther away than the near-distance of his thoughts. Forty-five years after he left Korea on a stretcher, he remains a "Soldier of the Night" wherein there is "no house, no lamp, no chimneyed curl / but only life outstepping night."

VII

If Magner is a reluctant Korean War poet, Reg Saner doesn't appear to be a Korean War poet at all. Most of his poetry reflects a man most at home when out of doors and fully engaged with the natural world around him: hiking, mountain climbing, skiing, camping under the stars. Much of his writing is inspired by the American West with its mountains and deserts and high plains stretching away to horizons distant enough to make a man reflect humbly upon the universe and his place in it.

Not one of the poems in his four books even uses the word "Korea," and if you didn't already know Saner fought in Korea, you would not likely ever suspect it from reading his books. "I have not really tried to write about Korea," Saner wrote in a January 1997 letter. "I wanted to forget."

To look at the body of his work, one might readily conclude that he's succeeded in forgetting. One *might* conclude that. And one might be wrong.

After graduating from St. Norbert College in 1950, Saner entered the army as an officer and served in Korea in 1952 and 1953, spending six months as an infantry platoon leader with the 25th Infantry Division and earning a Bronze Star. After the war, he earned M.A. and Ph.D. degrees from the University of Illinois before taking a position in 1962 with the English Department at the University of Colorado in Boulder, where he still teaches. His first book of poems, *Climbing into the Roots*, was chosen by William Meredith to receive the first Walt Whitman Award in 1975, and his second book, *So This Is the Map*, was selected by Derek Walcott for the 1981 National Poetry Series. His third and fourth books were published in 1984 and 1989.

From the first book, only "One War Is All Wars" deals with war at all, and Saner's description of the white crosses on soldiers' graves as "line after line after / line regular as / domino theory" suggests the Vietnam War at least as much as it does the Korean War (which, I imagine, is Saner's point, as the title implies).

1st Lieutenant Reginald Saner, 25th Infantry Division, U.S. Army, Korea, 1953. (Photograph provided by Reginald Saner)

From his second book, Saner himself says (again in that January 1997 letter) that "From Chief Joseph I Turn the Page" and "Doc Holliday's Grave" may be related to residual anger about Korea, and that "Talking Back: A Dream" is perhaps prompted "at least partly by survivor guilt," but the connections, such as they may be, exist only for Saner, not for the reader. Only "Leaving These Woods to the Hunters" makes anything like an identifiable reference to his Korean War service with its closing lines: "having never myself / killed anything / more beautiful than a man."

The poems in Saner's third book travel from Colorado to Egypt to Italy, but they don't go anywhere near Korea, and one of the two poems that touch on war in his fourth book, "Little Rituals," with its "men wearing guns, belted jackets," is, like "One War Is All Wars," entirely nonspecific.

"Re-Runs," however, the second war poem in *Red Letters*, is a bit different. It seems to suggest that Saner has not forgotten his war experiences, but only repressed them, and not entirely successfully. It may be presumptuous of me, but I think not, to assume that the "he" in the poem is Saner himself, "alone inside a nameless grief" where "what's buried won't cry / and won't go away." What troubles Saner, however, he will not say beyond "flying iron," "a torn head," "crossfire tracers." He tells us only that sometimes there are "odd nights."

I find it curious indeed that his two most personal and particular poems about the Korean War do not appear in any of his four books. The explanation for "Flag Memoir" may (or may not) be as simple as the fact that it was possibly not written until after his most recent book was published (it appeared in a 1991 issue of *Ontario Review*), but "They Said" has been around since at least 1976 when it appeared in *Demilitarized Zones*, predating publication of three of his four books. Both are quite unlike anything else in Saner's repertoire.

"They Said" is bitter and cynical and angry. When it comes down to it, the poem could well be about some other war than Korea—certainly Jan Barry and I thought it applied to the Vietnam War quite readily—but the vehemence of the sarcasm bespeaks something very personal here: an old grudge, a raw nerve, an unhealed wound. The repetition of the unnamed "they"; the Big Brother authoritarianism masquerading as benign paternalism; the smiling insistence upon conformity; the use of modifiers like "nicely," "suitable" and "quite," taken altogether, powerfully convey the poet's disapproval of, even revulsion at, what he describes. Most striking, perhaps, is Saner's implication that the wholesale destruction in the last stanza, where under the guise of supporting democracy "there is no need to vote," is made possible by

Poet, essayist, and Korean War veteran Reg Saner. (Photograph provided by Reginald Saner)

the years of conditioning that preceded it. And if there's any doubt that Saner rejects the end result, if only in retrospect and too late, there is that fascinating use of the word "almost" in the final line: "[we] wore our brass / stars of unit citation almost all the way home." Like Siegfried Sassoon before him and the Vietnam veterans of Dewey Canyon III after him, Saner rejects the decorations given for actions in which he can take no pride.

In "Re-Runs," Saner mentions "a torn head" among the things he revisits on "odd nights." In his stunning prose poem "Flag Memoir," we learn that the torn head belongs to the first man killed in action in Lieutenant Saner's infantry platoon: "the country boy," Barnett. Saner must identify the body, and he can "face the remains of his face [only] by saying inwardly, again and again, 'This isn't him, he's not here. He's elsewhere.'" The poem offers a series of tight, hard vignettes, very specific, very particular: this is Korea; this is Saner's war. He describes learning to fire single shots from a .50 caliber machine gun, "sucking lather-warm [beer] from cans, talking Red Sox and Yankees under summer shreds of something once like an orchard," seeing a skull hanging "from commo wire looped between tent poles," preparing for a Chinese assault in which the "third and fourth waves may carry scythes, hooks, farm tools, sticks" instead of rifles.

And all of this is "memoir," memory, called back by 4th of July municipal fireworks that "report to the eye as muzzle flash and sheared jaw, red teeth, clay dirt on the brains. Or maybe with one long zipper-pull some corporal exactly my age throws open a dark rubber bag, there yet, in any such zipper I hear…. A stadium anthem can do it, or flag at a ballpark…. The flag slowly dipping, lifting, over nobody there. Explaining. Trying to explain."

If Saner has not really tried to write about the Korean War, "Flag Memoir" suggests that he's forgotten nothing, and likely never will. "But to be completely honest, writing about it would make me cry, and I was raised to *know* that men don't cry," he writes in an unpublished 1997 essay titled "Why so little Korean War poetry?" Then he adds, "Therapeutic grief can go to hell."

VIII

Len Fulton, who published William Wantling's 1966 collection *The Source*, describes Wantling in a February 1997 letter as "a superbly unruly poet (and person)." If anything, that's an understatement.

Soon after graduating from East Peoria High School in Illinois, Wantling enlisted in the Marines, arriving in Korea in early 1953. Discharged from the Marines in 1955 with the rank of sergeant, he spent the next three years in southern California until he ran afoul of the law in 1958, possibly for narcotics and forgery, and was sent to the California State Correctional Facility at San Quentin.

It was in prison that Wantling discovered poetry and the poet in himself, and as early as 1959, he began publishing poems in *Wormwood Review*. After five and a half years, Wantling was released from San Quentin and returned to Illinois, eventually earning B.A. and M.A. degrees from Illinois State University. Wantling's poetry, meanwhile, had come to the attention of Fulton and others in the small press world, and by the mid-sixties (according to H. Bruce Franklin in *Prison Literature in America*), the anthologist Walter Lowenfels was calling him "the best poet of his age."

But Wantling was, finally, an unruly person. He never escaped a dependency on drugs and alcohol, in spite of repeated visits to Veterans Administration hospitals and psychiatric clinics. He lived at fever pitch, consuming prodigious amounts of morphine, heroin, codeine, alcohol, marijuana, LSD, barbiturates, and whatever prescription drugs he could get his hands on. In the spring of 1974, near the end of a one-year nonrenewable instructor's appointment at Illinois State, he was found unconscious in a pool of his own urine and feces. Every window of his apartment had been broken out. Not yet 41, he died a few days later. The official cause of death was heart failure, but in truth he had burned the candle from both ends until there was nothing left to burn.

Wantling's poetry conveys a strong sense of the poet—at least this poet—as outsider and rebel, which he mostly was. Except for his inclusion in several of Lowenfels' anthologies such as *Where Is Vietnam?* (Anchor Doubleday, 1967) and *Open Poetry* (Simon & Schuster, 1973), even in his heyday he published almost entirely in the smallest of the small presses and journals. Most of his books and chapbooks appeared in editions of fewer than 500 copies, some as small as 100. After 1966, though he published in Britain and New Zealand, no collection of his was published in the U.S. until after his death, and he has largely disappeared from the landscape of poetry.

Which is a shame because the best of his work is worth preserving. Interestingly, like Childress and Wilson, he has poems that deal with both Hiroshima ("It's Cold for August") and the Vietnam War ("Your Children's Dead Eyes"). Beyond that and the fact of his being a Korean War veteran, however, his poems bear little resemblance in style or subject to those of any of the other poets included in this discussion. They are frenetic and boisterous, full of restless energy. Much of his writing is drawn from his experiences with drugs, street life, crime and prison. As the sixties wore on, he also became increasingly aware of and responsive to the social and political issues that galvanized so many college campuses (remember, Wantling was an undergraduate and graduate student from

1966 through 1973, though he was well into his thirties).

Wantling's poem "Poetry," from *San Quentin's Stranger*, with its image of "bright pink, lung blood," is perhaps one of the greatest prison poems ever written, asking in the wake of a prison yard killing, "Now / what could consonance or assonance or / even rhyme do with something like that?" Both Franklin in *Prison Literature in America* and critic Robert Peters in *Where the Bee Sucks* are so taken with the poem that each reproduces it in full.

Like Magner and Saner, Wantling wrote only a handful of poems about the Korean War, all of them apparently written in fewer than five years in the early sixties. Because they appeared one or two or three at a time in multiple publications in various configurations and usually interspersed with many other poems as well, as with Childress but even more so, it's impossible to know how Wantling himself would have wished them to be arranged as a group, so once again I have organized my discussion as best I can thematically.

"Korea 1953" begins with "endless weeks of zero" and a "lurking bunker on a barren hill" where murder is "sanctioned" and men find "a certain inner logic to / our violence." Though they dream of returning to a "time of childhood / Grace," what men become in "that strange war that was not / a war" is "a pack of maddened dogs" tearing each other to pieces for "one small piece of rancid meat." It's as ugly an image of war as you will find, made especially haunting by Wantling's unusual use of rhyme.

As if to confirm the cold-blooded savagery of war, "The Korean" is summarily executed for "stealing from Americans." It happens quickly, without hesitation, the Korean with "arms folded / staring," accepting his fate as inevitable, knowing that no appeal will save him from men bent on killing.

But it's not as simple as that. War brutalizes but cannot fully exterminate conscience. In "Without Laying Claim," even as "we calmly" hurl grenades into a crowd, the men who do this have "a lump in our throats" and do not really believe their own self-justifications.

The tension between the rough, hard soldiers' exterior necessary to survive the ordeal of war and the innate inclination toward a broader range of human emotions is particularly evident in "I Remember," in which a tough lieutenant, finding the frozen body of a soldier who's been missing all winter, kicks the corpse, swears, and spits—but then stares directly into the sun to give himself an excuse in front of his men for the tears in his eyes.

By the time "the 6x6 [truck] bounces me down the / washboard roads" toward "Pusan Liberty," Wantling himself has dropped any pretense of toughness. He's had it with the "sun-eaten walls of Korea" where, while men die horribly and senselessly at the front, in the rear everything from jeeps to people is for sale. He buys heroin from an ex-soldier who "sits on his roller-skate cart / minus arms & legs," then resells some of it to "2 Chinese agents" and they get high together, "three angry boys lost in the immense / absurdity of War & State."

Though Wantling survived the Korean War, he couldn't escape it. Feelings of guilt and remorse dominate "Sure," while rage is the controlling emotion in "The Day the Dam Burst," in which he imagines himself running "headlong, frothing, haphazardly / hurling shrapnel grenades / into high-noon crowds." Tired of the "dead ugly ache of it / all," he wants to force those in whose name he and his comrades fought to pay some price for their ignorance and their complicity:

> O My, wouldn't I
> shine? wouldn't
> I shine then?

But instead of directing his rage outward, he turned it in upon himself, and eventually it killed him. For all his beatnik, hipster, hippy, ex-con, ex-Marine bravado—and his poems are full of all that—he could not reconcile his own nature to the world around him. In his most tender poem, "The Awakening," he describes a hopelessly mangled bee still struggling to fly. Holding the bee in his hand, he remembers "the agony on the face of wounded friends/and the same dumb drive to continue." Angered by "the unfair conflict suffered/by will and organism," he shouts at the bee:

> STOP THAT!
> Then it ceased to struggle, and somehow suddenly
> became marvelously whole, and it arose
> and flew away.

In the end, perhaps, it's as simple as this: Wantling wanted the bee to fly, and he could not accept that it wouldn't.

IX

"I was a regular Navy officer," Annapolis graduate Keith Wilson writes in a February 1997 letter. "I came from warrior stock, right out of the Highlands of Scotland, and the Welsh Marches." He went to Korea the first time as a 22-year-old ensign in 1950, and returned from his third tour in Korean waters in 1953. "I expected nothing from war. I was a professional. I didn't, however, expect to be lied to and betrayed. I was very proud of the U.N. flag at our masthead when we went in to launch attacks. I thought, and still do think, that the only way I can see for the planet to survive is to have an effective worldwide government. When I found out that Korea was all a very dirty and murderous joke, I was silenced for many years."

Wilson got out of the navy and returned to his native New Mexico, earning an M.A. degree from the University of New Mexico before commencing a career in academia. Now professor emeritus at New Mexico State University, where he taught for many years, he has also held visiting professorships and residencies at universities and arts centers in Kansas, New York, Ohio and Utah, as well as Canada and Romania.

He has also had a prolific career as a poet and writer, publishing over two dozen books and chapbooks since 1967. Among his many awards are a

U.S. Naval Academy Midshipman Keith Wilson and his dog Poochie, 1946. (Photograph provided by Keith Wilson)

National Endowment for the Arts fellowship and the Governor's Award for Excellence in the Arts from the State of New Mexico. A great deal of his work is rooted deeply in the American Southwest, especially New Mexico, and he has a particular interest in and affinity for Native American and Spanish-American cultures.

But Wilson's experiences in the Korean War provide the foundation for one of his most important books—arguably his most important: *Graves Registry*. "I started writing *Graves Registry* in the winter of 1966 in anger that our government was again fighting an undeclared war in a situation that I, from my experiences in Korea, knew we could never win. I was one of the first combat veteran officers to protest Vietnam because I knew it to be unlawful, and could only lead to another disgraceful stalemate. I led protest marches and read at them, [but] I had no poems about war at all—I had buried it inside.... It took the pressure of rage and fear for the young men like you that made me write it and it poured out, page after page."

First published by Grove Press in 1969 as *Graves Registry & Other*

Poems, it contained the Korean War poems along with poems about the Southwest. In 1992, Clark City Press published an updated edition called simply *Graves Registry* and containing the original Korean War poems; additional poems from his 1972 *Midwatch*, including a number that deal explicitly with the Vietnam War; and some fifty newer poems. Taken all together, they weave the literary and the political into a single tableau that moves across time and geography, but my attention here, of course, must necessarily be limited to the poems dealing with the Korean War, most of which are grouped together at the beginning of the book.

The sequence begins with what amounts to a love poem to his wife, "Echoes, Seafalls for Heloise," followed by three poems that deal more with the remnants and reminders of World War Two than they do with the Korean War (scattered throughout the Korean War sequence are a number of other poems that are related by locality, experience and circumstances, but that do not deal directly with the war in Korea—including a poem titled "Hiroshima").

The first Korean War poem is "The Captain," in which Wilson encounters a U.S. Army officer with "the kind eyes / of somebody's uncle." But as the captain describes the raids he and his Korean commando team conduct, Wilson records "what happened to his eyes":

> the changes when he spoke of their raids
> of villages flaming, women & children
> machinegunned as they ran
> screaming from their huts.

It isn't all blood and guts. One of the virtues of Wilson's poems is the way they traverse a wide range of experiences, all of them belonging to the war. In "*...ganz in Waffen*" ["clad wholly in armor"; throughout the sequence, Wilson includes quotes in German from Rainer Maria Rilke's *The Lay of the Love and Death of Cornet Christopher Rilke*], a deck officer, firmly but without humiliating, bolsters the courage of a young sailor on the verge of breaking as their ship comes under fire from enemy shore batteries. "The Singer" recounts an incidence of accidental gunshot (in any war, though for obvious reasons it is seldom given much attention, large numbers of soldiers are killed not by the enemy but by their own and their comrades' mistakes). "Waterfront Bars" in Japan offer temporary relief to sailors between 90-day battle cruises "north of the bombline." And in "The Mistress," an American sailor and a Japanese woman, each with his or her own sorrows and griefs, hold "each other / through horrors higher than language." The relationship is even more tenuous for "the girl / in an Inchon officers club" in "The Girl," whose "passion" is followed by "the crinkle of paper / passing hands." And in "Combat Mission," three officers "in a ruined merchant's house" ten miles behind the lines drink Scotch while squatting around an oilcan stove, lifting "their cups against / the darkness, the rumbles rolling forward."

But if it isn't all blood and guts, there is plenty and more than enough of both. In "Guerrilla Camp," Wilson is confronted first by the dead and wounded "from the / raid the night before," then by "a retired fighter" no older than himself whose hand has been ruined by a bullet and who demands to know "how a man / could farm / with a hand like that." In "The Circle," Wilson's ship steams for hours through hundreds of Korean bodies floating "in faded blue lifejackets," victims of a sunken troop ship, no survivors: "We sailed on. I suppose that's all / there is to say." But one body in particular remains fixed in his mind:

> ... God knows why
> but his ass was up instead
> of his head; no pants left,
> his buttocks glistened
> greyish white in the clear sun.
> the only one.

Whatever illusions of service and nobility Wilson entered the war with are evaporating. Even the masculine bravado of "High Noon," in which Wilson and two companions cavalierly risk *"the street. / lined with thin watchful men. / silent. eyes upon them, the / hatred, passive,"* rings ever more hollow. By "December 1952," once again "back in the combat zone," he recalls the heroism of great naval commanders of the past—Nelson, Farragut—and the grand enterprise to which he'd thought he himself was attached:

> A blue United Nations patch
> on the arm, a new
> dream. One World. One
> Nation.
>
> Peace.

Poet and Korean War veteran Keith Wilson. (Photograph by Everett Campbell)

But now he realizes that nothing has changed since the days of Nelson and Farragut, that "the old bangles" still work, allegiances are still bought, and "tracers hit a village, / the screams of women, children / men die." And while the New York stock market rises and "cash registers / click," Wilson is finally forced to confront

> ... the cost of lies, tricks
> that blind the eyes of the young. *Freedom.*
> Death. *A life safe for.* The Dead.

"Commentary" is equally scathing, a recitation of what has become, for Wilson, only the squandering of lives, especially Korean lives, in the name of Americans back home

> whose enemies
> are always faceless, numbers
> in a paper blowing in the
> Stateside wind.
>
> How many bodies would
> fill a room
> living room with TV, soft
> chairs & the hiss
> of opened beer?
>
> We have killed more.
>
> The children's bodies alone
> would suffice.
>
> * * * * *
>
> ... O,
> do not dream of peace while such bodies
> line the beaches & dead men float
> the seas, waving, their hands
> beckoning.

After "Truce," which concludes the first section of *Graves Registry*, only a few other poems touch on the Korean War directly: "The Ex-Officer, Navy," a poem much like Saner's "Re-Runs"; "The Poem Politic 4," reminiscent of Wantling's "Sure"; "Memory of a Victory," which reads about as hollow as victory can get; and "Corsair," an elegy for a friend who "refused / to machinegun civilians / on the Korean hillside / to bomb a courtyard / full of refugees" and who died for his decency.

Wilson's poems are not about the big battalions and the pitched battles, but about coastal operations and guerrilla raids, shattered villages and shattered ideals. They are peopled by Americans, yes, but also by Koreans and Japanese, refugees and cripples, and by warriors, yes, but also and more so by the defenseless and the innocent who always become the wreckage of war. They are Wilson's explanation of how he began his life expecting to kill people and ended up dedicating it to teaching people instead.

X

So there is indeed a body of work that can be called Korean War poetry. But to reflect upon these poems and these poets only brings one back to the question: why so few? I have thought for many years that the Korean War must have been a hellish frustration for those who fought it, especially in those last two long years when both the front lines and the truce talks barely moved while men died miserably for nothing but barren lumps of mud with holes dug into them, and one would think the soldiers came home as bitter and disillusioned as any of the 33 veteran-poets who contributed to the 1972 anthology *Winning Hearts and Minds: War Poems by Vietnam Veterans,* a book published even before the Vietnam War was over. But in the days of the House Un-American Activities Committee and Senator Joe McCarthy, it would perhaps have been impossible to say or write what Rafe Buenrostro could only put into words 25 years after the end of the Korean War: "What am I doing here?" In the fifties, the answer would have been, "Fighting Communism," and only a fool would likely have asked such a question loudly enough to be heard.

But I'm only guessing, and considering that I was not yet five years old when the truce was signed, I thought it might be useful to pose that question—why so few Korean War poets—to others whose opinions I respect, including but not only the poets themselves.

"Korea was a 'non-war,'" says William Childress in his June 1997 letter, "being alternately a 'police action' and 'Harry Ass Truman's war.' Korea was no war to inspire poetry or fiction. It lacked all nobility and didn't settle a damned thing. The line is still where it began and even after losing 40,000 men we're still patrolling the damned thing—millions and millions of dollars 40 years later. No resolution, and every good piece of writing needs a denouement."

"Why," asks Reg Saner in his unpublished essay, "out of the thousands over there, shooting and getting shot at in 'the land of the morning calm,' have so few poets turned to Korean War material? I don't have the answer. Rather, my answers are questions themselves. Is it because Korea wasn't officially a war, just bloody murder on both sides, while being officially termed a 'police action'? Is it because for a long time people referred to it as 'the Phoney War'? Is it because our betters in Washington supplied us with outdated, outworn weapons deliberately, and even gave us, often, ammo that had been corroding since before World War II? Is it because we were judged, from the Pentagon's strategic outlook, to be only a 'brush fire' distraction set ablaze by the Russians who would wait till enough U.S. troops and weaponry had been committed in Korea before making their European push? Is it because as soldiers in a 'police action' or 'Phoney War,' using up old ammo, supported by reconditioned, obsolete tanks, and eating literally leftover C-rations, we were nonetheless—in terms of patriotism and duty—enough the echo of World War II morale as to be unwilling to bitch in print? Or, finally and perhaps most likely, had World War Two made us small potatoes by inevitable comparison—among even ourselves?

"Despite all the ink spilt about poor public support for Vietnam veterans, I must say we Korean veterans got neither respect nor disrespect. Except amid our immediate families, there was no reaction. Even in Korea, I recall vividly [a lieutenant] in my infantry company saying sardonically, 'We're the second team.' Everybody knew it.

"Withal, however, I think the scant poetry written by Korean veterans ... probably resulted from two main factors. First, the ruckus raised by World War Two had barely subsided when the North Koreans poured across the 38th parallel. As I've already pointed out, World War Two, by being virtually global in scope, overshadowed the fighting in Korea, bloody as it was. Second, Vietnam split the U.S., creating in the process a vast readership for antiwar writing. The fact that major U.S. publishers were slow to print the stuff isn't relevant to anything but fiscal caution. Furthermore, readers generally, and readers of poetry *unanimously*, were militantly against continuing in Vietnam. The poetry 'be-in' and 'poetry happening' and 'open mike poetry protest' all became features of U.S. campus life. Nothing remotely resembling a split in U.S. society existed during or after Korea.

"Then there's that vogue word 'closure.' Once the truce was signed in Korea, everybody including combat veterans turned the page. The whole thing was over.... When I heard Tim O'Brien read from *The Things They Carried*, I was deeply impressed by his quality, yet puzzled, unable to understand how a man well past middle age could tolerate dwelling for years on his Vietnam experience. The title chapter of that book is easily the best war piece I've ever read. How could any reader not admire such depth and power? It's just that I don't get it. How can any writer go on recycling such horrors? As for me, you can have them. All of yours, of course, but especially all of mine. I do not want them."

The other poets did not hazard even a guess as to the answer to the question, but publisher Len Fulton, William Wantling's champion and himself a veteran of service in Japan from 1953 to 1955, suggests in a February 1997 letter that Americans "went into that John Foster Dulles 'cold war' freeze right after Korea, the Fifties, and a 'massive-retaliation' mentality that helped shut down the sort of cultural churn that heats up the thought processes and gets books written. And I think by the time that 'churn' came back to us we were ass-deep in Vietnam, rocket science, and rock and roll. Korea was sandwiched, you might say, between our great rise and our great fall. It was transitional, hence, somewhat transitory. You could argue—and some have—that it was a nexus between what we were and what we are. It was a lesson we should have learned, but which took the much longer and more arduous experience of Vietnam to make it sink in."

"War poetry is almost always about required suffering and the wreckage of men's lives," Gloria Emerson, winner of the National Book Award for *Winners and Losers: Battles, Retreats, Gains, Losses, and Ruins from the Vietnam War*, writes in a March 1997 letter, "so one reason that there may be so little American work on the Korean War is the monumental shadow of what others just before them had endured in World War Two. A second consideration is the possibility of being seen as 'disloyal' or subversive in an era of the witch hunt, the insistence on the most rigid patriotism, the specter of being 'un-American.' Poetry flourishes under oppression—always—but it does not thrive when people are thwarted in questioning why they were obligated to fight. Perhaps the level of political sophistication after World War II, and the fear of the Communists against whom Americans were fighting, also imposed artistic inhibitions and an uncertainty in the poets that they had the right to write. There was, because the Korean War came so soon after World War II, a general lassitude on the part of the public. The most piercing history of that war is in the photographs."

"Whenever I have talked about war poetry in public, the question [of why so little writing from the Korean War] has always been asked by the audience, and I confess that I don't know the answer," Paul Fussell, a World War Two veteran and author of *Doing Battle, Wartime,* and *The Great War and Modern Memory*, says in a February 1997 telephone message. "I always answer it this way by saying that that war was called a police action and there was a widespread decision, a silent decision, not to refer to it as a war. And a police action can't have any poetry. A thing that I think is truer is that it came so close to the Second World War that everybody imagined that the poetry emanating from that war would do for the Korean War as well. But my real, honest answer is that I don't know."

"I don't really know why Korea didn't become a 'literary' war the way that World War Two and the American Vietnam War did," Englishman

Jeffrey Walsh, author of *American War Literature: 1914 to Vietnam*, writes in a March 1997 e-mail. "Some wars are imaginatively productive; others seem to be eerily unpopular in a creative sense. If I had to speculate about why Korea wasn't written about much by poets, I'd suggest that it was perhaps because of its poor timing: it happened just when Europe and to a lesser extent the U.S. were exhausted by World War Two. I doubt if there was much mileage in Korea as a topic for commercial publishers. The war occurred just when a flood of books and films covering World War Two were coming out. Neither did Korea involve as many troops as World War Two or Vietnam, or last as long. It never was as glamorous a war as Vietnam became because it did not generate countercultural opposition or become 'a cause' as, say, the Spanish Civil War. It has remained a complex, distant Asian conflict, fought strategically for sterile Cold War objectives. Unlike Vietnam or the 1914-18 war, Korea did not signify 'futility' nor did it have the moral resonances of World War Two waged against evil genocidal powers. In retrospect, Korea seems especially dull, ideologically, bloody, a dirty, uncompromising conflict with few positive images." But, he adds, "I don't think any of this offers a persuasive explanation."

Maybe there isn't one. Or, more likely, probably it's some combination of all these things. Trying to explain what hasn't been written is a good deal more difficult than trying to explain what has, and certainly the question warrants more attention than anyone has yet given it. But so does the war itself, and the writing it generated. Even after nearly half a century, the Korean War largely remains "the Forgotten War," and its literature remains largely unknown, unread, and unexplored. I hope this essay will make some small contribution toward bringing an end to such inattention, lest, as James Magner, Jr., writes in "Elegy for the Valiant Dead":

> the eyes of night go out
> and are blind of men.

[Poems by all of the Korean War soldier-poets discussed in this essay can be found in *War, Literature, and the Arts*, v.9, #2, Fall/Winter 1997, and in *Retrieving Bones: Stories and Poems of the Korean War*, co-edited by W. D. Ehrhart and Philip K. Jason, Rutgers University Press, 1999. Section VIII on William Wantling has been revised since its original publication to take into account information not available at the time it was first published (see the two additional essays on Wantling in this volume).]

❖ ❖ ❖

"I Want to Try It All Before I Go": The Life and Poetry of William Wantling

"I want to try it all before I go," William Wantling wrote in a poem called "the great american novel" (*10,000 r.p.m. & digging it, yeah!*), and he very nearly did. In the course of his too brief life, he was wounded in combat as a Marine in Korea; did hard time in the California State Prison at San Quentin for forgery and possession of narcotics; married twice; earned bachelor's and master's degrees and taught college; was in and out of psychiatric and alcoholic wards repeatedly; published over a dozen books and chapbooks of poetry in the United States, Wales, England and New Zealand; and died of hard living at the age of 40.

And these are just the high points. Indeed, his desire—his apparently unquenchable and uncontrollable need—to try it all is what killed him. He regularly injected any and every drug he could get his hands on: morphine, heroin, codeine, alcohol, marijuana, hashish, LSD, barbiturates, peyote, and whatever prescription drugs happened to be within reach—as often as not, three, four and five different drugs simultaneously. "How do you know a poets been to yr house?" Wantling asked in another poem, "Style 4" (*7 on Style*), answering his own question, "yr medicine cabinets empty & yr dogs pregnant." If it was meant as a joke, the reality of Wantling's life made the laughter ring hollow.

"He reduced those who loved him to chemical pimps and puke wipers," John Pyros writes in *William Wantling: A Biography & Selected Works*. "The first thing he did when he walked in your house was gulp down everything in the medicine cabinet," said his friend Art Greenberg, "I mean everything" (Pyros). Said another friend, Sam Zaffiri, "Most of Bill's life was spent in a constant search for things which would get him drunk or high. He was a manipulator and all with whom he came in contact, whether best friend or casual acquaintance, were game for his wiles. He wheedled, begged, lied, and even stole from people to get the things he required to get stoned" (Pyros).

Yet critic and scholar H. Bruce Franklin, in *Prison Literature in America*, calls him "a master stylist." He inspired the great anthologist of the sixties and seventies Walter Lowenfels to describe him as "the best poet of his age" (Franklin). Small press legend Len Fulton wrote in his introduction to Wantling's collection *The Source*, "Bill Wantling is an Aristotelian man. He is a man of huge contrasts, a wrestler's physique, a Keatsian sensitivity, a genius reach." "Bill was a decent man," wrote A. D. Winans in Wantling's posthumously published *7 on Style*, while Edward Lucie-Smith, in his introduction to Wantling's *The Awakening*, attributed to him "a generosity of spirit," noting that "he suffers for others as well as for himself." Charles Bukowski—himself no stranger to hard living—wrote in *Dramatika*, eulogizing the recently deceased Wantling, that "everything he said lifted the game out of the muck, made it gently human." More recently, Kevin E. Jones, in a 1994 doctoral dissertation titled "Finding Jewels in the Awkward Mud," asserts that "despite character flaws and a number of excesses and weaknesses, [Wantling] deserves to be remembered as something more than a narrowly fuddled walk-on, an alcoholic junky-poet."

Nearly 25 years after Wantling's death, hardly anyone remembers him as anything at all. Most of his books and chapbooks were published by small presses in editions of a few hundred copies or less, and all of his publications are long since out of print. The best one might do is to find a poem or two in an anthology here and there, gathering dust on a library shelf. Even at the peak of his brief career, Wantling attracted only modest attention—one small star in a cosmos filled with stars, most of them very much brighter—and when his star burned out, few people even noticed the absence.

I for one had never heard of Wantling when I began researching American veterans' poetry from the Korean War a few years ago, but one of the books I came upon was an anthology edited by Korean War veteran Paul M. Edwards called *The Hermit Kingdom: Poems of the Korean War* that contained three striking poems by Wantling. "Korea 1953" begins:

> Endless weeks of zero
> A lurking bunker on a barren
>   hill
> Waiting to receive our orders
>   *Probe, Capture, Kill*
> As if one must recompense in
>   limbo
> For each probe which lacked
>   all sense[.]

Though Wantling briefly imagines that he and his comrades might be "returned to a time of childhood / Grace," by the end of the poem they are reduced to "a pack of maddened dogs[.]"

Edwards had found the three poems in a book of Wantling's called *The Source*. The 31 poems in that book range widely in form, quality, and subject, but they were compelling enough to induce me to search out more of his poetry and more of the man himself. And the more I learned, the more I began to feel a curious and powerful affinity with him, an odd but real sense that he was some sort of shadow older brother, and that but for the grace of God or the vagaries of Chance, his fate might have been mine.

Like Wantling, I had enlisted in the Marines at 17 and gone off voluntarily to fight what turned out to be a senseless Asian war (mine was in Vietnam). Like Wantling, I had been wounded in combat and had earned promotion to sergeant. Like Wantling, I had come home embittered and disillusioned, distrustful of my government and ill at ease in my native land. Like Wantling, I had systematically engaged in self-destructive behavior and the use of various drugs both legal and illegal over an extended period of time. Like Wantling, I had earned two degrees in English and wrote poetry. And the fact that I did not end up in prison has only to do with dumb luck and changing times.

Wantling was born in November 1933 in what is now East Peoria, Illinois (it was then the twin towns of Robein and Valley View). He played trombone in his high school band and was an underachiever as a student. Soon after graduating, he enlisted in the United States Marine Corps, serving in Korea in 1952 and 1953, where he was wounded gravely enough to spend ten days in a coma and another eight weeks in the hospital. After his discharge, he returned to Peoria only briefly before heading for southern California. There he mostly got by on peripheral jobs, street hustling and petty crime, struggling to support a narcotics habit he claimed resulted from being given morphine for his wounds in Korea. In 1956 he married a woman named Luana, who was also an addict. Two years later he was sent to San Quentin, apparently taking a rap for both himself and his wife ("riding the beef for her," as he says in one poem). Nine months after he arrived in San Quentin, Lee, as he called Luana, stopped writing, divorced him, and vanished from his life, taking their infant son with her.

Wantling first began to write while in prison, taking Saturday morning writing classes. By the time he was released five and a half years later, he had begun to make contacts in the small press world and was soon publishing regularly in *Wormwood Review, Second Coming, Small Press Review, Ole* and elsewhere. He returned to Peoria, where a chance encounter with a woman he'd known in high school—Ruth Ann Burton *nee* Cooper, now a divorced mother of two boys—blossomed. They were married in 1964.

In 1966, he and Ruthie and her boys moved to Normal, Illinois, where Wantling enrolled as an undergraduate student at Illinois State University, from which he eventually earned both his B.A. and M.A. At the time of his death in May 1974, he was separated from Ruthie and nearing the end of a one-year nonrenewable appointment as an instructor in the English Department at ISU, and Ruthie was in the process of filing for divorce.

So brief and simple a recitation of facts doesn't begin to convey the staggering turbulence of Wantling's life, the havoc he wreaked upon himself and others. But a lot of his poems do. In "poets are sensitive" (*10,000 r.p.m.*), he writes:

> I was drunk, stoned & speeding, leaning
> over the icebox spilling lunchmeat and milk
> on [Ruthie's] clean kitchen floor
> she kicked me in the shins, tried for the
> head & nuts
> I broke her nose & hitched out to
> Berkeley to see the girl that'd just had my
> baby daughter[.]

In "I wake up under a fig tree" (*10,000 r.p.m.*), after another binge, he says:

> 5 days later I've
> puked on everybody's rug
> shit in Jackies bathtub
> ripped off people I love[.]

Or this from "Style 4" (*7 on Style*):

> hungover, burntout & poisoned w/lush & drugs ... hadda spend the Xmas
> holidays inna hospital, drying out, I.V. bottles dripping glucose & vitamins
> into my punched-out veins.... I cant handle my own wife ... I cant even
> handle the day without a 6-pak & as many joints a hit or 2 of codeine.

But Wantling's writing isn't all a matter of self-absorption and self-destruction and the using and abusing of himself and others. As he apparently could be in his own life when he wasn't loaded, he was capable of thoughtfulness, sensitivity and empathy in his poetry. In "Christmasong" (*Five Poem Songs*), he writes:

> Born in a conquered land, I knew a meager shelter
> A mother's quiet pain, a poverty of the times
>   * * * * *
>   I knew cool mornings and rainbows, the sweet
> Love of a man called Peter
>   * * * * *
> I knew failure and a foolish death[.]

"Dirge in Spring" (*The Source*) recounts a rabbit's unsuccessful attempt to save her newborn and still-blind babies from a farmer's uncaring and oblivious plow. "In Zoology Lab" (*Obscene & Other Poems*) compares "tanks of frogs / cans of grasshoppers" and "a crate of embalmed cats" with "a Taiwan prison / a Czech prison / a Cuban prison" and a young American black man who "gets 99 years / for slipping an agent / the dope he so repeatedly begs for[.]" "[T]he street in front of our house" (*10,000 r.p.m.*) is a meditation on humanity's inability to learn from our mistakes, even after "3 million generations." And in "Style 2" (*7 on Style*), he describes in awful detail the death of an abandoned kitten:

> her eyes were pasted shut
> with infection
>   every bone
> showing through her dirty hide
> her stomach distended
> with worms & starvation
> too weak to stand
> she made a little noise at me[.]

It's difficult to trace Wantling's chronological development as a poet in any detail. He had a habit of publishing many of his poems repeatedly, and I have thus far been unable to obtain more than a small handful of poems from the half dozen early chapbooks Wantling published in 1964 and 1965; it's possible that at least some of the poems appearing in later publications may well have been written much earlier. Moreover, Wantling apparently tinkered endlessly and published multiple versions of poems. For example, the text of "Just Lately" in *The Source* reappears word for word in *The Awakening* only a year later—but is configured as two poems with two different titles on facing pages: "Just Lately" and "The Day the Dam Burst." Finally, Wantling's active writing life spanned only about fifteen years at most, and easily half of that seems to have been lived in the near-constant fog of intoxication in one form or another.

Others have identified a certain change over time that I find largely erroneous. In a 1969 letter cited in *7 on Style*, Bukowski wrote to Wantling, "Since you've been going through this college thing, babe, your writing has changed, softened." Wantling's "early work was tight and hard hitting," Winans wrote, also in *7 on Style*, but he "began to alter his style in the late 1960s. He became increasingly more aware of form and technique and perhaps unconsciously became a little too poetic."

It is true that writing doesn't get much tighter or hard hitting than Wantling's 1965 "All the fucking time" (*Down, Off & Out*), which begins:

All the fucking time
I was in San Quentin
I kept remembering my
stinking bitch of an
old lady and how I'd
rode the beef for her
and how she'd stopped
writing in 9 months
and served papers and
shacked up with some
Chicano in East L.A.

But a year *earlier*, in a fifteen-part chapbook poem called *The Search*, he'd written:

give us the pure distilled boredom of each hour
straining toward its goal of infinite mediocrity
show the deliberate sensualities, the mad
mixture of possibilities, the chaos called life,

which is "poetic" in the worst sense, and a string of clichés about as soft and flabby as it gets. Similarly, his awareness of form and technique aren't bound by any sort of chronological progression. Indeed, his 1966 collection *The Source* contains a number of metered and rhymed poems, and the subtlety of the rhyme and rhythm in "Korea 1953" is masterful:

We found a certain inner logic to
                    our violence
A game in which each player and
          his mate
                    understood all rules
(each sensing his brother's center)
And at expense of this—genius of
                              fools
One might purge oneself
          so clean
That love would come to our dead
          winter
                    for one cannot hold
                         an inner void
And if one's hate is utterly
                         purged
One's intuition told
          that love could enter
And we, bold, would become merged[.]

Conversely, his 1973 collection *10,000 r.p.m. & digging it, yeah!* is all but devoid of form and perhaps somewhat lacking in technique as well.

I would argue that the variations one sees in Wantling's work are not generally progressional and furthermore result from his never finding a single style that suited him fully, his remaining unsatisfied with any one voice or form or technique. And if much of his poetry, especially by the early 1970s, is less tight and hard hitting than it once was, that almost surely is less the result of "the college thing" than of the accumulated wear and tear of years of monumentally self-destructive living. A brain and a body can only take so much punishment, and Wantling punished his without mercy.

What caused Wantling to commit slow suicide, to squander every opportunity he'd been given, to waste his obvious talent along with the devotion and loyalty of those who loved him? Who can say? So much of what we are and what we become is in our genes, or lies in our early childhood, and little is known of either that would shed light on Wantling's subsequent life. Still, I think it would be hard to overestimate the impact of his Korean War experiences on what happened to him later.

Exposure to the modern battlefield—where death comes equally and at random to the brave and the cowardly, the skilled and the clumsy—utterly unhinges one's sense of order, cause and effect, fairness, justice, and the belief that one has any real control over one's own fate, and the younger one is at the time of exposure the more profound the impact. This general phenomenon was badly compounded by the sheer senselessness of the war Wantling fought, where for its final two years men suffered horribly and died miserably along a static front while diplomats sat at a table in Panmunjom and argued over the finer points of prisoner repatriation and most people back home went about their lives with little thought for "that strange war that was not a war" (as Wantling puts it in "Korea 1953") and that ended with the lines almost exactly where they had been when the killing had begun three years earlier.

It is true that tens of thousands of men saw combat in Korea, and most of them didn't end up as junkies—but most of them didn't end up as poets, either. For better or worse, Wantling possessed sensibilities that were and are, though not unique, certainly unusual. It is also true that one of the hazards of the use of morphine to treat the pain of battlefield injuries is the possibility of addiction. "When I was in Korea," Fulton quotes Wantling in the introduction to *The Source*, "they gave me my first shot of morphine. It killed the pain. It was beautiful." For a man in his early twenties, disillusioned and bitter, trying to understand what had happened to his world and how he fit in to what must surely have felt as alien a landscape as the moon, the temptation to kill the pain and make things beautiful must have been powerful indeed.

And then to end up in San Quentin, and to be abandoned by the woman you had sheltered from the same fate, and to have that woman successfully petition to strip you of any legal claim whatever to your own son (Wantling fought the petition from behind bars, but lost): that's a lot of bad stuff to cope with in the prime of your life. Nor did it help that, with his propensity for excess, he arrived on the campus of ISU just at the outset of the whole sixties counterculture underground antiwar protest scene when "drugs, sex and rock 'n' roll" wasn't just a cute phrase.

None of this excuses his behavior, but it may go some way in helping to explain it. Wantling was clearly haunted by what he'd seen and done in Korea. In "Without Laying Claim" (*The Source*), he writes:

> in the midst of that crowd
> we calmly pulled the pins
> from six grenades
> mumbling an explanation
> even we didn't believe[.]

In "The Awakening" (*The Awakening*), he can't help comparing the struggle of a crushed but still living bee to "the fatal struggle / the agony on the face of wounded friends / and the same dumb drive to continue[.]" In the poem, the bee is miraculously restored and flies out of Wantling's hand, but in real life the crushed, the mangled, the maimed, the broken in body and spirit could not be restored. "Sure" Wantling says in the poem of that name in *The Source*:

> I'd like to love
> altogether & believe
> absolutely in non-
> violence & make
> this a world
> where children
> no longer suffer
>
>   * * *
>
> but
> can you be a
> pacifist
> after you've killed
> too many
> & if one is too many
> where do I stand
> with *my* score?

And in "It Was Tuesday Morning" (*Sick Fly*), he writes: "I never wanted to be a poet / I'd carry a lunchbox like everybody else / if only the muttering would stop[.]"

God only knows where the muttering really came from, but it wouldn't stop, and in the end it left him unable even to be a poet. "If I cld only love, hate, write a poem, maybe I cld sleep," he wrote in "Style 4" (*7 on Style*). He was dead before the poem was published. A few days before his heart finally gave out, he was found in his apartment—Ruthie having finally thrown him out, unable any longer to cope with him—unconscious and lying in his own urine and feces, every window of the apartment smashed out. It was a sorry end for a man who, at his best, was both a good poet and, by all accounts, a good man. Better to remember him, as he himself writes in "ah, history!" (*10,000 r.p.m.*), this way:

> now, upon this awkward ball of Mud
> at certain times I see
> despite the poison raging through my blood
> all
> all is ecstasy[.]

[The bulk of the biographical information on Wantling comes from Pyros and Jones. See "Setting the Record Straight: An Addendum to the Life and Poetry of William Wantling" for important information not available at the time this essay was first published.]

Works Cited

Bukowski, Charles. "W. W. Goes." *Dramatika*, Fall 1976.

Edwards, Paul M., ed. *The Hermit Kingdom: Poems of the Korean War*. Dubuque, Iowa: Kendall/Hunt, 1995.

Franklin, H. Bruce. *Prison Literature in America*. New York: Oxford University Press, 1989.

Jones, Kevin E. "Finding Jewels in the Awkward Mud: A Reconsideration of William Wantling and His Poetry." Unpublished doctoral dissertation, Illinois State University, 1994.

Pyros, John. *William Wantling: A Biography & Selected Works*. Peoria, Illinois: Spoon River Poetry Press, 1981.

Wantling, William. *Five Poem Songs*. Torrance, California: Hors Commerce Press, 1964.

_____. *The Search*. Torrance, California: Hors Commerce Press, 1964.

_____. *Down, Off & Out*. Bensenville, Illinois: Mimeo Press, 1965.

_____. *The Source*. El Cerrito, California: Dustbooks, 1966.

_____. *The Awakening*. London, England: Rapp & Whiting, 1968.

_____. *Sick Fly*. Cardiff, Wales: second aeon publications, 1970.

_____. *Obscene & Other Poems*. Dunedin, New Zealand: Caveman Press, 1972.

_____. *10,000 r.p.m. & digging it, yeah!* Cardiff, Wales: second aeon publications, 1973.

_____. *7 on Style*. San Francisco, California: Second Coming Press, 1975.

❖ ❖ ❖

Howard Fast's "Korean Litany"

Though the Korean War did not produce a body of poetry comparable in size to that of either World War Two or the Vietnam War, contrary to both popular and scholarly perceptions it has served as a source of poetic inspiration for a number of writers, veterans and non-veterans alike.

In a previous essay called "Soldier-Poets of the Korean War" (*War, Literature, and the Arts,* v.9, #2, 1997), I discussed the poetry of William Childress, Rolando Hinojosa, James Magner, Jr., Reg Saner, William Wantling, and Keith Wilson. Most prominent among those poets who did not serve in Korea but who wrote poems about the Korean War are Thomas McGrath, whose "Ode for the American Dead in Korea" first appeared in *Figures of the Double World* in 1955, and Hayden Carruth, whose "On a Certain Engagement South of Seoul" first appeared in *The Crow and the Heart* in 1959.

One of the most ambitious attempts to address the Korean War in verse, however, is Howard Fast's *Korean Lullaby*, an undated fourteen-page pamphlet published by the American Peace Crusade and containing three poems. (While *Korean Lullaby* carries no date or copyright notice, the contents of the booklet itself clearly suggest that it was published sometime between the outbreak of the war in June 1950 and the signing of the truce in July 1953.)

When Georgina Murphy, La Salle University's immensely able collection Development Librarian, first brought the pamphlet to my attention, I dismissed Fast rather more hastily than I should have. At least part of his *Korean Lullaby* has more to recommend it than I initially recognized. I am grateful to Philip K. Jason of the U.S. Naval Academy, my co-editor on *Retrieving Bones: Stories and Poems of the Korean War,* for urging me to take a closer look.

All three poems are stridently antiwar, and not just in a general sense. Fast makes it clear that he quite specifically opposes American intervention in Korea. Anyone familiar with Fast will not be surprised by the stance he takes. A successful and prolific novelist, Fast had already published more than two dozen books by 1950 and would go on to write *Spartacus* and *The Immigrants*, both of which would become popular movies (the latter on TV), and scores of others (most recently *Greenwich*, which he published in 2000 at the age of 85). In 1943, however, he joined the Communist Party. Though he left the party in 1956, he was an active member during the Korean War, and since the war was being waged against North Korean and then Chinese Communists, it was a matter of Communist Party doctrine to oppose it.

Not surprisingly, the pamphlet's publisher, the American Peace Crusade, was denounced as a Communist front organization by Secretary of State Dean Acheson, an assessment that was largely accurate. (In fact, it probably was exactly what Acheson said it was. Though many prominent Americans involved in the American Peace Crusade were not members of the Communist Party—Cornell Professor Philip Morrison, for instance, who assembled the first atomic bomb on Tinian Island in 1945; Cal Tech professor Linus Pauling, who had been given the Medal of Merit for his World War Two contributions to rocket research; and former Minnesota Governor Elmer Benson—others such as Fast certainly were.) Acheson's assessment, however, is of no practical consequence in regard to Fast's poems, which are what they are regardless of the publisher.

Korean Lullaby seems to be Fast's only published excursion into the world of poetry, and the first and third poems in the pamphlet are strong arguments that one should be grateful Fast mostly avoided poetry. Both "Korean Lullaby," the title poem, and "A Song of Peace" are, says Jason, "undistinguished, manipulative rhymed verse," and "polemical" as well. In "Korean Lullaby," for instance, Fast twice rhymes four lines in a row, having the unintended and almost comical effect of bringing to mind Edgar Allan Poe's "The Raven." Elsewhere in the poem, he argues that the war is really being fought by western capitalists to fuel the economy and stave off depression, and he puts "free world" in quotes to make sure we get his point. "A Song of Peace" is not quite as ham-fisted with its politics, but as a poem it is no improvement over "Korean Lullaby."

Given these two poems, it is all the more startling to encounter "Korean Litany" wedged between them, for "Korean Litany" is as different from these other two poems as one could possibly imagine—in form, in content, in quality, and in impact. Written entirely in free verse, it is actually seven poems in one, each in the voice of a dead American soldier. Though Fast had no combat experience of his own—during World War

Two, he was assigned to the Office of War Information—the voices he assumes are for the most part both compelling and convincing. While one can see Fast's politics at work in these poems, their deceptive simplicity and heartbreaking humanity transcend ideology and make them truly works of art.

All in all, "Korean Litany" works so effectively one wonders how it could be possible for Fast to have written anything as bad as the two poems that precede and follow it in *Korean Lullaby*. However that happened, "Korean Litany" is a poem—really seven poems under one title—that deserves to be treated as a major contribution to Korean War literature. Instead, the poem has been all but lost. Only a few copies of the original pamphlet still exist, tucked away in research libraries. It is not in the Library of Congress, and a survey of rare book dealers I recently conducted turned up not a single copy. To my knowledge, no part of the pamphlet has ever been reprinted.

In the case of "Korean Litany," this is a shame that is happily and finally corrected. Here, with the kind permission of Fast himself, is the full text of "Korean Litany."

VERNON BLAKE, RIFLEMAN:

My age reads, as long as the wood lasts,
twenty-three, and read my name,
I, Vernon Blake, who died in action
from a sniper's bullet—and rests in peace,
or less than peace perhaps, in Korean soil.
And fortunate perhaps, for only one question
twists a little with the maggots.
You see, the American way of life
was all at one with me, ten generations on each side
all from this soil, and the house I lived in,
Chester, Vermont, white clapboard,
and easy with all those generations.
I ate, drank and slept and played,
studied a little, grew strong and tall and proud;
I saw it when my mother looked at me,
and my father's eyes were full of pride,
and I wrote to him, "I make a good soldier,
and all those days we tramped the fields
and brush together were not wasted—"
We went for rabbit and squirrel, and once a long shot
at a deer. How my mother loved us both!
"Two men," she said, "the Bible notwithstanding,

my own prescription for a happy home."
And I fought her when she wanted my college diploma,
framed in the livingroom—why didn't she
have four children, tall and strong and proud like me?
I would have answered her question eventually,
for I had no doubts and no questions.
It was in her that the doubts grew, like a cancer,
"Why, why, why, why? Why are you there, my son,
and not with me?" I would have framed the answer,
given time, framed it proudly for her to hang on the wall—
for there must be an answer.

HARRY MORGAN, MACHINE GUNNER:

My old man never had much sense,
working on an assembly line all his life,
the candle burned at both ends, squeezed in the middle,
and always yapping of the pride of class
a worker has. "What future where the world is yours?"
I'd ask him. "You got only a past, old man,
and the smart money goes to the smart fingers.
Get smart, old man, get smart.
I'll take a buck and you—you keep your commie line."
He could have said a lot of things,
and talked of damn young punks,
but it wasn't easy for him to put in words
the things he felt, and the one letter he sent,
I never answered. "Only remember," he wrote,
"the men you fight are your brothers,
working with their own hands, as I work with mine,
and you with yours." Where are my hands,
old man? Both of them blown off by a mortar shell,
and me looking at the stumps as I bled to death.

ARTHUR DEMBROWSKI, CHEMICAL WARFARE:

Dug up quickly, you would see,
snub nose, sandy hair and a broad face;
we never like what we see in our own mirror,
and I only started shaving three months before the service.
A girl would like or not like that face,
making a better judgment than mine—
but even love was postponed, this crazy kid
making a pal of a three year old, my brother,

sixteen years between him and me,
me the child of my mother's youth,
and he of her last bearing time.
The way it was, I never loved anything
the way I loved that kid,
and we were better friends than most brothers.
With his little fat hand in mine,
we'd walk on my furloughs, and they'd say,
"There's Dembrowski and his buddy."
I was a flame thrower, and out of one burning house
crawled a Korean child, blistered and singed
all over his skin. I picked him up
and cradled him in my arms, talking to him
when a bullet blew off the back of my head.

AL CARLTON, MEDIC:

When I crawled up to a Korean wounded
to heal him, and got a bullet in my gut,
I hated for the first time in nine months,
dying wastefully and painfully, whimpering,
"Oh Jesus—what a lousy way!"
And he, with one arm torn off,
lay watching me and whispered,
"Hey, Yank—what for you come here?
Go home. Go home." And then we bled together,
blood mixing with blood,
and the last thing I thought of
was blood brothers, and then I died
by the side of the man who killed me.

GERALD CARTWHEEL, TANKMAN:

The day my tank rolled through a village,
flattening those flimsy houses,
I saw a woman caught under a beam,
screaming as the tank rolled over—
on that day, I wrote to my congressman,
my free and democratic right,
"Was I sent here to do this kind of thing,
or tell me why, or have I no right to know,
or do you know?" I sought no easy answer,
knowing—as others don't—
that things are not all black and white.
Others ribbed me, scoffed, and said,

"Tell it to the chaplain, bub."
I wonder what the answer would have been,
and whether I would have felt at ease,
cooking in a burning tank
and screaming for my mother.

AARON KLEIN, RIFLEMAN:

I did what I did, and followed orders through,
and died with one hundred and sixteen men,
all together, brave men who fought and died,
and left a wife and child, and a mother
who will die too, this being too much pain
for her to take and live with,
and I was brave, and asked no questions,
and never asked to know what I,
a Jew and kin to those six million
whom Hitler slew, was doing here, in this strange land,
making a desert and a graveyard
of a sunny place where people lived and worked—
and never asked what good dead children did
in freedom's struggle. And if I thought,
am I or the man across the ridge and facing me,
fighting freedom's fight? I never changed
the thought to words or deeds—
then why do I rest so poorly,
in this strange soil?

JAMSIE ANDERSON, QUARTERMASTERS:

I used to laugh and say,
"I got no future, but lots of past."
Well, take my past and put it you know where,
all of it, cleaning toilets and shining shoes—
not like them that sat and sighed
for a glass of beer at five o'clock,
just that to walk on them soft heaven clouds.
That ain't no heaven for me,
promoted to driving a half-track through Korean mud;
and then they'd say, "You're turning evil, Jamsie,
evil as all hell." Oh, no, never, not no evil
in me now, but just a little plain damned common sense.
"Then keep it to yourself," they said. "Black man's
got no business talking common sense."
But never was a man could take his common sense
and force it to behave, and mine kept plaguing me.
Oh, what a lot of questions I could ask

of them strange men who blew me all apart.
Not white men, boss men,
no southern accent there,
but colored men like me,
with eyes as full of pain—
lifted me tenderly,
and buried me in Korean soil. I'd ask them calm and gentle,
not evil, but just with common sense.

❖ ❖ ❖

From the Halls of Montezuma to the Chosin Reservoir

For most Americans, the Korean War is "the Forgotten War." One of the better histories of the war, by Clay Blair, is even titled *The Forgotten War*. In his book *The Fifties*, David Halberstam writes, "America tolerated the Korean War while it was on but could not wait to forget it once the war was over." Who wanted to remember a war in which the U.S. Army was handed its hat by a bunch of peasants in sneakers not once but twice in six months, and thereafter raged on for another two and a half years only to end up pretty much where it had started—minus 37,000 dead Americans (not to mention a couple of million Koreans). Only in recent years, with the approach of the 50th anniversary of the Korean War, have Americans begun to acknowledge this unacknowledged war, most visibly with the 1995 dedication of the Korean War Veterans Memorial.

Little of this, however, applies to the United States Marine Corps, which was not handed its hat by anybody, not in Korea at least. Historian Bruce Cumings, an otherwise persistent critic of the war, acknowledges in his book *Korea's Place in the Sun* that the initial North Korean successes in the summer of 1950 were halted only when "the American First Marine Division stiffened the defense." It was the Marines who spearheaded the Inchon landings and the recapture of Seoul in September 1950. And while the U. S. Eighth Army fell back pell mell in the face of the Chinese onslaught in November 1950, the First Marine Division decimated an estimated ten Chinese divisions during its fighting withdrawal from the Chosin Reservoir (actually the Changjin Reservoir; Chosin was the Japanese name for it). Whatever the military and political ramifications, mystifications, and obfuscations of the Korean War for the rest of America, Marines have never forgotten or tried to forget their role in it.

In the realm of literature, as in the culture at large, the Korean War has been overwhelmed by the wars which come immediately before and after it, but in fact a little digging reveals a much richer body of work than most people realize. And, interestingly enough, a disproportionate part of this literature is written by former Marines. Among the best of the memoirs are James Brady's *The Coldest War* (Orion Books, 1990) and Martin Russ's *The Last Parallel* (Rinehart, 1957), while the best works of fiction include William Styron's *The Long March* (Random House, 1952), set in the United States but very much a Korean War novel, and Gene Coon's *Meanwhile, Back at the Front* (Crown, 1961).

Indeed, the body of Korean War literature is still growing, and one of the most recent additions is Edwin Howard Simmons's novel *Dog Company Six* (Naval Institute Press, 2000), a book that is of particular interest because its author is a retired Marine Corps brigadier general, a three-war veteran who commanded a weapons company during the first year of the Korean War and took part in both the Inchon/Seoul and Chosin campaigns. It's not every day that a general-grade officer turns his hand to novel-writing. Aside from Simmons, the only other person who comes to mind is William Chamberlain, an army brigadier who took up writing after he retired in 1946, publishing a number of novels and short stories, many of them about World War Two and the Korean War.

Captain Edwin H. Simmons, U.S.M.C., North China, 1946. (Photograph provided by Edwin Simmons)

Simmons, who directed the Marine Corps History and Museum Division for 24 years after retiring from active service, has been a prolific writer over the years, his titles including *The United States Marines: A History* and *The Marines,* but *Dog Company Six* is his first foray into the realm of fiction. And it's an impressive first novel in any case, not just because its author is a septuagenarian general. Well written and very readable, it's a page-turning story that keeps a brisk pace from beginning to end. And while clearly relying on many of Simmons's own experiences in Korea, the book is decidedly not—as are many first novels—merely a thinly disguised autobiography.

Dog Company Six (military parlance for the commanding officer of Company D) is Captain George Bayard, a non-combat veteran of World War Two called back to active duty at the outbreak of the Korean War and assigned—largely due to a shortage of qualified personnel—as a rifle company commander. Because the United States demobilized so rapidly and thoroughly at the end of World War Two, his was a situation faced by a great many World War Two veterans who chose to remain in the reserves, never imagining the United States would be involved in another major war so soon after World War Two. (Indeed, the same dilemma lies at the heart of Styron's *The Long March*, published 48 years ago.)

Simmons doesn't follow a straight-line narrative. Beginning and ending the book in a convalescent hotel in Japan in the late spring of 1951, he moves around in time, following Bayard and his battalion from North Carolina to Inchon and Seoul, Chosin, and finally central Korea. Along the way, the narrative goes back to Bayard's pre-war upbringing in Columbus, Ohio, and his post-World War Two life as a school teacher in Baltimore.

But the heart of the story is Bayard's struggle to turn himself into a competent infantry commander and to prove himself both to his rigidly demanding battalion operations officer and to the skeptical regular officers and noncommissioned officers of Dog Company:

"If I'm going to make the grade," Bayard says to his far more experienced (though junior in rank) executive officer, "if I'm going to do even a half-way decent job, I'll need all the help I can get. Particularly from you, Gibson."

"You'll have it," Gibson replies. "One more thing, sir, I think you should know: there's no plot against you. Nobody wants you to fail. The officers and men, they want you to turn out to be a good company commander."

Whether Bayard succeeds or fails I will not say. That would spoil the fun. But I will say that this is not quite the book one might expect from a man who spent a total of fifty-four years of his life in or working for the Marine Corps. Simmons throws in all sorts of surprises. Though the washed-up-battalion-commander-living-on-his-glorious-reputation rather predictably turns out to be the equal of his reputation after all, the good guys don't always win—in war or in love—and on more than one occasion, when you think you know what's coming next, it turns out that you don't.

Simmons also presents the war with remarkable balance and perspective. While we see the atrocities of the North Koreans, for instance, he pointedly makes clear that atrocities occurred on both sides of the lines. And while Bayard and his men fight with unquestioning professionalism and tenacity, Bayard also realizes that "you can't export made-in-America democracy the way you can automobiles or fountain pens. You can't even give it away like you can machine guns and dollars."

Just as fascinating is Simmons's willingness to challenge accepted wisdom. While history has generally remembered Douglas MacArthur's Inchon landing as his most brilliant moment,

Brigadier General Edwin H. Simmons, U.S.M.C. (Ret.), veteran of World War Two and the Korean and Vietnam wars, historian, and novelist, 2000. (Photograph provided by Edwin Simmons)

Simmons has Bayard's battalion commander (known as "the Red Snapper") observe, "Today was the goddamnest landing I've ever seen in the twenty-five years I've been a Marine. You couldn't have fouled it up more if you tried. If the enemy had been the Japanese you wouldn't have gotten a goddamn' man ashore alive. You'd be out there face down in the mud with the crabs feeding on you."

Another accepted truth, one that Marines love to trumpet, is that Marines never leave their dead behind. In reality, while Herculean efforts were made to avoid doing so, during that terrible winter withdrawal from the Chosin Reservoir, a number of the dead simply had to be left, and Simmons does not shy away from that harsh reality. As Bayard's company prepares to withdraw, Bayard asks, "What about the dead?"

"'They must be left,' said the Old Man. 'We'll have barely enough able-bodied men to carry the wounded.'"

"'Just leave them?' he asked shakily."

"'Son,' said the Red Snapper gently, 'we're going to need every ounce of energy we can muster to get ourselves and our wounded out of this place.'"

It is touches like this that make *Dog Company Six* not just an action-packed adventure story—though it is that, to be sure—but a starkly realistic portrait of infantry combat.

Finally, Simmons is not just a good storyteller but a good writer as well. Time and again, his language and imagery are startlingly alive: "Dog Company shook itself into what amounted to a long skirmish line…. Yesterday the shelling of Inchon had been a pageant of fire and smoke; today it was ten thousand homeless families."

That is just good writing. And *Dog Company Six* is a good book. More than that, it is a valuable contribution to the much-neglected literature of the Korean War. And perhaps with the 50th anniversary of that war now upon us, and the nation as a whole finally willing to examine that critical episode in American history, Simmons's novel will get the attention it deserves.

❖ ❖ ❖

Tarnishing the Glory of the Corps

Perhaps the most glorious episode in the glorious history of the United States Marine Corps is the 1st Marine Division's fighting withdrawal from the Chosin Reservoir during the Korean War.[*] Numerous histories of the Chosin campaign have been written over the years, among them Jim Wilson's *Retreat, Hell!*, Eric Hammel's *Chosin: Heroic Ordeal of the Korean War*, and Martin Russ's *Breakout: The Chosin Reservoir Campaign*. Joseph Owen's *Colder Than Hell: A Marine Rifle Company at Chosin Reservoir* is an excellent memoir.

A number of fictionalized accounts of the campaign have also been published, most notably Pat Frank's *Hold Back the Night*, Ernest Frankel's *Band of Brothers*, and William Crawford's *Give Me Tomorrow*. A portion of Edwin Simmons's recently published *Dog Company Six* also takes place on the road to and from Chosin. To this list of novels, James Brady, Marine veteran and Korean War memoirist (*The Coldest War*), has added *The Marines of Autumn* (St. Martin's Press, 2000).

Brady's story revolves around Captain Thomas Verity, who grew up in North China as the son of an American businessman, went to Yale but dropped out after Pearl Harbor to join the Marines, fought at Guadalcanal,

---

[*]*The Korean name for the reservoir is actually Changjin. American military forces in 1950 had access only to Japanese maps of the area, which called the reservoir Chosin.*

went to officer candidate school and subsequently fought at Okinawa, returned to North China with the Marines in 1946, earned a doctorate from Harvard after mustering out, and is teaching at Georgetown University when the Korean War begins. Though still an inactive reservist, he is initially spared call-up in the summer of 1950 because he is also a widower with a daughter not yet three.

But because he can speak and understand several dialects of Chinese, he is finally called up and sent to Korea that autumn, tasked with monitoring Chinese radio traffic as the 1st Marine Division advances north toward the Yalu River. The adventures of Captain Verity, his radio operator, Gunnery Sergeant Tate, and his driver, Corporal Izzo, are interspersed with a running historical account of the advance and withdrawal.

Unfortunately, this novel will add no glory to the Chosin campaign or its literature. For starters, Verity's dead wife, whom we see in a series of flashbacks and reminiscences, is too perfect to be believed. Young (17 when he—at 26—marries her; 20 when she dies giving birth to a second child, who also dies), beautiful, rich, she is also practical, sexy, adventurous, spontaneous, liberated—you name it, she's got it: "Elizabeth would astonish her husband with an imaginative lust good girls weren't supposed to demonstrate and few wives could."

But now that she is dead, Verity must raise little Kate alone with only the help of Madame, a full-time nanny. This is a burden which weighs heavily on Verity as he fights for survival against the Chinese and the cold because he has promised to dance with Kate on the bridges of Paris (as he had once done with Elizabeth), just like in the little song he and Kate sing together in French.

Brady relies heavily on smarmy sentamentalism and transparent irony to carry the book, devices which might work in a Danielle Steele novel, but are downright insulting in what purports to be serious literature. With combat against the Chinese imminent, Verity writes to Kate that "some Chinese gentlemen I used to know might be coming to visit us soon." When Madame tells Kate it is snowing where her father is, Kate innocently exclaims, "Oh, I hope they have sleds." In the midst of Marines struggling with the terrible cold and snow of North Korea, Brady has Kate respond to the first snowfall in Washington, D. C., "Oh, I wish Poppy could see it. He loves snow, too." And immediately on the heels of Verity's death, he has Douglas MacArthur say to his wife, "Yes, Jean, home is of all destinations sweetest."

These sorts of cheap tricks and melodramatic juxtapositions are just the beginning of the book's problems, however. For another thing, Brady repeats himself endlessly. Twice he tells us about MacArthur's meeting with Harry Truman on Wake Island in October, and twice he describes the

Chinese attacks of late October and early November, each succeeding time as if he had not told us before. Four times he tells us that Verity has not been in a firefight or killed anyone in five years. At least that many times he tells us that Verity was not afraid to die in World War Two, but now that he is a father and a widower, he's afraid. Four times he tells us that Gunny Tate, who had been a prisoner of the Japanese, would rather die than be taken prisoner again.

And speaking of gunnery sergeants, in the course of the novel Brady tells us that "Gunnies were notoriously difficult to please," "Gunnery sergeants know where to draw the line," "It takes a lot to unsettle a Marine gunny," "Gunnery sergeants take care of each other," and "It wasn't in the nature of gunnery sergeants to show emotion." It is as if all Marine gunnery sergeants are cut out of sheet metal, each the same as the next.

And, of course, they are stalwart and true, as are most of the Marines Verity encounters. Reading page after page of lines like "We're a ferocious little confraternity, we Marines" and "Marines were nothing if not pragmatic" and "*Hell*, Verity thought, *they look like … Marines*" (ellipsis in original), it is as if Brady fears we'll forget just how special Marines are if he does not remind us every few pages. Even his bashing of the U. S. Army in general and General MacArthur in particular, entertaining at first, begins to take on the quality of kicking a dog that's already down.

Other problems include Brady's putting Kate in kindergarten at age three, her classmates also being a dozen other "three- or four-year olds" with nary a five-year-old among them; telling us at one point that Yale granted Verity a bachelor's degree even though he never finished, but later telling us that Verity went back to Yale to finish after World War Two; having Corporal Izzo repeatedly use the word "frigging," as if this novel were being published in 1950 instead of 2000; having Verity use the term "peace process" with regard to truce negotiations between Mao Tse-tung and Chiang Kai-shek in 1946; and perhaps most egregious of all, having George Washington's Continental Army break its winter encampment at Valley Forge to attack the British and Hessians at Trenton.

One of the most disturbing elements of the book is Brady's three references to black soldiers. Since black soldiers play no part at all in the novel, except in these odd little digressions, the references are puzzling, to say the least— and each impugns the fighting qualities of black soldiers. Here is one:

> At Kunu-ri in the west, in I Corps, Lt. Col. Melvin Blair, commanding the Third Battalion Twenty-fourth Infantry, fled the field. Colonel Blair blamed his black troops, claiming they said 'Bugout Boogie' was their official regimental ditty. The black soldiers said their colonel ran first and they only followed.

What on earth is this doing in a novel about Marines at the Chosin Reservoir?

There's a lot more, but you get the idea. Any few of these problems might have been tolerable, but the cumulative impact of all of them, page after page after page, produces first irritation, then anger, and finally disgust. At Verity's funeral, in the book's final sentence, Brady has Kate ask Madame, "And who will take me now to France to see the bridges?" After 274 pages of such heavy-handed attempts to manipulate the reader's emotions, the word that comes to mind is not pathos, but pander.

❖ ❖ ❖

Pennridge High School and the Vietnam War

One of the more delicious ironies of my life occurred in November 1965 during my senior year at Pennridge High School in Perkasie, Pennsylvania. I was taking Margaret Geosits's public speaking class that fall, and as part of the course, we had to do "for and against" presentations in an all-school assembly. Partners, topics, and points of view were all chosen at random, and I ended up having to argue against the war in Vietnam while Timmy Moyer argued in support of the war.

I spent several weeks preparing, and when the big day came, I got up in front of a thousand students, faculty, and administrators and made my case: that years of civil unrest in South Vietnam's cities, most graphically epitomized by Buddhist self-immolations, demonstrated that the Vietnamese had neither faith nor confidence in their government or ours; that the numerous coups and countercoups of the South Vietnamese army generals demonstrated that our allies neither understood nor cared about democracy and were furthermore incapable of governing themselves under any system; that every U.S. escalation of force had only led to continuing stalemate at ever higher levels of death and destruction; that we'd picked the wrong place to take a stand beside the wrong ally, and we ought to cut our losses and get out while the getting was good.

Maybe not the most sophisticated analysis, but not bad for a 17-year-old from a rural Republican community in 1965, and I was closer to the truth than I ever imagined at the time. That's where the irony comes in: I didn't believe a word of what I said that day. I believed the problem was that the U.S. wasn't using anywhere near enough force in Vietnam. I believed those Buddhist monks and nuns were either Commie dupes or Commie agents. I believed the civil unrest was fomented and perpetrated by the Communists. I believed it was impossible to build a democracy until we had defeated the Viet Cong.

Indeed, when I'd first received my topic, I'd argued long and hard with Mrs. Geosits. I didn't want to argue against a war I believed to be right, but she insisted that it was all just an academic exercise, that arguing persuasively for what one believed was easy, that the real test of my skills would be to argue well for something I didn't believe in, and that in any case, if she made an exception for me, the whole exercise would turn into a personal preference free-for-all.

I have often wondered, in the years since, if my ending up with that topic and that point of view were really as random as it appeared, or if Mrs. Geosists had somehow managed to engineer it in the hope that I might learn something to give me pause. That doesn't seem possible because it would be another month before I would begin to consider delaying college and joining the Marines instead, and another four months before I would share the knowledge of that decision with anyone. But I wonder. Did she see the path down which I was headed even before I saw it? For once I made my intentions known, I realized later, she had indeed tried to give me pause.

I liked Mrs. Geosits, in spite of her assignment, and in the spring I took her journalism class as well. By then I was full of myself and my future. For every assignment she gave—feature writing, editorials, hard news—I wrote about the Vietnam War. I ended an editorial in which I staunchly defended the U.S. war in Vietnam by concluding, "What more noble a cause can a man die for, than to die in defense of freedom?" Her comment was, "I hope your feelings are strengthened along these lines but not to the point where you no longer see the whole picture." I ended a feature assignment about my impending departure for Parris Island by saying, "Only after I complete the twelve-week training course will I be a full-fledged United States Marine. Her response was, "To your satisfaction? To the satisfaction of the USMC? Be careful of the 12 week package; there's no guarantee."

I suspect Mrs. Geosits would like to have slapped me up aside the head and said, "Hey, wise up! This is not a good idea." But she was young, not a native of the community, in her first year of teaching at Pennridge, and undoubtedly far more aware than I was at the time that the limits of acceptable dissent in Pennridge High School and the larger community it served (four small boroughs and four rural townships) were very narrow. Lyndon Johnson was too liberal by half for the majority of folks in Perkasie—which had voted heavily for Barry Goldwater in 1964—and the only public dissent on the Vietnam War came from people who thought Johnson was too timid in his prosecution of it. If anyone in Perkasie thought that Johnson's war policy was too hawkish, they kept it to themselves. There was no antiwar movement in Perkasie, nor would there ever be. Whatever Mrs. Geosits might have thought, she had to be careful about what she said.

The student body of Pennridge High School, not surprisingly, was very much a reflection of the community. I received polite applause for my presentation that day in November 1965, but for his defense of the war, Timmy Moyer received a raucous outburst of approval. (Therein lies a second irony of the day: barely more than a year later, I was tromping through the ricefields with 70 pounds of gear on my back and leeches in my boots while Timmy Moyer was tromping from psychology class to philosophy class with a pile of books under his arm, and to my knowledge he never spent a day in uniform, let alone in Vietnam—though whose fault is that, anyway?)

We were, of course—the student body of Pennridge High School— teenagers, rebellious by definition, but our rebellion against our elders took the most traditional of forms: underage drinking, smoking cigarettes (not marijuana—there was no marijuana in Perkasie in 1965, or speed or acid or coke), partying in whichever house the parents were gone for the weekend, long hair of the early Beatles variety (if your hair overhung the nape of your nack and touched your collar, you would be sent home from school until you got it cut), berets and madras shirts and whatever else we thought was cool from year to year. We listened to rock 'n' roll music by the Rolling Stones, Paul Revere and the Raiders, Mitch Rider and the Detroit Wheels. Some of the hippest among us, myself included, also listened to Peter, Paul & Mary, Bob Dylan, and Donovan. I could get misty-eyed and wistful listening to "Blowin' in the Wind," but it never occurred to me—to any of us really, except maybe Eric Royer, who eventually became a Lutheran minister and spent the early years of his career at an inner city church in West Philadelphia—that the problem might be us at least as much as it was the Russians.

Our assumption that the Russians were the bad guys—an assumption pretty much shared by most Americans, not just the good folks of Perkasie—was not entirely groundless, one needs to remember. Among my earliest memories of a world beyond my own family and community are newsreels of Soviet tanks crushing the Hungarian Revolution of 1956. As a youngster, I watched Nikita Khrushchev banging his shoe on the podium at the United Nations while shouting, "We will bury you!" And I came home from school one afternoon when I was 14 to find my parents sitting ashen-faced in front of the television set, looking at reconnaissance photographs of nuclear missile sites in Cuba, and I knew that what was happening was, quite literally, deadly serious. For two weeks, I waited to die in a nuclear Armageddon.

Our high school history teachers, I learned only years later, of course had not taught us that the U.S. had handed eastern Europe over to Joseph Stalin and his minions even before World War Two had ended. Nor had they mentioned that the Soviet Union was completely ringed by American nuclear missiles, those in Turkey and Iran and Alaska closer to Russian soil than the Cuban missiles were to American soil.

There were lots of things we were never taught by either our his-

William D. Ehrhart, Pennridge High School, Perkasie, Pennsylvania, Class of 1966. (Photograph provided by W.D. Ehrhart)

tory teachers or anyone else responsible for our education, but I did not come to know this until much later. So when sober-faced men like Lyndon Johnson and Dean Rusk and Robert McNamara told us the Communist threat must be met in Vietnam, I had every reason to believe them and no reason not to. It seemed perfectly clear to me. Thus, while I grooved on "Masters of War" and "Where Have All the Flowers Gone," it didn't occur to me that there was any contradiction between my fondness for these songs and my decision to join the Marines. A man's gotta do what a man's gotta do.

My senior English teacher, John Diehl, saw the contradiction and, like Mrs. Geosits, tried to warn me. He was a cool guy, Mr. Diehl. He would let us come over to his house in Blooming Glen for coffee, and while we were there at least, we were allowed to call him "John" instead of "Mr. Diehl," an absolutely unheard of liberty that made us feel privileged and sophisticated and adult. Once he brought into class a full-page ad from the *New York Times* that had been placed by a single individual—a Japanese businessman, I think. The ad was a plea to end the war in Vietnam. Mr. Diehl wanted us to see that here was someone who believed so strongly in something that he was willing to spend thousands of dollars of his own money to be heard. I realize now that he was trying to get us to consider another point of view that was heard not at all at Pennridge High School, but I remember thinking: Wasn't that something? Only in America could a Japanese businessman express himself so openly without fear of reprisal. To me, the whole exercise only served as further proof that America was the greatest country on earth. You certainly couldn't run an ad like that in Russia!

One day in April 1966, Mr. Diehl asked me if I could stop by his house that night. I had been there on a number of occasions, but always with Eric or Larry Rush or someone else, and always we'd invited ourselves. I was very excited, and wondered all day what the occasion for the invitation was. I knew Mr. Diehl had been a Marine during the Korean War. Maybe he was going to give me some inside advice.

Which, it turns out, was true, though it wasn't the kind of advice I'd been expecting. Mr. Diehl suggested that I might be wiser to go to college first, then if I still wanted to join the Marines, I could go in as an officer. He never told me he thought the war was wrong or the U.S. government wrongheaded—he had more seniority than Mrs. Geosits, though again I understood only well after the fact that he too had to be cautious—but he politely suggested that I was perhaps acting precipitously and without all the facts, and a few years' delay might be prudent. He couched his argument in terms of the advantages of being an officer rather than an enlisted man, but given what I later learned about the brief life expectancy of an infantry platoon commander in combat—something he must have been fully aware of himself—he was clearly hoping to buy time for the war to end or me to come to my senses.

Alas, his efforts were futile. I had dreams of glory, a lifetime of certitude, and a whole community four-square behind me. I was going to be a Marine, just like John Wayne in *The Sands of Iwo Jima*, just like my favorite teacher had been. I did learn that night, however, that while Mr. Diehl had been in the Marines during the Korean War, he had never left the U.S. I remember it made me feel a little sorry for him, for what's a Marine in wartime who hasn't been to war? I resolved to make damned sure so embarrassing a turn of events did not happen to me. I made it clear to my recruiter, Staff Sergeant Robert Bookheimer, that I was joining the Marines to fight in Vietnam, and he assured me that the Marine Corps would be happy to accommodate me.

Given what I've said about the community in which I grew up, it will come as no surprise that Pennridge High School, and the older Sell-Perk High it superseded, had always supplied its share of recruits for the armed forces of the United States. Every Armed Forces Day, the school held an all-school assembly at which representatives from all the services—recruiting sergeants, in fact—would take the stage in their fanciest dress uniforms and pitch their respective branches. For many boys who would spend the rest of their lives at the U.S. Gauge plant in Sellersville, or Hendricks' Dairy in Perkasie, or working the family farm in Hilltwon Township, a few years in the service would likely be their only chance for a little adventure and travel and status. The idea of dying in Vietnam—even after Randy Moore died there in the spring of 1966—was no real deterrent to a 17- or 18-year-old kid with an itch in his pants and a bellyful of woodshop, and our school guidance counselors weren't likely to try to discourage him either. Quite the opposite, in fact.

So my enlistment was unusual only in that I had long before been pegged by the school system as college material. The curriculum was divided into academic, general, commercial, and vocational sections, and I had always been in the top academic section. Of that group—about 60 kids, 30 boys—I was the only one to join the service instead of going to college. But even at that, when I announced my decision, only Mr. Diehl and Mrs. Geosits offered anything resembling reservations. Many of my teachers quite explicitly congratulated me and heartily suggested that I was doing a fine thing. It was—though no one said it in so many words, or had to say it—the American thing to do, the patriotic thing. Had I not, after all, begun each day of my twelve years in public school by covering my heart with my hand and reciting the Pledge of Allegiance to the Flag and to the Republic for which it stands? My photograph appeared in the local weekly paper, the *News-Herald*, me shaking hands with SSgt. Bookheimer, he in his dress blue uniform. And wasn't it a dandy uniform, too? In a few months, I'd be wearing a uniform like that. And wouldn't the girls at Pennridge High think "wow" when they saw me in it?

I never did own a dress blue uniform. I have a portrait of me wearing one that was taken at Parris Island in the summer of 1966, but it's only a posed shot for our boot camp platoon book. The photographer had a few hats of varying sizes, and the jacket I appear to be wearing is really just a one-size-fits-all shoulder drape held in place at the back of the neck with a springloaded clothespin. When I came home on leave a few weeks after boot camp, my mother gave me $50 to buy a set of dress blues (they were only issued to enlisted personnel who required them: embassy guards, recruiters, seaborne detachments; everyone else had to buy them because they were just for show anyway). But the Marine supply depot in South Philadelphia didn't have my size in stock the day I went there, and by the time the sun went down, I had spent the money on a day in the big city with my high school sweetheart, who would send me a Dear John letter a year later while I was in Vietnam.

A lot of things happened to me while I was in Vietnam, but I've already written elsewhere and at length about all that (if you're curious, see *Vietnam-Perkasie: A Combat Marine Memoir*), so I won't try to explain any of it here except to say that it became clear within a few days of my arrival in

February 1967 that what was happening there was not at all like what Lyndon Johnson and *Time* and my high school history teachers had told me. And by the time we came upon that woman down on Barrier Island during Operation Pike in August 1967 with her chest torn wide open and her dead baby blue in her arms and her house blown flat by heavy artillery only our side possessed that far south of the demilitarized zone, I was sick in my soul of the whole damned thing and wanted nothing except to get out alive. And by the time I got back to Perkasie in March 1968, I still didn't understand what the hell was actually going on in Vietnam—I wouldn't begin to learn the truth until after the Ohio National Guard murdered four kids at Kent State University and wounded nine others, and I finally realized I'd sure better find out what was going on and damned quick—but I understood enough to know that I'd been sucker-punched by somebody, and it hurt like hell. It hurt more than anything I'd ever imagined.

While I was home on leave that March, 1968, I was invited to visit a class of elementary school children who had adopted me while I was in Vietnam. The teacher had wanted the kids to write to someone—the home-

Corporal William D. Ehrhart, 1st Battalion, 1st Marines, Vietnam, 1967. (Photograph provided by W.D. Ehrhart)

town front doing its bit—and one of the kids had an older sister who was a friend of mine, so I got picked. They all wrote me letters in January 1968, and I wrote back to each one of them, about 35 letters in all. Now they wanted to have a welcome home party for me.

Truth be told, I was flattered by the attention. For the most part, each of us went to Vietnam alone and came home alone, and certainly my own homecoming had been a solitary and even melancholy affair stripped of anything but the mere fact of having survived. So on the day of the party, I put on my winter dress green uniform and drove to the school, and when I entered the classroom, the children cheered. They had made a huge banner that hung above the blackboard from one side of the room to the other. It said: "Welcome Home, Corporal Bill!" And it was all I could do to keep from crying in front of a bunch of fifth graders.

We ate cupcakes and drank lemonade, and then the teacher asked if the children could ask me questions, and I said yes. They asked me things like what was the weather like, and what kind of food did we eat, and did I see any snakes. And what was it like on patrol. And guard duty. And did I throw grenades like they did on *Combat* (a popular television show about World War Two starring Vic Morrow), and had I killed anyone. And it began to dawn on me that these children—especially the boys, but not only the boys—thought what I'd been doing in Vietnam had been exciting and fun and really neat, and they were sitting there imagining themselves doing what they imagined I had done and could hardly wait for their turn to do it, too. And what for a few moments had been the only happy day I'd had in what seemed like as long as I could remember became one of the saddest days of my life, before or since. I was 19, and I did not know how even to begin to explain to these ten-year-olds and their teacher what was going awry with their little party, and I did not have the heart to try. It was all still too raw and broken inside, and would stay that way for a long time before I finally began to find my voice. I wanted only to get away from them and their banner as quickly as I could, and that is what I did.

During that same leave immediately after my return from Vietnam, I was inducted into the local Forrest-Post Lodge of the Veterans of Foreign Wars. Only a month after my arrival in Vietnam, my father had written to say that some of the men had approached him about my becoming a member. It would cost me nothing because it was traditional to waive the membership fee for anyone on active duty. I felt a little strange becoming a veteran of a foreign war while I still had nearly a year to serve in that foreign war, but the drinking age in Pennsylvania was 21, and I would be only 19 when I came back from Vietnam, and I knew the local VFW had a bar where the only card the bartender asked to see was your VFW membership card, so I figured it would be a place I could drink without getting hassled.

I already had my card before I got back to Perkasie, but I still had to go through an official ceremony. There were a dozen or so men present— these were all men I knew, the fathers of my childhood playmates and class-mates, including two who were teachers at Pennridge High, all of whom were veterans of World War Two—and what I had to do (I had not known this in advance) was put my left hand on the Bible and raise my right hand and swear to defend my country and my government against all enemies foreign and domestic. It was, in fact, the same oath of allegiance I'd sworn when I'd been inducted into the Marine Corps. And I remember looking around at this room full of middle-aged men I'd known all my life, and thinking about that mortally wounded mother with her dreams dead in her arms and a whole lot of other misery that my country and my government and I had inflicted upon people who had never done harm to any of us, and suddenly I realized that I needed a drink, but not here, not here, and I left as quickly as I could, and I never went back.

I could not go and visit Mr. Diehl or Mrs. Geosits while I was home. I did not, as I've said, then understand who had sucker-punched me—did not dare to understand, perhaps—but I knew somebody had, and I real-ized dimly that each of them had seen it coming and had tried to warn me, and I had not listened, and now I could not bring myself to look either of them in the eye, so damned cocksure of myself I had been.

Instead, I got away from Perkasie entirely, reporting to my next duty station fully two weeks before I was due. I served out the remaining 15 months of my enlistment in North Carolina, Okinawa, Japan, and the Philippines. I came back to Perkasie in June 1969 only for a few weeks before, as chance alone would have it, I ended up spending much of that summer as a deckhand on the Irish coastal freighter M/V *Marizell*, where I was when Neil Armstrong stepped onto the surface of the moon and—I may be the only member of my generation who does not claim to have been at Woodstock—Jimi Hendrix cranked out the only beautiful version of the Star-Spangled Banana I've heard in thirty years (thanks to the miracle of audio recording).

I entered Swarthmore College that September of 1969, where one of the very first things I saw was a Viet Cong flag flying from a third-floor window of Parrish Hall. That, too, is a story I've already told (once again, if you're curious, see *Passing Time: Memoir of a Vietnam Veteran Against the War*). Suffice it to say here that, whatever else happened to me during my four years in the midst of that campus hotbed of leftist, radical, anti-war activity, no one ever spit on me or called me "baby killer."

Meanwhile, after Randy Moore was killed in Vietnam, Pennridge High School lost Oscar Benevento, Kenny Worman, Clifford Van Artsdale, and as the war dragged on year after year, other younger boys who had not even been in high school when I'd enlisted. My childhood playmate Maynard Hager survived 25 months as a Marine in Vietnam, but died in a motorcycle accident on Main Street in Sellersville in the summer of 1971. He must have been driving his Harley at very high speed because he had clearly still been airborne sixty feet from his motorcycle when his body struck the telephone pole that stopped his flight. He had not been wearing a helmet, though it is doubtful that would have mattered much. It was nighttime and dark, but he had not had his lights on; the driver of the car that backed out of the driveway into Maynard's path never saw him. The *News-Herald* noted the irony of Maynard's surviving two years in Vietnam only to die on a hometown street, but the article did not mention the word suicide and offered not the slightest suggestion that what had happened to him in Vietnam and what happened to him on Main Street might have had anything to do with each other.

A year or two before Maynard died, the world beyond Perkasie had finally begun to seep in. As archaic school dress codes fell to legal challenges all over the country, bell-bottomed trousers and love beads and long hair came to Pennridge High School, and even marijuana, I suppose. I certainly had occasion to smoke it with old high school friends of mine, and I imagine their younger siblings were smoking it, too. At least a few of my friends, who were then just graduating from college, were none too keen on the war, and I wrote a letter in support of John Pifer's application for a conscientious objector's deferment from the draft (his application was successful—I like to think at least in part because an ex-Marine sergeant and Vietnam veteran with a Purple Heart and two Presidential Unit Citations vouched for him).

But John Pifer and all my classmates were long since gone from Pennridge High School, and what they thought and felt and said did not register in the halls of our alma mater, which continued to hold Armed Forces Day assemblies, and begin each day with the Pledge of Allegiance, right on through the end of the war and to this very day. Whatever doubts that long and unhappy war in Vietnam raised among the students and faculty and administration of Pennridge High School and the community the school served, they were slow in coming and quick to disappear once the ugliness vanished from the daily headlines. Even before the end of the war, it was as though the war had never happened.

By then, Margaret Geosits had moved on, I know not where but I can guess why, and before the decade's end John Diehl would suffer two nervous breakdowns and leave not only Pennridge but the profession of teaching— a terrible loss, in my opinion, and in my opinion occasioned by the unbearable stress of trying to teach kids to think critically in an atmosphere where critical thinking was deemed disrespectful, impudent, and treasonous.

Here's another irony: a dozen years after I graduated, the theme of the official Pennridge School District calendar for 1988-89 was "Notable Pennridge Graduates." If you turn to page 8, the month of December, you will find a photograph of me, along with a biographical sketch noting my service in the Marines and in Vietnam, my college degrees, some of my literary achievements, and the titles of a few of my books.

What you will not find is any mention of my participation in Vietnam Veterans Against the War, my contributions to the antiwar anthology *Winning Hearts and Minds: War Poems by Vietnam Veterans*, my co-editorship of the companion anthology *Demilitarized Zones: Veterans After Vietnam*, or any other indication that I am other than a native son who rallied to the flag and then went on to do his alma mater proud.

But while Pennridge High School held an all-school assembly in the spring of 1991 to pay homage to a later Pennridge grad who had been shot down during the Gulf War and held prisoner for several weeks in Iraq, not once in all the years since 1966 have I ever been invited to share my writing or my ideas with the students of Pennridge High School. It is one thing to allow dissent when the speaker is a student compelled to express a point of view everyone knows he doesn't believe, but quite another to allow it—let alone invite it—from an articulate speaker who can bring to bear the force of conviction and the weight of experience, even if that speaker is a notable Pennridge graduate.

❖ ❖ ❖

The Poetry of Bullets, or: How Does a War Mean?

[Originally presented as the keynote address to the Conference on War in Memory, Popular Culture & Folklore sponsored by the Center for the Study of the Korean War and the National Archives and Records Administration – Central Plains Region, Kansas City, Missouri, February 25, 2000.]

It's a catchy title, isn't it? Has a nice ring to it. A bit of intrigue to get your attention. A touch of dissonance. And a literary allusion, too: many of you, especially the English literature Ph.D.s, may recognize the reference to John Ciardi's classic book *How Does a Poem Mean?* But what does my title have to do with my talk, you must be wondering. What will be the substance of a talk with such a title?

I must confess that I have been dreading this moment since mid-January because I'm not at all sure what my talk has to do with my title. Possibly nothing. Six weeks ago, Tim Rives from the National Archives and Records Administration asked me for the title of my talk, which he needed for preconference publicity. Title, I thought; geez, I don't even have a talk yet. But he needed a title, so I gave him this one. It took me about five minutes to think up, and I was rather pleased with it, actually, though I have been worrying ever since about how I am going to live up to it.

The fact is that bullets thudding into a human body, as those of you who have heard the sound need no reminder from me, are not poetry at all but only murderous and cruel and insensible to the damage they do. What's more, I've never read Ciardi's famous book, so I've not a clue what he has to say or how I might, by whatever intellectual gymnastics, relate his ideas to mine.

I do know, however, that Ciardi was a combat veteran of World War Two, and he wrote some very good poetry out of that experience. One poem called "A Box Comes Home" begins like this:

> I remember the United States of America
> As a flag-draped box with Arthur in it
> And six marines to bear it on their shoulders.

After ruminating on how other countries and other cultures in other times might have remembered their war dead, Ciardi returns to the present:

> Once I saw Arthur dressed as the United States
> Of America. Now I see the United States
> Of America as Arthur in a flag-sealed domino.
> * * *
> ... I would pray
> An agreement with the United States of America
>
> To equal Arthur's living as it equals his dying[.]

But Ciardi finally gives the reader little expectation that the United States of America will either make or keep such an agreement.

It is not exactly the kind of poem one might expect from what has by now become utterly fixed in the American cultural and historical landscape as "the Good War." But if World War Two was a good war, it certainly did Arthur no good, nor did it do much good for Randall Jarrell's more famous ball turret gunner who "woke to black flak and the nightmare fighters" and who was washed "out of the turret with a hose" when he died. It did no good for Van Wettering or Averill, "gone to early death" in Richard Eberhart's "The Fury of Aerial Bombardment." In what way was World War Two—which devastated Europe and Asia and cost the lives of some 40 million human beings, the majority of them not even armed combatants—in what conceivable way was World War Two a good war, and for whom was it good?

Perhaps we could call it "the Necessary War." But wait! New America Foundation senior fellow Michael Lind, who was five years old when I was fighting in Vietnam, says that the war *I* fought in was *The Necessary War*, so we can't use that moniker for World War Two. Tom Brokaw says that the generation that fought World War Two was *The Greatest Generation*, so maybe we should call it "the Greatest War." ("Say, wasn't the Super Bowl great this year?" "Yeh, but not as great as World War Two.")

Meanwhile, historian Clay Blair calls the Korean War *The Forgotten War*, a label that is becoming almost as synonymous to the Korean War as "the Good War" is to World War Two. But James R. Kerin, Jr., of the United States Military Academy argues persuasively that we can't call it "the Forgotten War" because "there are too many cultural artifacts [in the form of histories, novels, memoirs and films] for that characterization to be acceptable." Kerin points out that a good many people, especially Korean War veterans themselves, have lately taken to calling the Korean War "the Forgotten Victory," which is an interesting interpretation, but I haven't time here to pursue that one.

And speaking of good wars and bad wars, Colonel Kerin also writes—this is in 1994—that "the proposition that the war in Vietnam was certainly *not* a 'good' war will by now meet relatively little opposition." Yet only last October, at a reunion of my old battalion from the Vietnam War, I heard Marine Corps Major General Ray Smith say that in his whole long career he was proudest of his service in Vietnam as a young lieutenant, and that furthermore we had won the Vietnam War because the United States of America is still here but the Soviet Union is no more. And he's not the only one from whom I've heard such an argument in recent years. In other words, the Vietnam War was a good war after all. How you can be run out of town at gunpoint and still insist that you've won is a mystery to me, but there you are.

That's the trouble with how we remember things. Memory is a faulty instrument, unstable and constantly changing, prone to distortion and breakdown and utter falsification, often without the person remembering even being aware that his or her memories bear little or no resemblance to what is being remembered. A former army captain, a man who had served as an infantry company commander in Vietnam, said in the course of the 1983 documentary *Vietnam: A Television History* that the men he'd served with were the finest men he'd ever known, and he was proud to have commanded them. He got tears in his eyes, and it was very touching. Over the years, I have frequently heard men speak and write this way of those they served with in wartime, especially in combat.

And maybe it's true, but it certainly wasn't my experience. I knew some really fine people in Vietnam, sure, undoubtedly among the best people I've ever known or ever will know. But I knew men who were real scoundrels, too. And men who were liars and thieves and blowhards and shirkers and all kinds. A few of the men I knew in Vietnam were so pathological that they actually seemed to enjoy hunting and killing other human beings. Most of us were just a bunch of pretty ordinary young men armed to the teeth and scared to death, trying to do the best we could in miserable circumstances and secretly wishing our mothers could somehow come and get us out of this mess.

As a group, the men I served with were neither superior nor inferior to the people I went to high school with, or the people I met in college, or people I worked with over the years, or people I've met anywhere else. You put a bunch of people together and it is the nature of things that some of them will be diamonds and some of them will be dirtbags and most of them will be spread out somewhere between those two extremes. Yet a good many veterans, as the years pass, increasingly remember the people they served with in war as uniformly the finest men they ever knew. This defies logic, but that is no obstacle to memory.

Forgive me if I'm stepping on toes here, but this is, after all, a conference on war and memory, and I think war is always better in memory than it is in person. When I was a kid, I used to watch awestruck every Memorial Day as the fathers of my childhood playmates—the grocer, the shoe repairman, the teacher, the dentist, men I saw every day of my young life, men in whose houses I played—marched up Fifth Street toward the town's little war memorial in their VFW uniforms, there to fire a 21-gun salute to their fallen comrades. It was all so thrilling to a young boy. Next to Christmas, it was my favorite day of the year. And my favorite moment was when they fired those rifles. I waited every year for that moment.

I wouldn't have used the word then, wouldn't have known to use it in that fashion, but it was *romantic*, for Godsake. I wanted to *be* those men. I wanted to do what they'd done and know what they knew. But when I finally did, all I could think was: *You bastards. You knew it would be like this and you never told me?!* I swore I would not do that to another generation of children. And I am not the only Vietnam veteran who felt that way. In 1979, the commander of the New Jersey Veterans of Foreign Wars, Thomas Blesedell, lamented, "We're concerned that Vietnam veterans are not joining [VFW], are not having concern for the flag." Yet twenty years later, Vietnam veterans are major players in VFW, and the American Legion, and even have their own organization, Vietnam Veterans of America. And when I see them on ceremonial occasions, I watch the children watching them, and all I can do is wonder what those veterans remember that makes them want to dress up in uniforms and march around and salute things.

Such is the nature of memory. And popular culture, which this conference is also about, isn't much more reliable. Remember the Spice Girls? *The Mod Squad*? How about Hula-Hoops? During the war I fought in, Sly and the Family Stone's "Everyday People" was a protest song, a celebration of counterculture life in the face of the faceless Establishment. Now it's the sound track for Toyota car commercials on TV. Or is it Honda ads? Whatever. That's popular culture for you.

Popular culture imagines that every GI who came home from World War Two got to have a parade, and every soldier who came home from Vietnam got spit on and called "baby killer." Popular culture, moreover, doesn't even know there was such a thing as the Korean War. Ask any ten people at random which war Hawkeye Pierce and the 4077th MASH fought in, and see what answer you get. One might make a reasonable argument that popular culture is a contradiction in terms, a practical impossibility, but so what? Popular culture allows us to think that *Catch-22* is a hilariously funny book. Popular culture allows Sylvester Stallone to earn millions and millions of dollars from the Vietnam War without ever spending ten minutes in the service of his country. What can you do with popular culture?

And as for folklore, with Lydia Fish in the audience, I'm not going to say one nasty word about folklore. She is a folklorist, and I'm not sure what that means, but she's got a Ph.D. and hers are one set of toes upon which I do not wish to step, so I'm just going to skip folklore entirely and get on to my next point, which is that all my adult life I have relied on poetry to do what neither memory nor popular culture can do: that is, to show me the world as it really is.

Having spent my entire adult life writing poetry, of course, I may be open to charges of bias in touting the virtues of poetry. I suppose it's a bit like Ben and Jerry saying that Ben & Jerry's is the best ice cream in the world. On the other hand, Ben & Jerry's *is* the best ice cream in the world. But don't just take my word for it. Consider Lorrie Smith of St. Michael's College, who believes that because "poetry occupies a marginal position in the larger canon of [war] literature and in the culture at large, this position may actually assure its literary vitality and freedom from cultural hegemony."

While Dr. Smith is writing about the Vietnam War in particular, her argument clearly extends to poetry from the Korean War and World War

Two as well. And while she uses certain language such as "literary vitality" and "cultural hegemony" that tends to give academics a bad name, the heart of her argument seems all but irrefutable: while other writers, artists, and commentators sometimes can and do receive fame and fortune from what they do or create or say, and therefore are constantly having to hedge their vision of the truth against what they think their potential audience will buy, both figuratively and literally, poets have no audience to speak of, no serious prospect of fame or fortune no matter what they say or write, and therefore they can say and write exactly what they think and feel.

Consider that a best selling novel might reach 100,000 readers. A hit movie might be seen by millions of viewers. How many people watched television's *Combat* in the 1960s or *China Beach* in the 1980s during those two popular shows' lifetimes? But even our best Pulitzer Prize-winning poets are lucky to sell 4,000 copies of a book of poems, and most poets would drool at sales figures that high.

As for self-censorship, consider the fate of the only American-made Vietnam War movie I've ever thought was any good: *Go Tell the Spartans*. It was released the same summer as *The Deer Hunter*. It portrayed the Vietnam War as an unnecessary, unwinnable, hopeless morass forced upon the Vietnamese by arrogant, ignorant, insufferable foreigners. The bad guys in the movie are the Americans, however well-meaning they imagine themselves to be. *Go Tell the Spartans* was withdrawn from commercial distribution within three weeks of its release, an utter box office failure. Meanwhile *The Deer Hunter*, in which wholesome American boys are brought to ruin by wantonly evil Vietnamese sadists, won a truckload of Oscars and earned millions of dollars at the box office. *The Deer Hunter* was a vision of the Vietnam War that Americans could live with; *Go Tell the Spartans* was not. The lesson of those two movies was not lost on anyone inclined to make an honest movie about the Vietnam War, and there have been no honest movies made about the Vietnam War since.

Had Norman Mailer insisted on using the word "fuck" in *The Naked and the Dead* instead of "fug," his book would never have seen the light of day. Those of you who have served in the military know perfectly well that not only does no soldier go around saying "fug," but that the actual one-syllable four-letter F-word is almost polite compared to the kind of language scared teenagers trying to act tough regularly use in their daily discourse. Mailer was willing to compromise with reality in order to reap the rewards successful publication and reception of his novel held out to him, and his compromise paid off handsomely. Does it matter? Am I being too nitpicky here?

Okay, would Ron Kovic's *Born on the Fourth of July* have been so well received if he had made it clear that at the time he was wounded he had already served one full 13-month tour in Vietnam, come home to America, and then volunteered to go back for a second full 13-month tour? Does Kovic obscure this fact in order to present himself in a more sympathetic light, to make himself appear to be the naive kid suddenly struck down in his innocence instead of an experienced veteran who knew what he and his country were doing, thus to make his book more appealing? If that is not the reason, how else does one explain Kovic's disingenuousness? Did he just forget to mention it?

Anyone who aspires to being a poet, on the other hand, quickly abandons any notion of material success and popular acceptance or quickly abandons the desire to be a poet. This is an awkward dilemma for those of us who are neither tenured university professors nor able sellers of life insurance, but it does, as Dr. Smith points out, give poets a remarkable freedom because we almost literally have no one to please but ourselves.

Well, of course there are the petty jealousies and the jockeying for status and the struggles to get published by this press and reviewed in that journal and all the other junk that seems to be inherent in human discourse—especially among people egotistical enough to take seriously a form of expression that for the general populace ranks well below smoke signals or skywriting. Nevertheless, any poet who pulls his or her punches in the interest of pleasing the minuscule audience that actually reads poetry in America is sad beyond pathetic. For the most part, poetry is honest because there is nothing to be gained by being anything other than honest. And war poetry, at least since the Great War—that is, the one fought between 1914 and 1918—is where you will find, in my opinion, the truest relationship between war and memory.

My knowledge of American soldier-poetry from the Great War—the poems of Alan Seeger and Joyce Kilmer, both killed in action, and poems written well after the fact by e. e. cummings, Archibald MacLeish, Malcolm Cowley, and John Peale Bishop—is simply too limited for me to attempt to make generalizations. But I have read hundreds of poems from the Second World War, several hundred poems from the Korean War, and thousands of poems from the Vietnam War, and what is most striking about these poems is that, almost to a poem, they have nothing good to say about the experience of war. Furthermore, whether a poet is writing about the war we won, the war we tied, or the war we lost, the tone, the feel, the sensibilities of the poetry from war to war bear remarkable similarities, uncannily so.

Popular culture remembers the end of World War Two as a sailor exuberantly kissing a nurse in Times Square amid tickertape and happy crowds. Not so Howard Nemerov, who remembers it this way in "Redeployment":

> They say the war is over. But water still
> Comes bloody from the taps, and my pet cat
> In his disorder vomits worms which crawl
> Swiftly away. Maybe they leave the house.
> These worms are white, and flecked with the cat's blood.

Later in the poem, Nemerov mentions a man he knows "who keeps a soldier's dead blue eyeballs that he found / Somewhere," a grisly souvenir that anticipates the popular culture image of American soldiers collecting human ears in Vietnam (an image that is largely—perhaps almost wholly—fiction, by the way), and in any case the poem is hardly celebratory. Indeed, is it much different in what it has to say than John Balaban's "April 30, 1975"?

> The evening Nixon called his last troops off,
> the church bells tolled across our states.
> We leaned on farmhouse porch pilings, our eyes
> wandering the lightning bug meadow thick with mist,
> and counted tinny peals clanking out
> through oaks around the church belltower.
> You asked, "Is it peace, or only a bell ringing?"
>
> This night the war has finally ended.
> My wife and I sit on a littered park bench
> sorting out our shared and separate lives[.]

He goes on to describe an urban American landscape that seems "a city at war," where a ski-masked man who tried to attack a girl is, in his own turn, attacked by yet another predator, and where "kids have burnt a bum on Brooklyn Bridge."

Despite each being about the end of a war—different wars at that, with seemingly different outcomes—in neither poem does one come away with any sense of peace. Both poets suggest a world still out of kilter. Both poems are possessed of a profound sadness. Even their closing lines, in both imagery and intent, are strikingly similar, though the poems were written thirty years apart:

> I heard the dust falling between the walls.
> - - - - - - - - - - - -
> By the Lo waterfalls, free and high,
> you wash away the dust of life.

Nor does the passage of time seem to bring with it any greater peace. Consider Reg Saner's "Re-Runs":

All that flying iron was bound to hit something.
His odd nights re-visit a stare, let a torn head
trade looks with him, ...

                    * * *

... alone inside a nameless grief holding
nothing: their faces, grass shrapnel—which some field
on the world's other side bothers with. Like seed,
the shapes that won't go away without tears.
They just lie where they fell, and keep going.

Or Keith Wilson's "The Ex-Officer, Navy":

the man, in whose eyes gunfire
is a memory, a restless dream
of stuttering mouths, bright flame
a man, who no matter how long the days
faces still the combat, the long night's terror—

If you are not already familiar with Saner or Wilson, could you tell
which war either man fought in? Both happen to be Korean War veterans,
but does that even matter? Both men would surely know instinctively
exactly what Gerald McCarthy is talking about in "The Sound of Guns":

At the university in town
tight-lipped men tell me the war in Vietnam is over,
that my poems should deal with other things:
earth, fire, water, air.

                    * * *

I don't know what it is that's kept me going.
At nineteen I stood at night and watched
an airfield mortared. A plane that was to take
me home, burning; men running out of the flames.

Seven winters have slipped away,
the war still follows me.
Never in anything have I found
a way to throw off the dead.

No doubt, McCarthy could change his fourth to last line to read
"thirty-three winters have slipped away," and the poem would still be just
as true. He could change the word "Vietnam" to "Korea" or "Guadalcanal"
or "Salerno," and the poem would still be just as true.

For Hayden Carruth in "On a Certain Engagement South of Seoul,"
a newspaper story about a battle in the Korean War triggers a reverie of
his own experiences in the Second World War:

> we were a few,
> Sprawled on the stiff grass of a small plateau,
>
> Afraid. No one was dead. But we were new—
> We did not know that probably none would die.

He describes in moving detail the terrible fear of these young soldiers before shifting his attention to "another campaign ... in another land," admitting that this brief account of an engagement in Korea "can make my hand tremble again." Of the men who were with him on that small plateau, "one limps. One cannot walk at all." One has nightmares. Carruth concludes:

> Is this a bond? Does this make us brothers?
> Or does it bring our hatred back? I might
>
> have known, but now I do not know. Others
> May know. I know when I walk out-of-doors
> I have a sorrow not wholly mine, but another's.

Carruth is not the only poet to make connections between and among the three major American wars of the mid 20th century. While his poem touches on both the Second World War and Korea, in "The Long March" William Childress connects Korea to Vietnam:

> North to Pusan,
> trailing nooses of dust,
> we dumbly followed
> leaders whose careers
> hung on victory.

Childress seems haunted by the misery of war, especially the suffering of children who line the roads, begging, many of whom, nothing more than "bones in thin sacks," will be picked up by "the dead-truck" in the frozen dawn. "A soldier fished a bent brown stick/from a puddle," Childress writes, "the arm of someone's child," before concluding:

> Not far away, the General
> camps with his press corps.
> Any victory will be his.
> For us, there is only
> the long march to Viet Nam.

As if to bring the three wars full circle, Joseph A. Soldati associates the Vietnam War with World War Two in "Surroundings." Ostensibly a poem about the destruction of Soldati's old neighborhood, including the house he and his brother grew up in, it takes us back to 1944, when the poet and his brother were five and three, before returning to the present:

> Long trains were going to Asia then,
> And still are. Two small boys,
> Who rushed to see them pass, are men—
> Have been there and come home again.

Well, I could read poetry to you all night long, but I don't suppose anyone is much interested in having me do that, least of all me. It is a pity, however, that more people don't read poetry because our culture and our nation would be a good deal better off if we did. For all its supposedly realistic cinematography, *Saving Private Ryan* really isn't much more than an updated version of a cowboy western, complete with the 7th Cavalry arriving to save the day just in the knick of time. If Alan Alda occasionally rails against the stupidity of war while performing meatball surgery on some wounded GI, there are always plenty of laughs thrown in to break the tension. And if Michael Herr's *Dispatches* is a brilliant piece of writing, in the end it is only the story of a journalist who went to Vietnam to find his manhood and thinks he succeeded.

In my introduction to an anthology of war poetry called *Carrying the Darkness*, I wrote that "time may play tricks with human memory. Scholars and politicians, journalists and generals may argue, write and re-write 'the facts.' But when a poem is written, it becomes a singular entity with an inextinguishable and unalterable life of its own. It is a true reflection of the feelings and perceptions it records, and as such, it is as valuable a document as any history ever written." Fifteen years later, I would amend that statement only to include not just histories but all the many forms in which we remember our individual and collective past.

There are those among us tonight who undoubtedly carry their military service with great pride, who genuinely make of necessity a virtue, and who sincerely consider the war they fought in a necessity. There are those here who have not served, but who believe that those who have *should* be proud. And there was a time when I would have dismissed such people without a second thought, but I have finally reached a point in my life where I am capable of recognizing that reasonable people can reasonably disagree, and that each of us—myself included—builds whatever defenses he or she must build in order to go on living.

I find it remarkable, however—indeed, truly astonishing—that among all the poets who have faced the ordeal of war and lived to write about it with any seriousness of purpose, the prevailing themes to be found in their

poems are sorrow, loss, anger, fear, pain, dislocation, isolation, emptiness. There is nothing uplifting about the poetry of war in the 20th century, but I would argue that this is because there is nothing uplifting
about war, and the poetry only reflects what is. It is our memories playing tricks with us when we imagine, as British General Sir John Hackett
put it with remarkable candor, that war is anything other than "being in
a strange and terrible nightmare from which you [long] to wake up and
[can] not."

Nor is this, I suppose, the most uplifting keynote address you've ever
heard, though I hope it has been somewhat better than a strange and terrible nightmare. I will stop now, except to leave you with one last poem,
one of my own if I may be so self-indulgent, that has—to my mind—much
to do with war and memory. It's called "Beautiful Wreckage":

> What if I didn't shoot the old lady
> running away from our patrol,
> or the old man in the back of the head,
> or the boy in the marketplace?
>
> Or what if the boy—but he didn't
> have a grenade, and the woman in Hue
> didn't lie in the rain in a mortar pit
> with seven Marines just for food,
>
> Gaffney didn't get hit in the knee,
> Ames didn't die in the river, Ski
> didn't die in a medevac chopper
> between Con Thien and Da Nang.
>
> In Vietnamese, Con Thien means
> *place of angels*. What if it really was
> instead of the place of rotting sandbags,
> incoming heavy artillery, rats and mud.
>
> What if the angels were Ames and Ski,
> or the lady, the man, and the boy,
> and they lifted Gaffney out of the mud
> and healed his shattered knee?
>
> What if none of it happened the way I said?
> Would it all be a lie?
> Would the wreckage be suddenly beautiful?
> Would the dead rise up and walk?

NOTES

The full texts of the poems by World War Two veterans quoted in this essay can be found in *Articles of War*, Leon Stokesbury, ed., University of Arkansas Press, 1990, except for Hayden Carruth's, which is taken from his collection *The Crow and the Heart*, Macmillan, 1959. Likewise, the poems by Korean War veterans can be found in *Retrieving Bones: Stories and Poems of the Korean War*, W. D. Ehrhart & Philip K. Jason, eds., Rutgers University Press, 1999. The poems by Vietnam War veterans can be found in *Carrying the Darkness: The Poetry of the Vietnam War*, W. D. Ehrhart, ed., Texas Tech University Press, 1989, except for my own concluding poem, which is taken from *Beautiful Wreckage: New & Selected Poems*, Adastra Press, 1999. Colonel James Kerin is quoted from his unpublished University of Pennsylvania doctoral dissertation, "The Korean War and American Memory." Major General Ray Smith made his remarks at the October 2, 1999, reunion of 1st Battalion, 1st Marine Regiment held at the Detroit Marriott Renaissance Center. New Jersey VFW Commander Thomas Blesedell is quoted in the Morris County *Daily Record* of December 12, 1979. Dr. Lorrie Smith is quoted from "After Our War: Poets of the Vietnam Generation," an essay published in the June 1989 issue of *Poetry Wales*. General Sir John Hackett is quoted in Paul Fussell's *Wartime*.

❖ ❖ ❖

Setting the Record Straight: An Addendum to the Life and Poetry of William Wantling

In a 1998 essay called "'I Want to Try It All Before I Go': The Life & Poetry of William Wantling," I wrote that Wantling had been a Marine Corps sergeant who had been seriously wounded in combat in the Korean War, that he had been given morphine for his wounds, that he had subsequently become addicted, and that he had ended up in the California State Prison at San Quentin as a result of his addiction.

In that same essay, Samuel Zaffiri, who had known Wantling in the late 1960s and early 1970s at Illinois State University, said of Wantling, "He was a manipulator and all with whom he came in contact, whether best friend or casual acquaintance, were game for his wiles. He wheedled, begged, lied."

I should have seen in Zaffiri's observation a warning, and eventually I did—but only after I kept encountering comments similar to Zaffiri's and those of Wantling scholar Kevin E. Jones, who wrote in a May 1999 e-mail to me that "Wantling lied, cheated, ripped off his friends, shat in their bathtubs." By the time I became suspicious, however, and began to dig deeper into the life of this fascinating but deeply troubled man, I had already repeated—in print and on more than one occasion—a number of falsehoods concerning Wantling that I had picked up from other published sources. Indeed, a good deal of what little we thought we knew about Wantling turns out not to be true.

We do know that he was born on November 7, 1933, in what is now East Peoria, Illinois (it was then the twin towns of Robein and Valley View). After graduating from high school, he enlisted in the U.S. Marine Corps, serving in Korea for most of 1953. Released from active duty in 1955, Wantling soon settled in southern California. He married a woman named Luana and they had a son. He ran afoul of the law and in 1958 was sentenced to serve time San Quentin. While he was in prison, Luana divorced him and he lost custody of his child. He also began to write poetry, taking creative writing classes offered at the prison. Released in 1963, he returned to Peoria, marrying Ruth Ann Burton nee Cooper—a woman he'd known in high school, herself now divorced and with two sons—in 1964. In 1966 he enrolled as a student at Illinois State University in Normal, earning B.A. and M.A. degrees over the next seven years. He was teaching at ISU, apparently on a one-year nonrenewable appointment, at the time of his death on May 2, 1974.

The official cause of death was heart failure, but this was certainly brought on by years and years of massive drug and alcohol abuse, for Wantling's post–San Quentin life in Illinois, according to Zaffiri, was "a constant search for things which would get him drunk or high." What Wantling did to get sent to prison in the first place, however, we do not know. Both Jones, in his 1994 doctoral dissertation from Illinois State University, and Wantling biographer John Pyros, in his 1981 *William Wantling: A Biography & Selected Works* (the source of the two Zaffiri quotes above), say it was for possession of narcotics. In a November 1999 letter to me, A. D. Winans of Second Coming Press, who published Wantling's posthumous collection *7 on Style*, mentions narcotics possession and possibly forging prescriptions. The ultimate source of this information, however, seems to be Wantling himself. In a letter to Edward Lucie-Smith, quoted in Lucie-Smith's introduction to Wantling's 1968 collection *The Awakening*, Wantling said he was "imprisoned for forgery and narcotics."

Wantling claimed that his addiction and subsequent incarceration were the result of combat injuries he sustained during the Korean War, further implying that his later drug problems also stemmed from that initial addiction. "When I was in Korea," Wantling is quoted in the introduction to his collection *The Source*, "they gave me my first shot of morphine. It killed the pain. It was beautiful. Five years later I was in San Quentin on narcotics." War injuries led to addiction led to prison and a lifetime of problems, according to Wantling.

But what happened to Wantling in Korea? Len Fulton of Dustbooks, who published Wantling's book *The Source*, said in a February 1997 e-mail, "I think he got hit with a flamethrower but I'm not sure. I think he was the youngest sergeant in Korea (17)—or I remember him writing that somewhere." In his letter to Lucie-Smith, quoted in *The Awakening*, Wantling wrote, "Enlisted US Marine Corps age seventeen. Volunteered for combat duty and sent to Korea War Nov. 1952. Was youngest Marine Sgt. in combat (eighteen) during winter campaign '52-'53 ... Morphine in Korea field hospital due to burns[.]" "Wounded in Korea," Pyros writes in his biography, "ten days in a coma, eight weeks in a hospital, a leg which remained permanently scarred[.]" More recently, Zaffiri wrote in a December 1999 letter that Wantling "had a large scar on his leg. He claimed he got it when the jeep he was riding in hit a landmine, which also caused a 50-gallon barrel of gasoline on the jeep to ignite, burning him. He claimed then that he got hooked on morphine recovering from his wounds. This, in turn, he always claimed, caused him to get hooked on heroin."

But again the sole source for all of this information is, finally, Wantling himself. Fulton, Lucie-Smith and Pyros all published accounts of Wantling's Korean War service. These accounts were then accepted at face value by anthologist Walter Lowenfels, scholar H. Bruce Franklin, critics Robert Peters and Rich Manglesdorff, doctoral candidate Jones—and myself—and reproduced in one form or another in a number of other published sources spanning more than thirty years. Everyone, until now—again, myself included—simply took Wantling at his word, and this in spite of the fact that at least some of these people knew Wantling to be, however likeable, a liar.

Wantling's own military records, which I obtained in 1999 under the Freedom of Information Act from the National Personnel Records Center in St. Louis, Missouri after my suspicions were finally—if belatedly—aroused, reveal that Wantling enlisted in the Marine Corps on January 23, 1952—when he was 18 years old, not 17 as he claimed—and did not actually begin active service until March 4, 1952. He was trained and deployed as an aircraft radio repairman. He did not arrive in Korea until January 7, 1953, at which time he was assigned to Marine Composite Squadron 1. According to the squadron's command diaries, provided by the Archives Unit of Headquarters Marine Corps in late 1999, the squadron was engaged in electronic countermeasure warfare. Wantling himself was not on flight status and did not serve as air crew. The squadron was based at an airfield designated K-3, which was located at Pohang, a city on the southeastern coast of Korea about 150 miles south of the 38th parallel and the front lines, which had become fixed and static by mid-1951.

Wantling, therefore, served "in combat" only in the most loosely defined sense of that word, since all of Korea was considered the war zone. His claim to have been in a jeep that struck a landmine is doubtful. While a certain amount of Communist guerrilla activity did take place behind the lines in the earlier stages of the war, most guerrilla activity had been eradicated by 1953. In addition, had he been wounded in combat or as a result of enemy action of any kind, he would automatically have been awarded a Purple Heart Medal, but his decorations are listed as these: the National Defense Service Medal, the Korea Service Medal, the United Nations Service Ribbon, the Korean Presidential Unit Citation, and the Good Conduct Medal. There is no Purple Heart. Lastly, the record indicates that Wantling spent his entire time in Korea—January through November 1953—as a private first class; he did not make corporal until January 1954, and did not earn his sergeant's stripes until October 1954.

It is within the realm of possibility that Wantling sustained some sort of non-battle injury that led to hospitalization and the administering of morphine (his medical records from the Marine Corps are not available under FOIA, being subject to federal privacy laws), but even this is questionable at best. In any case, we now know with reasonable certainty that he was never wounded in battle, that he was never a sergeant during the Korean War—let alone the youngest Marine combat sergeant—and that he greatly embellished his wartime experiences in relating them to those who knew him only well after the fact.

Indeed, those who have tried to reconstruct Wantling's biography prior to his return to Peoria, Illinois, after his release from San Quentin in 1963 have relied entirely on Wantling himself and on those who knew him after he returned to Illinois. A good deal of what happened to him in the last eleven years of his life can be verified by people who knew him in those years, but of the years Wantling spent in the Marines, in southern California, and in prison, there is no one to offer corroboration.

Wantling did serve time in prison, this is certain. Though I have been unable to obtain any court records for Wantling, and thus cannot ascertain what he was charged with or convicted of, the California Department of Corrections does have an inmate number for him (A45522) and a discharge date (September 1963). Various letters and documents among Wantling's papers—which are housed at the McLean County Historical Society in Bloomington, Illinois—corroborate his incarceration and the fact that he took courses and began writing in prison. As to Wantling's first marriage and subsequent divorce while in prison, Jones writes in a 1999 e-mail, "There are a series of letters in the archives in which Wantling, post divorce, pleads for custody of Cardo [his son]. Probably wisely, the state of CA sent him to foster care."

Wantling's later behavior would certainly suggest an addictive personality, but whether he became a heroin addict in the mid-1950s, how and why he became an addict, and what exactly got him sent to prison, we simply do not know and may never know. Contrary to his own accounts, however, his later behaviour was almost certainly not the result—directly or indirectly—of combat injuries sustained during the Korean War. Dave Roskos of Iniquity Press, in a January 2000 letter, quotes James Harbaugh of *Dionysos: The Journal of Literature & Addiction*, thusly: "It's not unusual for people who abuse pain medication to make up lies like that."

Does any of this invalidate Wantling's poetry, especially his Korean War poetry? Not necessarily. It is possible that Wantling was indeed affected by his Korean War service, even if he never heard a shot fired in anger. "Many vets feel a sense of guilt to this day because they did not share the sufferings of the grunts [infantrymen]," Patience H. C. Mason writes in her book *Recovering from the War*. "I discovered that [many veterans] often had extremely painful traumatic experiences or entire tours, but feel that by comparison with the grunts, it was nothing—so they have no way to deal with the pain except to discount it, and, by discounting it, bury it."

Did Wantling actually see a Korean civilian summarily executed, as he suggests in his poem "The Korean"? Did other Marines tell him stories about their own fighting experiences that Wantling transformed into art, as Bryan Alec Floyd did so successfully in his collection of Vietnam War poems *The Long War Dead*? Maybe Wantling was simply able to apply his own imagination creatively and effectively. Certainly Wantling came closer to war than Stephen Crane had at the time Crane wrote *The Red Badge of Courage*. And Korean War poet William Childress readily admits that he was never in combat, yet we value his Korean War poems no less for that.

The difference, perhaps, is that Crane and Childress and Floyd never tried to represent themselves and their own actual experiences as anything other than what they were; they did not conflate their personal lives and the art they created. "It is always dangerous to confuse the various voices of poetry, to insist that the speaker of the poem is indeed the author of the poem, and that the persona is the person," warns Jones in his dissertation. Yet he too falls prey to that confusion, as has everyone else who has written about Wantling until now, as did I in a number of the inferences and conclusions I drew in "I Want to Try It All Before I Go."

Perhaps even Wantling himself began to believe his own stories. "I'm not at all surprised you found some bullshit on Wantling," Fulton wrote in May 1999 when apprised of Wantling's actual service record. "He was a long-tall-story teller trying to lift lying up to mythmaking." Be that as it may, it is no excuse for bad scholarship, and I offer none. I can only try to correct the erroneous record I have helped to perpetuate.

Among the poems Wantling left behind at his untimely death are more than a few that are worth keeping alive, and some that should be treated as genuine classics. "Initiation" is a harrowing poem about the life of an addict. "Poetry" is one of the best prison poems ever written by anyone, compelling enough to be quoted in full by both Franklin in *Prison Literature in America* and Peters in *Where the Bee Sucks*. And "Korea 1953" and "I Remember" are among the most memorable poems of the Korean War. Nevertheless, it is important to set straight the historical record on Wantling because what little we know about his life has already become distorted and mythologized, fiction made fact by constant repetition.

NOTE

"Initiation," "Poetry," and "Korea 1953" first appeared in Wantling's 1965 collection *Down, Off & Out* from Mimeo Press. "I Remember" first appeared in Walter Lowenfels' 1967 Anchor anthology *Where Is Vietnam?* The two Korean War poems can readily be found in *Retrieving Bones: Stories and Poems of the Korean War*, W. D. Ehrhart & Philip K. Jason, eds., Rutgers University Press, 1999, along with "The Korean" and five other Korean War poems by Wantling.

❖ ❖ ❖

"In Cases Like This, There Is No Need to Vote": Korean War Poetry in the Context of American Twentieth Century War Poetry

The Korean War is the least remembered and least acknowledged of all of America's wars. Even as it was being fought, ordinary Americans were aghast to find the country at war again so soon after World War Two; they found it profoundly embarrassing to be put to rout twice in six months by what they perceived to be a rabble of Asian peasants; and they did not understand a war in which total victory was not and could not be the goal. "America tolerated the Korean War while it was on," writes David Halberstam in *The Fifties*, "but could not wait to forget it once the war was over." And once it was over, the Korean War all but vanished from the American landscape.

Just as the war has vanished, so too has its literature. Keith D. McFarland, in *The Korean War: An Annotated Bibliography*, lists 33 Korean War novels. Arne Axelsson, in *Restrained Response: American Novels of the Cold War and Korea*, identifies over forty Korean War novels. Colonel James R. Kerin, professor of English literature at the United States Military Academy, has found "some five dozen published novels" about the Korean War. And Philip K. Jason, professor of English literature at the United States Naval Academy, lists 66 stories by 42 different authors on his internet web site "Short Fiction of the Korean War." Yet Paul Fussell is typical of most critics and scholars in arguing, as he does in his *Norton Book of Modern War*, that the Korean War "generated virtually no literature worth preserving for its own moral or artistic sake."

Kerin counters with the observation that literary critics have failed "to locate and acknowledge quality where it exists," but when he considers the poetry of the Korean War, he too falls into the same trap as those he takes to task for failing to locate and acknowledge quality where it does exist. Responding to the prevailing assessment that the Korean War did not produce much in the way of imaginative responses, Kerin replies, "Only in the realm of poetry does the charge of literary vacuity hold almost literally true." In his doctoral dissertation "The Korean War and American Memory," he reserves less than two pages of commentary for Rolando Hinojosa's 35-poem sequence *Korean Love Songs*, and notes in passing only one other poem, Edith Lovejoy Pierce's "Heartbreak Ridge," while lamenting "the absence of any notable poetry" from the Korean War.

Other scholars, critics, and editors (including Axelsson and McFarland) have done no better. In the preface to his 1994 study of Vietnam War poetry, *Radical Visions: Poetry by Vietnam Veterans*, Vince Gotera mentions the Civil War, World War Two, the Vietnam War, and the Gulf War, but not the Korean War. In the body of his text, he refers to poets Alan Seeger, Joyce Kilmer, and e.e. cummings from the Great War, and to John Ciardi, Richard Wilbur, Richard Eberhart, and Randall Jarrell from World War Two, but does not name a single Korean War poet. Jeffrey Walsh, in *American War Literature: 1914 to Vietnam*, includes discussion of poets from the Great War, World War Two, and the Vietnam War, but not from the Korean War. Subarno Chattarji's *Memories of a Lost War: A Study of American Poetic Responses to the Vietnam War* includes a lengthy chapter on World War Two poetry, but nothing about Korean War poetry. Neither

Jon Stallworthy's *Oxford Book of War Poetry* nor Kenneth Baker's *Faber Book of War Poetry* includes a single poem from the Korean War, though both include poems from World War Two and the Vietnam War.

Carolyn Forche's *Against Forgetting: Twentieth Century Poetry of Witness* does include four poems by Etheridge Knight, whom Forche identifies as a Korean War veteran, but none of Knight's poems deals with the Korean War. Indeed, it turns out that while Knight did serve in the army during the early months of the Korean War, he never served in Korea nor was he wounded in combat (both of which he claimed), never getting closer to Asia than Ft. Knox, Kentucky.[1] Meanwhile, Forche does not include any of the Korean War poets who actually are Korean War poets.

And there *are* Korean War poets, as well as poems about the Korean War by people who did not serve there. And if the body of Korean War poetry is relatively small (which it is)—and some of that is of questionable quality (which it is)—all of it is valuable as documentary history and cultural commentary. Moreover, Fussell's opinion notwithstanding, the best of it possesses both moral and artistic value.

Howard Fast (of *Spartacus* fame) wrote a short but powerful sequence of seven poems called "Korean Litany" that was published as part of his *Korean Lullaby* even before the war ended. Both Hayden Carruth and Thomas McGrath, World War Two veterans and major American poets, wrote individual poems about the Korean War as early as the mid–1950s that both men continued to include in subsequent collections of their own for the rest of their lives. Carruth's "On a Certain Engagement South of Seoul" first appeared in *The Crow and the Heart,* and subsequently appeared in *The Selected Poetry of Hayden Carruth* and *Collected Shorter Poems.* McGrath's "Ode for the American Dead in Korea" first appeared in *Figures of the Double World,* and subsequently was reprinted in *New & Selected Poems, The Movie at the End of the World,* and *Selected Poems 1938-1988.* (In the latter two books, which post-date the Vietnam War, McGrath changed the title to "Ode for the American Dead in Asia.")

In the early 1960s, Korean War veteran William Childress began publishing in the highly respected magazine *Poetry,* as well as in *Harper's,* and within a few years he would be joined on the pages of *Poetry* by fellow veteran Keith Wilson, whose long sequence of Korean War poems was published as *Graves Registry and Other Poems* in 1969 and reprinted in an expanded version as *Graves Registry* in 1992. Childress's own two books, *Burning the Years* and *Lobo,* each of which contains Korean War poems, came out in 1971 and 1972 respectively and were reprinted together in 1986 as *Burning the Years & Lobo: Poems 1962-1975.*

Meanwhile, the ubiquitous anthologist of the 60s and 70s Walter Lowenfels included one of former Marine William Wantling's Korean War poems in his 1967 *Where Is Vietnam?* Hinojosa's *Korean Love Songs* appeared in 1978, and was reprinted in a bilingual edition in Germany in 1991. Jan Barry and I included Reg Saner's "They Said" in our 1976 anthology *Demilitarized Zones*, Saner's "Re-Runs" appeared in his own 1989 *Red Letters*, and his "Flag Memoir" was published in *Ontario Review* #34, 1991. In 1995 Paul Edwards edited *The Hermit Kingdom: Poems of the Korean War*. While the quality of the poems in the Edwards anthology is uneven, there are good poems by Korean War veterans James Magner, Jr., Wantling, and Wilson, along with a number of poems by younger writers who still find the Korean War a source of creative energy, notable among them David Biespiel, John Jacob, and Patricia Monaghan.

Nevertheless, most editors, critics, and scholars have persisted in believing, as Gotera asserts, that the Korean War has "not produced a significant body of poetry." Because this belief is so widely held and so unquestioningly accepted, it has never been seriously examined. Evidence to the contrary either goes unnoticed or is routinely disregarded. Not until 1997 was there even so much as a single scholarly critical essay on Korean War poetry, and that was my own "Soldier-Poets of the Korean War." Little has changed since then. Editors continue to publish anthologies, and critics continue to publish studies, that only reinforce the prevailing assumption, which is then passed on to the larger reading public. The poetry of the Korean War, for the most part, is and always has been all but invisible on the American literary landscape, even that part of the landscape reserved for American war poetry.

What constitutes "a significant body of poetry," of course, is debatable. If we look at the four major American wars of the twentieth century—the Great War, World War Two, the Korean War, and the Vietnam War—the poetry of the Korean War comes out a distant third when comparing the number of poets or the number of poems resulting from each of these wars. The list of soldier-poets from World War Two reads like a Who's Who of mid-twentieth century poetry: Hayden Carruth, John Ciardi, James Dickey, Alan Dugan, Richard Eberhart, Anthony Hecht, Richard Hugo, Randall Jarrell, Lincoln Kirstein, Thomas McGrath, William Meredith, Howard Nemerov, Karl Shapiro, Louis Simpson, W. D. Snodgrass, and Richard Wilbur. Among those who did not serve in the military, but who wrote about the war are Robert Lowell and William Everson (Brother Antoninus), both of whom were conscientious objectors, Archibald Macleish, Carl Sandburg, Edna St. Vincent Millay, Stephen Vincent Benet, and Vachel Lindsay.

Likewise, the number of poets to have come out of, or written about, the Vietnam War is extensive. A short list of soldier-poets includes Doug Anderson, Jan Barry, R. L. Barth, D. F. Brown, Michael Casey, Horace

Coleman, David Connolly, Bryan Alec Floyd, David Huddle, Yusef Komun-yakaa, Gerald McCarthy, Walter McDonald, Marilyn McMahon, Basil Paquet, Dale Ritterbusch, and Bruce Weigl, along with John Balaban, who spent several years doing alternative service in Vietnam as a conscientious objector. Among the many others who wrote poems about the Vietnam War are Philip Appleman, Robert Bly, Allen Ginsberg, Samuel Hazo, Daniel Hoffman, June Jordan, Galway Kinnell, James Laughlin, Denise Levertov, Sharon Olds, Joel Oppenheimer, and David Ray.

On the other hand, the Great War, which cost the U.S. 80,000 dead (significantly more costly in American lives than either the Korean or Vietnam Wars), left far less poetry of any importance than did the Korean War. Mark Van Wienen, in his anthology *"I Have a Rendezvous with Death" and Other American Poems of the Great War*, includes over 125 poems by 100 different poets, and argues that these are only a small sampling of the "many hundreds, and then many thousands" of poems written between 1914 and 1920. The table of contents includes names such as Carl Sandburg, Vachel Lindsay, Wallace Stevens, Amy Lowell, Edith Wharton, and Edgar Lee Masters, along with the likes of C. Arthur Coan, Ellen Winsor, Lola Ridge, and Arthur Brisbane, but the poems themselves support the contention of bibliographer James Hart, quoted in Van Wienen's introduction, that "although thousands of minor American authors felt moved to write about the First World War, none was transformed by the conflict into a true poet. More important writers, of course, composed a few war pieces, but none produced a major poem."

Only seven (possibly eight[2]) of Van Wienen's poets served in the military or as civilian ambulance drivers, only two of these—Alan Seeger and Joyce Kilmer—are names we recognize today, and both are, in Walsh's words, "curiously genteel and conservative writers who were seemingly unaffected by the new energies at work in American poetry at this time." In *The Great War and Modern Memory*, Fussell argues that American writing about the Great War "tends to be spare and one-dimensional. The best-known American poem of the war, Alan Seeger's 'I Have a Rendezvous with Death,' operates without allusion [to any poetic tradition]. It is unresonant and inadequate for irony[.]"

And yet a number of poems from the Great War survive: Alan Seeger's "The Aisne," "Champagne, 1914-1915," and "Rendezvous"; Kilmer's "Rouge Bouquet" and "The White Ships and the Red"; e.e. cummings's "i sing of Olaf glad and big"; John Peale Bishop's "In the Dordogne"; Archibald MacLeish's "Memorial Rain"; and Malcolm Cowley's "Chateau de Soupir, 1917."

We remember Seeger and Kilmer, in spite of their deficiencies as poets, because they were immensely popular at the time (Kilmer had already published three books of poetry before he enlisted; Seeger's *Poems* was a national bestseller and remained in print through World War Two), because they died romantically in battle (Seeger with the French Foreign Legion, Kilmer leaving a wife and children), but perhaps most of all because we remember the war they fought in. And while cummings, Bishop, MacLeish, and Cowley have more to recommend them literarily than Seeger or Kilmer, it is doubtful that any of their Great War poems would have survived were the Great War as unacknowledged, unexamined, and unknown as the Korean War is.

That the poetry of the Korean War has been deemed insignificant and even nonexistent is as much a reflection of attitudes about (and ignorance of) the Korean War itself as it is a reflection on the poetry. Surely any number of Korean War poems possess as much or more moral and artistic value than any American poem of the Great War, and some of them can hold their own against much of the poetry from World War Two and the Vietnam War. Still, trying to characterize and generalize about Korean War poetry, and assess just where and how it fits into the artistic and aesthetic progression of twentieth century American war poetry, is not an easy exercise.

One can fairly safely say about American Great War poetry that it tends "to stress the heroism and sacrifice of the troops" and views "war as a purifying experience," as Walsh argues, adding that poets such as Seeger and Kilmer "deploy an aesthetic that is pre-modernist." Edwards observes that it is a poetry "lacking in personal comment, and strangely removed from immediate experience." Not until cummings began to write about the Great War, Walsh writes, do we "encounter a modernist sensibility at work, demythologizing, taking war out of the laudatory tradition of verse, and enacting a complete break with past war writing in the United States."[3]

The revolution in war poetry wrought by such British soldier-poets as Charles Hamilton Sorley, Siegfried Sassoon, Isaac Rosenberg, Robert Graves, Wilfred Owen, and Edmund Blunden did not reach across the Atlantic Ocean until the 1920s. Seeger was dead, for instance, before Sassoon even wrote "The Redeemer," of which Jean Moorcroft Wilson, Sassoon's biographer, says, "Here at last is War poetry based on actual experience." MacLeish, Cowley, and Bishop all wrote their most important Great War poems in the 1920s and 1930s. But by the beginning of World War Two, the whole enterprise of English-language poetry had changed enormously—the result of such innovative and groundbreaking poets as cummings, Ezra Pound, T. S. Eliot, Wallace Stevens and William Carlos Williams—and within that larger world, the apprehension of both war and war poetry had also changed. Those changes are readily apparent in the poetry to emerge from World War Two.

"The Second World War," writes Kerin, "has come to be known for the most part by a single characterizing label: 'the good war' ... the last American war to be considered then, and remembered now, as a 'good war' in the consensus of the American people." At the same time, he notes that World War Two poetry has "an edge lacking in the verse of American soldier-poets of World War I." Chattarji takes Kerin's line of thought even farther. "American poets were not as triumphalist as the rest of their society," he observes. "While the political establishment projected World War II as the 'good war', the poets ask for an honest reappraisal of the major military conflict of their time."

Consider, for instance, John Ciardi, who writes of his dead friend in "A Box Comes Home":

> Once I saw Arthur dressed as the United States
> Of America. Now I see the United States
> Of America as Arthur in a flag-sealed domino.

It is hardly a triumphalist image, but if World War Two was a good war, it certainly did Arthur no good. Nor did it do much good for Randall Jarrell's ball turret gunner who "woke to black flak and the nightmare fighters" and who was washed "out of the turret with a hose" when he died. It did no good for Van Wettering or Averill, "gone to early death" in Richard Eberhart's "The Fury of Aerial Bombardment." Louis Simpson's master-sergeant, captain, and lieutenant all end up dead in "Carentan O Carentan." And Alan Dugan's foot soldier—"an accomplished murderer"—"smelled bad and was red-eyed with the miseries / of being scared while sleepless."

While American popular culture may remember the end of World War Two as a sailor exuberantly kissing a nurse in Times Square amid tickertape and happy crowds, Howard Nemerov, in "Redeployment," remembers it this way:

> They say the war is over. But water still
> Comes bloody from the taps, and my pet cat
> In his disorder vomits worms which crawl
> Swiftly away. Maybe they leave the house.
> These worms are white, and flecked with the cat's blood.

Even twenty years after the war's end, James Dickey, in "The Fire-bombing," is still haunted by the memory of himself as "some technical-minded stranger with my hands" preparing to drop "the fire developed to cling / To everything" on a town where "five thousand people are sleeping."

Walsh writes that "the diversity of [World War Two] poetry, written by both civilians and combatants alike, resists facile summary or definition," but argues that "the most typical Second World War poets wrote like John Ciardi, in an ironic and slightly self-mocking tone. The new war poets often wrote from a common standpoint of subversive irony." Fussell, in his foreword to Leon Stokesbury's World War Two poetry anthology *Articles of War*, notes that the World War Two poets "preferred to speak in wry understatement, glancing less at the center of a topic than at its edges, proceeding by hints and indirections rather than open straight-forward declaration," often relying on "the wry mock-elegy or mock-epitaph." In *Wartime*, Fussell is highly critical of the poetry written by such noncombatants as MacLeish, Sandburg, Millay, Benet, Lindsay, and a great many others who wrote "patriotic drivel" because they were "persuaded that the war effort required the laying aside of all normal standards of art and intellect," but—again in Stokesbury—he argues that the soldier-poets adopted "a general skepticism about the former languages of glory and sacrifice and patriotism."

But while the World War Two poets may wrestle with "the horrors and ambiguities of war," as Chattarji says, or "regard the military conduct of the war with considerable skepticism," as Walsh writes, or rage "against war in the abstract," as Edwards suggests, or feel as if "it had all been gone through before" only a generation earlier, as Fussell contends in *Wartime*, what one does not find in the poetry of World War Two is any challenge to the need to fight this particular war. It may have been ugly, it may have been brutal, it may have been butchery and mayhem and stupidity and madness, it may have exacted a hideous price from everyone engaged in it, but one need only consider the alternative to not fighting—Adolf Hitler and the Japanese Imperial General Staff—and the debate is over. No American poet of World War Two has ever written, or ever said, "We should not have gone to war against Germany and Japan." It was necessary. It was unavoidable.

Herein lies a major difference between the poetry of World War Two and the poetry of the Vietnam War. "One quickly sees the anger expressed in the poetry of the Vietnam War," writes Edwards, "This poetry is full of rage and despair which seems to arise from an utter disbelief in the events taking place. [It is] lacking any respect for national interests." "Vietnam taught us our limitations and taught us that we had outlived the usefulness of our myths," says poet and Vietnam veteran Dale Ritterbusch, "This is one of the primary lessons of Vietnam. And the poets insist on teaching us this lesson." "Of all the writing to come out of the Vietnam War," critic and Vietnam veteran Philip Beidler observes, "Vietnam poetry remains a political genre. [T]his is what [the Vietnam War poets] tell us. We did not have the faintest notion of who we were and what it was, this awful, insanely misguided, yes—evil—thing we were doing." John Clark Pratt, in his foreword to the Vietnam War poetry anthology *Unaccustomed Mercy*, sees new themes in Vietnam War poetry, among them "the essential stupidity and causelessness of the war."

Just as Fussell criticizes the "patriotic drivel" of homefront poets in World War Two, scholar Lorrie Smith dismisses much of the homefront antiwar poetry of writers such as Levertov, Ginsberg, and Bly, writing that "many protest poems written during the war seem destined to fade from view." But she contends that the most effective poems of the Vietnam War are "invaluable for bringing home the war's horror and absurdity to complacent America" and attest to "the catastrophe of the Vietnam War."

Smith argues that "[W. D.] Ehrhart is guided by moral and political outrage," that John Balaban "helps counteract the invisibility of the Vietnamese in most American treatments of the war," that Bruce Weigl "shows the war's persistent nightmare presence in American culture," that D. F. Brown denies "comforting resolution, transcendence, or reconciliation," and that Lowell Jaeger (a conscientious objector who neither went to Vietnam nor served in the military) "reminds us that [the war's] legacy belongs to all Americans, that we cannot deny, forget, or refuse responsibility for it." Summing up, she concludes that, "having witnessed an unspeakably futile and vicious war, [Vietnam War poets] attest to the utter bankruptcy of myths celebrating the war's heroism and mystique."

Much of this assessment might seem to apply equally to World War Two poetry. But while these poets may and do express moral outrage on occasion, political outrage—the idea that the government and the nation are wrong—is absent. Nor do the World War Two poets suggest that either the American government or the American people were somehow responsible for World War Two. While the World War Two poets write about the lingering individual ghosts of their wartime experiences, they do not suggest that the nation itself continues to be haunted by their war.

Moreover, it is inconceivable that any World War Two veteran would spell "America" with a "k" instead of a "c" as Charles Purcell does in "The Walk":

> Take the war out of the T.V.s and put it in the complacent streets
> Kick Amerika awake
> Before it dies in its sleep.

Or consider Jan Barry, who compares Americans in Vietnam to "13th-century Mongol armies" in "In the Footsteps of Genghis Khan." Or David Connolly, who, in "To the Irish Americans Who Fought the Last War," writes of his service in Vietnam that "we became the hated Black and Tan, / and we shamed our ancestry." Or Gustav Hasford (whose novel *The Short-timers* became the basis for Stanley Kubrick's *Full Metal Jacket*), who writes in "Bedtime Story":

> Sleep, America.
> Silence is a warm bed.
>   * * *
> Bayonet teddy bear and snore.
> Bad dreams are something you ate.
> So sleep, you mother.

Of course, Vietnam War poetry "resists facile summary or definition," to use Walsh's words, every bit as much as does World War Two poetry. And there are many affinities the two groups of poetry share; modern war is both transforming and degrading, and the particulars of any given war don't make much difference to individual human beings down at the level of the firefight or the dogfight or the naval duel. What sets Vietnam War poetry apart is the unavoidable realization that all this suffering and death and destruction was for nothing. Just nothing. As Gerald McCarthy writes in "The Hooded Legion," a poem about the Vietnam Veterans Memorial in Washington, D. C.:

> There are no words here
> to witness why we fought,
> who sent us or what we hoped to gain.
>
> There is only the rain
> as it streaks the black stone,
> these memories of rain
> that come back to us—
> a hooded legion reflected in a wall.

Differences, too, exist in the form of the poems, the nuts and bolts of how the poetry is constructed. "The crucial thing to notice is the obvious devotion of [the World War Two poets] to poetry and the enterprise of poetry," says Gotera. "These artists pay devout attention to poetics (often to rhyme, meter, and inherited forms) in an attempt to extend the poetic corpus. In other words, they are cognizant and deliberate in writing fine *literature*. Vietnam-veteran poets would call these assumptions into question." The poetry of the Vietnam War, adds Edwards, "is personal, immediate, self-directed, and lacking much of the abstraction traditionally found in poetry." "With only a few exceptions," Pratt contends, Vietnam War poems "are essentially 'non-literary'; that is, they require little explication; they come from no recognizable tradition; [and] they usually invent their own forms[.]"

To some extent, this is a function of continuing changes in post-World War Two American poetry in general. But it is also the result—often will-fully so—of choosing to reject the values of the World War Two genera-tion that sent the Vietnam generation off to war, including their literary values. "Nearly all the poems on the Vietnam War," writes Smith, "strug-gle on some level—thematically, formally, or stylistically—to break down conventional social meanings rather than reflecting or accommodating them."

One really does have to be careful, of course, with generalizations, keeping in mind that there are always exceptions. Vietnam War poet R. L. Barth, for instance, writes almost entirely in closed forms, using both rhyme and meter, and David Huddle has written a fine sequence of sonnets about the Vietnam War. Not all of the poetry of non-veterans should be dis-missed out of hand, either. Philip Appleman, Christopher Bursk, Michael Stephens, Frank Stewart, and a number of other writers—including Car-ruth and McGrath—have written excellent poems inspired by the Vietnam War. And while Fussell rightly blasts the "patriotic drivel" written by non-combatants during World War Two, it is hard to find fault with Robinson Jeffers's "Pearl Harbor," or Winfield Townley Scott's "The U.S. Soldier with the Japanese Skull," or Weldon Kees's "June 1940."

Still, if generalizing about the poetry of either World War Two or the Vietnam War is difficult because in each case the body of work is so large, even more difficulty arises from Korean War poetry because the body of work is, relatively, so small. While dozens of individual poems of varying quality were written by various poets, only a small number of poets (most importantly Childress, Fast, Hinojosa, Saner, Wantling, and Wilson) have written more than half a dozen poems about the Korean War, and only Hinojosa and Wilson have produced larger sequences based on the war.

Because most scholars and critics don't even acknowledge the exis-tence of Korean War poetry, they of course make no attempt to general-ize about it. Gotera, for instance, who writes that "a wide gap of poetic philosophy may yawn between the soldier-poets of World War I and World War II and those of Vietnam," never considers the possibility that this gap might be at least partially filled by the poetry of the Korean War, a poetry he has already concluded does not exist. Only Edwards makes even a stab at characterizing Korean War poetry. "Caught like a shadow between World War II and Vietnam," he writes, "the Korean War was a very different war, and one which reflected a transition in war poetry." But instead of mak-ing any attempt to explain what he means by calling it transitional poetry,

Edwards, not a literary scholar but a historian, turns to the war itself, saying that "it was the first of the non-patriotic wars, a war during which participants expanded to an art form the idea that 'getting it over' was more important than 'getting it done,'" which may be true but does nothing to explain or illuminate the poetry.

It would seem logical that Korean War poetry should be a kind of transitional poetry, serving to "fill the gap" between World War Two poetry and Vietnam War poetry, and to some extent it does, sharing many of the themes of the poetry that comes both before and after: fear, pain, guilt, loss, sadness, dislocation, isolation, transformation in the most negative sense, disgust with war in general. Rolando Hinojosa captures the bleakness of war with these lines from "New Battery Position":

> The earth reveals patches of green here and there,
> But we'll soon fix that. What the gun crews don't trample,
> The shells and supplies will.... It doesn't take long.

William Childress's sad recognition, in "Soldiers," that "soldiers can't be soldiers and be human," is not limited to the Korean War. And Darien Cobb's shocked surprise, in a poem called "News," is surely universal:

> I did not understand
>   about time and space,
>
> Until pieces of an old tin roof
>   as big as the hands of
> God demanded the space
>   where your chest had been.

In "Re-Runs," Reg Saner grapples with almost every emotion in the list above:

> Odd nights, a clay pit or two may waken him
> still, alone inside a nameless grief holding
> nothing: their faces, grass shrapnel—which some field
> on the world's other side bothers with. Like seed,
> the shapes that won't go away without tears.

Some of this Korean War poetry, however, also anticipates the explicit anger of the Vietnam War poets, especially the soldier-poets, not at (or not only at) war as a general phenomenon, but at this war in particular, and at those whom the poets hold responsible for it. In "The Eighth Army at the Chongchon," Hinojosa makes fun of the rationale he and his comrades have been given for fighting in Korea:

Creating history (their very words)
by protecting the world from Communism. I suppose
One needs a pep talk now and then[.]

Childress is no more convinced of the cause than Hinojosa, writing in "Burning the Years":

Goodbye to the slim youth
in paratrooper garb,
with boots like mirrors
and ribbons straight as his spine.
He knew all there was to know
about honor and duty.
But duty changes with each job,
and honor turns ashes soon enough.

The vehemence of the sarcasm in Saner's "They Said" is almost palpable, driving the poem through two previous stanzas to its harsh conclusion:

They said, "Democracy is at the crossroads everyone
will be given a gun and a map in cases like this
there is no need to vote." Our group scored quite
well getting each of its villages right except
one but was allowed to try again on a fresh village
we colored it black and then wore our brass
stars of unit citation almost all the way home.

The use of the word "almost" in the poem's final line leaves no doubt that Saner takes no pride in what he and his country have done in and to Korea. And Keith Wilson's critique of Wall Street is scathing in "December 1952." After describing how "stabbing / tracers hit a village, / the screams of women, children / men die," he concludes:

Casualties are statistics
for a rising New York Stock Market—
its ticker tapes hail the darkeyed
survivors, and cash registers
click, all over the nation, these men
deceive themselves. War is for. The dead.

Fast (who is not a Korean War veteran) explicitly indicts the government itself in "Gerald Cartwheel, Tankman":

> The day my tank rolled through a village,
> flattening those flimsy houses,
> I saw a woman caught under a beam,
> screaming as the tank rolled over—
> on that day, I wrote my congressman,
> my free and democratic right,
> "Was I sent here to do this kind of thing,
> or tell me why, or have I no right to know,
> or do you know?"

Fast also seems to anticipate the racial tensions of Horace Coleman's "OK Corral East: Brothers in the Nam" when he has black soldier "Jamsie Anderson, Quartermasters" say: "Well, take my past and put it you know where, / all of it, cleaning toilets and shining shoes"—this after being told by white soldiers, "Black man's / got no business talking common sense." Just as John Balaban works to counter the invisibility of the Vietnamese, James Magner's "To a Chinaman, in a Hole, Long Ago" acknowledges the humanity of those faceless "Asian hordes" who swept out of the bitter Manchurian winter and died by the tens of thousands. Speaking to a Chinese soldier he has just killed, Magner wishes he could

> bequeath my life to you
> that you might fly the Yellow Sea
> to your startled matron's arms

but sadly recognizes that

> marbled you lie
> —and I, somewhat alive—
> this rock-white silent day
> of our demagogue damnation.

Certainly Lowell Jaeger holds the American people no more accountable for the consequences of the Vietnam War than does Wilson for the Korean War. In "Commentary," for instance, Wilson writes:

> deaths. lists of victims
> in a language the uncle
> back home couldn't read
> if he saw it, whose enemies
> are always faceless, numbers
> in a paper blowing in the
> Stateside wind.

How many bodies would
fill a room[?]

* * *

We have killed more.
The children's bodies alone
would suffice.

The women, their admittedly
brown faces frozen in the agony
of steel buried in their stomachs,
they too would be enough

but aren't, are
finally not piled high enough
the cost of war must be paid, bullets
made for firing, fired.

And one can hardly get more political than Childress, who writes in "For My First Son" that flamethrowers, trenchfoot, gangrene, and shrapnel are the

gifts of male birthdays,
wrapped in patriot slogans,
and sent by lying leaders.

In form, one can see movement away from what Gotera calls "attention to poetics" toward what Pratt calls "non-literary" poetry. While both Carruth's "On a Certain Engagement South of Seoul" (written in *terza rima*) and McGrath's "Ode for the American Dead in Korea" (a combination of rhymed and blank verse) are highly structured, and Paal Ramberg and Jerome Miller employ a variety of traditional forms (alongside of a prose-like free verse) in their 1950 collaboration *Hell's Music: A Verse Narrative of the Korean War*, most Korean War poetry is written in various styles of free verse from the prose-poetry of Reg Saner's "Flag Memoir" to the staccato lines of William Wantling's "Sure." Among the soldier-poets, only Childress attempts to use closed forms,[4] and then only in a few instances such as "Korea Bound, 1952," "The Soldiers," "Combat Iambic," and "The War Lesson."

This, too, however, may be as much a reflection of general trends in poetry as it is a result of deliberate artistic—and political—choices by the poets. None of the soldier-poets began writing poetry about the Korean War until the 1960s. Wilson says that his writing was heavily influenced by Charles Olson's essay "Projective Verse," which he did not read until 1960.

Childress stayed in the army until 1959 and did not attend the Iowa Writers Workshop until 1966. Wantling only began to write poetry while taking a creative writing class at San Quentin Prison in the late 1950s. By then, such new trends as the New York School, the Black Mountain Poets, and of course the Beats were helping to shape the course of American poetry.

Moreover, by the time Childress and Wilson were publishing the bulk of their Korean War poetry, Vietnam War poets like Balaban, Barry, and Basil Paquet had begun to write and publish. And though there is no evidence that Hinojosa was influenced by it, a significant body of Vietnam War poetry already existed by the time he began to write *Korean Love Songs* in 1976. Indeed, by the very nature of its being a novel-in-verse, in a number of ways *Korean Love Songs* may have as much in common with Peter Bowman's World War Two novel-in-verse *Beach Red* or McAvoy Layne's Vietnam War novel-in-verse *How Audie Murphy Died in Vietnam* as it does with the Korean War poems of any of the other authors in this study.

Finally, whatever parallels and foreshadowing one might manage to discern in Korean War poetry, one has to recognize that there is no direct line of connection from World War Two poetry to Vietnam War poetry through Korean War poetry. While Vietnam War poets regularly display their debt to earlier wars and earlier generations of war poets—sometimes quite explicitly as in Balaban's "On a Photograph of Schoolchildren Wearing Gas Masks. Rheims. World War I" or Paquet's "Mourning the Death, by Hemorrhage, of a Child from Honai"—in all the body of Vietnam War poetry there seems to be not one reference to the Korean War or its poets. Because Korean War poetry, like the war itself, has been so thoroughly overlooked, dismissed, and ignored, it did not and could not serve as an influence on those poets who came after.

This is not, however, a reason to continue to overlook, dismiss, and ignore it. As Philip K. Jason and I wrote in our introduction to *Retrieving Bones: Stories and Poems of the Korean War*, the Korean War produced "a literary heritage possessing power, beauty, and humanity" that "can teach us a great deal about an important experience in American history that shaped the nature of the Cold War that shaped the world we live in today. If we continue to neglect this literature, we do so at our own peril. It is time and long past time to open our minds and broaden our vision in ways that only literature can help us to do."

While we were writing about Korean War literature in general, all of this most assuredly applies to the war's poetry. The fiftieth anniversary of the Korean War (1950–1953) has brought renewed attention to the war—some would argue it has brought real attention to the war for the first time. One can only hope that some small part of this attention might be directed toward the poetry, which collectively deserves a better fate than it has thus far received.

Authors & Works Cited or Referenced

Appleman, Philip. *Open Doorways*. New York: W. W. Norton, 1976.

Axelsson, Arne. *Restrained Response: American Novels of the Cold War and Korea, 1945–1962*. Westport, CT: Greenwood Press, 1990.

Baker, Kenneth, ed. *The Faber Book of War Poetry*. London: Faber & Faber, 1997.

Balaban, John. *After Our War*. Pittsburgh, PA: University of Pittsburgh Press, 1974.

_____. *Locusts at the Edge of Summer*. Port Townsend, WA: Copper Canyon Press, 1997.

Barry, Jan, Basil Paquet & Larry Rottmann, eds. *Winning Hearts and Minds: War Poems by Vietnam Veterans*. Brooklyn: 1st Casualty Press, 1972.

Barry, Jan & W. D. Ehrhart, eds. *Demilitarized Zones: Veterans After Vietnam*. Perkasie, PA: East River Anthology, 1976.

Barry, Jan, ed. *Peace Is Our Profession*. Montclair, NJ: East River Anthology, 1981.

Barry, Jan. *Veterans Day*. Richford, VT: Samisdat, 1983.

Beidler, Philip. "Situation Report: American Writing About the Vietnam War." In *The Vietnam War: Its History, Literature and Music*, Kenton J. Clymer, ed. El Paso, TX: Texas Western Press, 1998.

Bishop, John Peale. *Selected Poems*. New York: C. Scribner's Sons, 1941.

Bowman, Peter. *Beach Red*. New York: Random House, 1945.

Brown, D. F. *Returning Fire*. San Francisco: San Francisco State University, 1984.

Bursk, Christopher. *Place of Residence*. West Lafayette, IN: Sparrow Press, 1983.

Carruth, Hayden. *The Crow and the Heart*. New York: The MacMillan Company, 1959.

_____. *The Selected Poetry of Hayden Carruth*. New York: MacMillan, 1985.

_____. *Collected Shorter Poems*. Port Townsend, WA: Copper Canyon Press, 1992.

Chattarji, Subarno. *Memories of a Lost War: A Study of American Poetic Responses to the Vietnam War*. Oxford: Oxford University Press, 2001.

Ciardi, John. *Selected Poems*. Fayetteville: University of Arkansas Press, 1984.

Childress, William. *Burning the Years*. New York: The Smith, 1971.

_____. *Lobo*. New York: Barlenmir House, 1972.

_____. *Burning the Years and Lobo: Poems 1962-1975*. East St. Louis, IL: Essai Seay Publications, 1986.

Cobb, Darien. "News." See Edwards.

Coleman, Horace. *In the Grass*. Woodbridge, CT: Viet Nam Generation, Inc. & Burning Cities Press, 1995.

Connolly, David. *Lost in America*. Woodbridge, CT: Viet Nam Generation & Burning Cities Press, 1994.

Cowley, Malcolm. *Blue Juniata*. New York: Viking, 1968.

cummings, e.e. *Complete Poems, 1913–1962*. New York: Harcourt Brace Jovanovich, 1972.

Dickey, James. *Poems 1957–1967*. New York: Collier Books, 1968.

Dugan, Alan. *New & Collected Poems, 1961–1983*. Hopewell, NJ: The Ecco Press, 1983.

Eberhart, Richard. *Collected Poems 1938–1986*. New York: Oxford University Press, 1988.

Edwards, Paul M., ed. *The Hermit Kingdom: Poems of the Korean War*. Dubuque, IA: Kendall/Hunt, 1995.

Ehrhart, W. D., ed. *Carrying the Darkness*. Lubbock: Texas Tech University Press, 1989.

_____. *Unaccustomed Mercy*. Lubbock, TX: Texas Tech University Press, 1989.

Ehrhart, W. D., guest ed. *War, Literature, and the Arts*, v.9, #2, Fall/Winter 1997.

Ehrhart, W. D. & Philip K. Jason, eds. *Retrieving Bones: Stories and Poems of the Korean War*. New Brunswick, NJ: Rutgers University Press, 1999.

Fast, Howard. *Korean Lullaby*. New York: American Peace Crusade, undated (probably 1950 or 1951; no later than mid–1953).

Forche, Carolyn, ed. *Against Forgetting: Twentieth Century Poetry of Witness*. New York: W. W. Norton, 1993.

Fussell, Paul. *The Great War and Modern Memory*. Oxford: Oxford University Press, 1975.

_____. *Wartime: Understanding and Behavior in the Second World War*. Oxford: Oxford University Press, 1989.

Fussell, Paul, ed. *The Norton Book of Modern War*. New York: W. W. Norton, 1991.

Gotera, Vince. *Radical Visions: Poetry by Vietnam Veterans*. Athens: University of Georgia Press, 1994.

Halberstam, David. *The Fifties*. New York: Fawcett Columbine, 1993.

Hasford, Gustav. "Bedtime Story." See Barry, Paquet & Rottmann.

Hinojosa, Rolando. *Korean Love Songs*. Berkeley, CA: Justa Publications, 1978. Reprinted as *Korean Love Songs/Korea Liebes Lieder*. Osnabruck, FRG: Osnabrück Bilingual Editions of Minority Writers, 1991.

Huddle, David. "Tour of Duty." In *Pig Iron* #12, 1984.

Jaeger, Lowell. *War on War*. Logan: Utah State University Press, 1988.

Jarrell, Randall. *The Complete Poems*. New York: Farrar, Strauss & Giroux, 1969.

Jason, Philip K. "Short Fiction of the Korean War": http://www.illyria.com/kor_shortfic.html

Jeffers, Robinson. *The Double Axe & Other Poems*. New York: Random House, 1948.

Kees, Weldon. "June 1940." *The Complete Poems of Weldon Kees*. Lincoln: University of Nebraska Press, 1975.

Kerin, James R. "The Korean War and American Memory." Unpublished doctoral dissertation, University of Pennsylvania, 1994.

Kilmer, Joyce. *Joyce Kilmer: Poems, Essays & Letters*. New York: Doubleday, Doran & Co., 1940.

Layne, McAvoy. *How Audie Murphy Died in Vietnam*. Garden City, NY: Anchor Books, 1973.

Lowenfels, Walter. *Where Is Vietnam? American Poets Respond*. New York: Anchor Books, 1967.

MacLeish, Archibald. *The Collected Poems*. Boston: Houghton Mifflin, 1962.

Magner, James, Jr. *The Dark Is Closest to the Moon*. Cleveland: The Ryder Press, 1973.

McCarthy, Gerald. *War Story*. Trumansburg, NY: The Crossing Press, 1977.

McFarland, Keith D. *The Korean War: An Annotated Bibliography*. New York: Garland, 1986.

McGrath, Thomas. *Figures of the Double World*. Denver: Swallow Press, 1955.

_____. *New & Selected Poems*. Chicago: Swallow Press, 1964.

_____. *The Movie at the End of the World*. Chicago: Swallow Press, 1972.

_____. *Selected Poems 1938-1988*. Port Townsend, WA: Copper Canyon Press, 1988.

Nemerov, Howard. *The Collected Poems*. Chicago: University of Chicago Press, 1977.

Olson, Charles. "Projective Verse." In *The New American Poetry*, Donald M. Allen, ed. New York: Grove Press, 1960.

Paquet, Basil. "Mourning the Death, by Hemorrhage, of a Child from Honai." See Barry, Paquet & Rottmann.

Pierce, Edith Lovejoy. "Heartbreak Ridge." In *Where Steel Winds Blow*, Robert Cromie, ed. New York: David McKay Co., 1968.

Purcell, Charles. "The Walk." See Barry, Paquet & Rottmann.

Ramberg, Paal & Jerome Miller. *Hell's Music: A Verse Narrative of the Korean War*. New London, MN: Green Spires Press, 1950.

Ritterbusch, Dale. "Lessons Learned and Unlearned." In *The United States and Viet Nam from War to Peace*, Robert M. Slabey, ed. Jefferson, NC: McFarland & Company, Inc., 1996.

Saner, Reg. *Red Letters*. Princeton: Quarterly Review of Literature, Poetry Series IX, v.XXVIII–XXIX, 1989.

Scott, Winfield Townley. *Collected Poems*. New York: Macmillan, 1962.

Seeger, Alan. *Poems*. New York: Charles Scribner, 1916.

Simpson, Louis. *A Dream of Governors*. Middletown, CT: Wesleyan University Press, 1959.

Smith, Lorrie. "After Our War." *Poetry Wales*, v.25, #1, June 1989.

Stallworthy, Jon, ed. *The Oxford Book of War Poetry*. Oxford: Oxford University Press, 1984.

Stephens, Michael. *After Asia*. New York: Spuyten Duyvil, 1993.

Stewart, Frank. "Black Winter." See Barry, *Peace Is Our Profession*.

Stokesbury, Leon, ed. *Articles of War: A Collection of Poems About World War II*. Fayetteville: University of Arkansas Press, 1990.

Van Wienen, Mark W., ed. *"I Have a Rendezvous with Death" and Other American Poems of the Great War*. Forthcoming from University of Illinois Press.

Walsh, Jeffrey. *American War Literature: 1914 to Vietnam*. New York: St. Martin's Press, 1982.

Wantling, William. "Sure" and "Korea 1953." See Ehrhart & Jason.

Weigl, Bruce. *Song of Napalm*. New York: Atlantic Monthly Press, 1988.

Wilson, Jean Moorcroft. *Siegfried Sassoon: The Making of a War Poet*. New York : Routledge, 1998.

Wilson, Keith. *Graves Registry and Other Poems*. New York: Grove Press, 1969.

_____. *Graves Registry*. Livingston, MT: Clark City Press, 1992.

NOTES

1. Copies of Knight's military records were obtained by Thomas C. Johnson, a graduate student at Butler University, and made available to WDE on October 27, 1997. While the original records were partially damaged by fire, careful inspection of what remains makes it all but certain that Knight never served in Korea and was never wounded. He served from June 1947 to June 1949, then re-enlisted in February 1950 and served until November 1950 when he was medically discharged for chondromalacia, a degenerative knee problem. He was awarded neither the Purple Heart Medal for wounds received in combat nor any of the Korean War service medals routinely given to anyone serving in Korea.

2. The status of one poet, J. Eugene Chrisman, is unclear. His poem "Poppies" suggests that he may be a veteran. It begins: "Poppies?/Not for me, buddy!/Buds o' Hell I'd call 'em," ending: "Then the Jerries cut loose … Got old Slim—got him right!/Down in the poppies he goes—kickin—clawin'!/Don't talk poppies to me … If you'd seen old Slim—Boy, he died *wallerin'* in poppies!/Poppies—/Hell!" Originally published in a 1921 issue of *Literary Digest*, it certainly does not share the gentility and conservatism (as Walsh puts it) of Seeger and Kilmer.

3. One might argue that some of the poems in Walt Whitman's *Drum Taps*—"The Wound-Dresser," for instance—demythologize and "take war out of the laudatory tradition of verse," but this is not the venue for such a discussion. For the most part, Walsh's observation holds true.

4. The one exception to this generalization is William Wantling's "Korea 1953," which contains an intricate and intriguing sequence of internal rhymes; aside from this poem, however, Wantling wrote exclusively in free verse.

❖　❖　❖

"The Madness of It All": A Rumination on War, Journalism and Brotherhood

I celebrated Thanksgiving Day 1967 in a sandbagged underground bunker at a Marine outpost called Con Thien on the southern edge of the

Vietnamese demilitarized zone. It wasn't much of a celebration. I'm told that in Vietnamese *Con Thien* means "place of angels," but at the time I was there, it was just a muddy rat-infested collection of bunkers, trenches, and concertina wire only big enough for a Marine battalion with supporting arms. If there were angels in that place, they did not reveal themselves to me.

But there was fire from the heavens. Because Con Thien was well within range of North Vietnamese heavy artillery dug in on the far side of the Ben Hai River dividing what was—quite temporarily, as it turned out—two Vietnams, we were shelled every day by 152-millimeter howitzers, along with 120mm and 82mm mortars fired from closer range, with the occasional 122mm rocket thrown in for good measure.

We seldom ventured beyond our own perimeter, and when we did, we were usually ambushed by NVA infantry or mortars, for Con Thien was constantly under observation by the NVA, and we did not come or go without their knowing it. Mostly we stayed inside our bunkers inside our wire and hoped that nothing big landed on top of the bunker we happened to occupy. All in all, being at Con Thien was a thoroughly unpleasant experience.

The outpost had been under almost constant pressure since the spring of 1967, and because it was so dangerous and demoralizing a place—even within the dangerous and demoralizing context of what the entire Vietnam War had become—the Marine Corps rotated its battalions in and out of Con Thien roughly once a month. The First Battalion of the First Marine Regiment spent thirty-three days at Con Thien, from 20 November to 23 December, which is how I ended up in a sandbagged underground bunker on Thanksgiving Day.

We did not like leaving the relative safety and protection of the bunkers unless we really had to, but on this Thanksgiving Day, somebody or other somewhere far up the chain of command—President Lyndon Baines Johnson himself, for all we knew or cared—had ordered that all of America's gallant fighting men should get a hot turkey dinner complete with all the trimmings. Ours had been flown in by helicopter and was, we were informed by our intelligence chief, waiting for us at the battalion aid station.

None of the inhabitants of my bunker—in addition to myself: Sgt. Floyd Graves, Cpl. John Wallace, and Cpl. Roland Maas—was eager to take the president up on his kindness since it meant slowly and precariously slogging several hundred meters through sucking mud a foot and more deep, all the while leaving us exposed to death or dismemberment from enemy artillery fire. We were content to stay home and eat C-rations spiced with Louisiana Red Rooster hot sauce, the latter bartered from Navy Sea-Bees.

But the gunny informed us that this was not actually an invitation, but rather an order. And so the four of us—with much grumbling and profanity, this to hide our fear as much as to show our indignation—donned our helmets and flak jackets, grabbed our mess kits, and set off down the aptly named Death Valley to the aid station, where all the bounty of the pilgrims and their Indian friends was heaped into one indistinguishable pile in our too tiny mess kits. Then we carried it back to the bunker.

It rained all the way down and all the way back. The journey took a long time, and the only good part was that we did not get shelled along the way. But we returned to the bunker with food that was stone cold and heavily diluted with rainwater. The four of us sat there on the duckboard floor, our boots and legs thickly caked with mud up to our knees, too overcome by the enormity of the little disasters piled in front of us to say much.

While we were still in a state of whatever state we were in—shock, disbelief, wonder at the strangeness of life in wartime—a man we had never seen before stuck his head into our bunker and said cheerily, "Happy Thanksgiving, fellas! Mind if we interrupt your meal for a few moments?" Without waiting for an answer, he crawled in, no doubt eager to get under cover. He was wearing a jungle utility uniform, our basic work clothes, but carried no insignia or rank of any kind. Close on his heels came a similarly dressed man with several cameras dangling from his neck. Both had flak jackets and helmets on, but neither was armed.

I remember Graves saying flatly, "Whadda you want?" It was phrased as a question, but it sounded like an accusation. Taking a notepad out of his breast pocket, the man explained that they were journalists on assignment for some magazine or other to do a story about Thanksgiving at Con Thien. To this, Graves said something to the effect of: "A little something to warm the hearts of the home folks, huh?" To which the journalist replied, "Yeh, something like that."

I remember the journalist gave an odd little half-smile, his discomfort obvious in the face of the quiet menace in Floyd's voice. And then Graves said, "Get the fuck out of our house. Now." The two men seemed to disappear into thin air. We got a good laugh at the rapidity of their departure. It wasn't all that funny, really, but when you're having no fun at all, every little bit helps.

We did not like journalists very much. They would come to a place like Con Thien by helicopter or by truck, stay a few hours, and then go away again, back to places with silverware and mixed drinks and clean sheets, leaving us to our misery. They got paid a lot more than we did. They got all the perks of officers, and then some. They came and went as they pleased. Even the most experienced of journalists, those that knew what to do when things got hot, were mostly just a burden. When they were with you, you had to look out for them and take care of them and help them if they were injured, but they did not carry weapons and did not fight and therefore could not defend you.

Moreover, by November 1967 I had long since come to realize that what I was reading in *Time* and *Stars 'n' Stripes* and the *News-Herald* bore no resemblance at all to what I was seeing and doing day in and day out. I did not then yet understand just exactly what was happening in Vietnam, but I knew what I read in the papers wasn't even close. I don't recall ever reading a single article that didn't end with the implicit or explicit conclusion that we were making progress, moving forward, winning the war.

Neither of the men who visited our bunker that Thanksgiving Day was John Laurence, the CBS television correspondent who covered the war off and on for long stretches between 1965 and 1970 and whose memoir *The Cat from Hue: A Vietnam War Story* was published in 2002 by Public Affairs Press. But one of them could have been. In his memoir, he describes a visit (his second of three) to Con Thien in September 1967. The visit lasted several hours. Together with cameraman Keith Kay and a Vietnamese sound technician, Laurence rode into Con Thien by truck from Dong Ha, got some not-very-good footage of a company beyond the wire getting hit by the NVA, took some incoming artillery fire, and then left a few hours later.

Laurence writes that "the biggest reason for going back to Con Thien was that Kay and I wanted to show Americans how costly the war had become, how brutal and wasteful it was, what it was doing to the individual young men who were trapped in it." Having come to know Laurence in recent years, I have every reason to believe his explanation. As his memoir makes clear, Laurence, after extensive exposure to the war, came to be thoroughly repulsed by it and driven to try to bring its horrible truth to the attention of the American people in whose name it was being fought. National Book Award-winning Vietnam War correspondent Gloria Emerson, when I first asked her in 1998 who Laurence was (for I had never heard of him until then), described him as "the best TV reporter of the entire Vietnam War." That is high praise indeed, for Emerson has seldom had anything complimentary to say about most of those who covered the Vietnam War.

Yet reading his memoir, much to my surprise and consternation, touched off a firestorm inside of me, renewing my deep-seated (however irrational) resentment of journalists. For instance, just prior to Laurence's first trip to Con Thien, he writes that CBS correspondent Harry Reasoner "sat in his room at the Caravelle [Hotel in Saigon]. He could not stop his hands from shaking. Nothing in his life had been as terrifying, he said, as the few hours he [had just] spent in Gio Linh [another Marine outpost similar to and just east of Con Thien]."

A few hours. A few hours? I spent 792 hours at Con Thien. While I was there, my best friend Gerry Gaffney had his knee shattered by NVA artillery while crossing Death Valley, and it was over three years before I saw or heard from him again; my bunker companions Graves and Wallace were both wounded by shrapnel and spent six weeks in the hospital before being returned to the line. Another scout, Mike Bylinowski, was hit in the head by shrapnel and died on the medevac chopper. The one time I went outside our wire, on a company-sized patrol, I ended up lying facedown in an open field while the NVA, who had the field pre-plotted and the hedgerows on three sides sown with explosive boobytraps, hammered us with mortars while all around me Marines screamed and shouted and cried for their mothers.

And when I left Con Thien, I and the rest of my battalion did not repair to the air-conditioned bar of the Caravelle Hotel, there to drink gin and tonics and tell green reporters how tough it was at Con Thien; we merely took up new positions south of Quang Tri. It was good to be free of the NVA's bigger guns and the mud, but the war was still the war. Within five weeks, I would be fighting in the streets of Hue. I would be wounded there by shrapnel from a rocket-propelled grenade. I would be temporarily rendered stone deaf, in which condition I fought on for another week until my 395-day tour of duty was completed.

So what am I supposed to think when Laurence tells me how frightened Harry Reasoner was by his few hours at Gio Linh? When he tells me how frightened he himself was on more than one occasion during his brief and always voluntary forays into harm's way? When he shares with me his sorrow at the death of his dear friend Sam Castan? His sadness at the disappearance of the dashing Sean Flynn and Dana Stone? Professional journalists all. There by choice. In harm's way, when they went in harm's way, in order to get that story and get it before the other guy does, getting paid well, getting bylines and headlines, advancing their careers—and able to quit the field and quit Vietnam any time they decided they'd had enough. Am I really supposed to give a rat's ass?

You should know that I did not set out to write this essay. *An* essay, yes, but not *this* essay. It grows out of Staige Blackford's asking me if I might want to write something about the 2000 Public Affairs Press reprint of Ward Just's memoir of the Vietnam War, *To What End*, originally published in 1968. At first I declined the offer, telling Blackford something to the effect that I didn't think very well of journalists and didn't really care what they had to say about the war. When he offered the fact that Just had been wounded while on a patrol as proof of Just's *bona fides*, I replied so snippily that even I was taken aback. Knowing that Laurence was working on a memoir of his own because he had shown me sections of it, and eager to read it because Laurence is my friend and I was curious about his experiences, I suggested to Blackford that perhaps I could do a discussion of both books, to which he agreed.

But when I began to read Laurence's book—though in recent years I have been a frequent guest in his house, like and admire him deeply, understand that his ideas and feelings about the war are not much different from my own, and know him to have been as profoundly changed by the Vietnam War as any combat soldier I have ever known—up came all those feelings of scorn and resentment and anger and helplessness and contempt and a welter of other emotions too numerous to be sorted out, let alone explained, even to myself. For all that I am now 53 years old and 34 years removed from the war in Vietnam, there is still a wounded place deep inside of me that will forever be the 18-year-old Marine watching journalists come and go as they please while I and my friends must stay where we are until we have served our time, or are severely wounded or crippled, or get killed.

I must tell you also that it embarrasses me to say some of these things. No doubt I demean the professionalism and dedication of at least the better journalists who covered the war by disparaging their experiences, and I demean myself by belittling their genuine hardships and losses. Reporters like Just and Laurence often put themselves at much greater risk than many rear echelon soldiers ever encountered, and if some of that was self-testing bravado and byline-seeking ambition, which it undoubtedly was, much of it was also for reasons as lofty as my own had been when I first enlisted.

If I am to be honest, you should also bear in mind that whatever explanations and excuses I might offer for how and why it happened, I volunteered for the Marines and I volunteered for Vietnam, and I did therefore in fact choose to be in the circumstances in which I found myself, no less so than Just or Laurence. And if, once I discovered that perhaps I had made the biggest mistake of my young life, I could not extricate myself from my predicament merely by the asking, as the journalists could, this was part of the chance I took when I enlisted.

Moreover, as Blackford argues, "If it had not been for their reporting, the American people would have never known what a fiasco we had gotten ourselves involved in. It was people like Ward Just and Jack Laurence who showed the war to be the disaster it was." Certainly, through the long course of the war, the reportage of the likes of David Halberstam, Malcolm Browne, Neil Sheehan, Jonathan Schell, Gloria Emerson, and others—including Just and Laurence—helped shape public opinion and public perceptions in ways that discomfited and confounded the Washington powerful.

Indeed, in the wake of the Vietnam War, the Washington powerful—more convinced than ever before of the need to keep secret from the

American people what they were up to and why, believing that the media (a term now more accurate than "the press") had betrayed them by printing and broadcasting the truth—set about to make sure that war reporters would never again have access to the truth. In consequence, we shall never again in my lifetime see genuine war correspondents genuinely going about the job of finding and reporting the news. If you think I am overstating the case, consider the docile press pools and fawning reporters who "covered" the absurd invasion of Grenada, the illegal invasion of Panama, and the inflated invasion of Iraq. Of Gulf War coverage, former CBS News president Fred Friendly said at the time that reporters should have been ashamed of themselves for putting their bylines on what were from start to finish, in reality, press releases written by the Pentagon.

All of this is even more remarkable when one considers just how little of the total news coverage from the Vietnam War was in any way negative. For every Ward Just or Jack Laurence, there were many other journalists who questioned nothing. Laurence writes that "the majority of American TV correspondents in Vietnam were on short assignments of three to six months and were reluctant to challenge the slick upbeat propaganda of the American political and military establishment." In a personal letter, he goes even farther: "Ninety-five percent of what was written and broadcast from Vietnam by American news agencies reinforced the official position of the United States government and military that the enemy was being bombed into submission, that its troops were suffering heavy casualties, that the war was being won. Informative or not, ultimately all that copy helped to prolong the war, and that is a good reason to get angry."

Moreover, even some of the most acclaimed journalists of the war deluded themselves—and their readers—into thinking they understood the experiences of ordinary soldiers and Marines. Michael Herr, a correspondent for *Esquire* and *Rolling Stone* whose book *Dispatches* is considered by many to be one of the great classics of the Vietnam War, wrote that "I was in many ways brother to those poor, tired grunts, I knew what they knew now, I'd done it and it was really something." And this delivered with a straight face after stating earlier in the same piece, "Sometimes you couldn't live with the terms any longer and headed for air conditioners in Danang and Saigon." Maybe Herr felt like a brother to those poor tired grunts, but I doubt that any of those poor tired grunts ever felt like a brother to Herr.

Even Laurence and Just occasionally fall victim to what I can only call the "Soldier Wannabee Syndrome." Speaking about the men of Charlie Company, 2nd Battalion, 7th Cavalry, with whom he and his camera crew spent time in the spring of 1970, Laurence writes: "In our way, we had become part of the squad." Though he acknowledges that "we weren't soldiers and we didn't pretend to be and we wouldn't fight in combat with them," he insists that "we were honorary members of their team, at least part of the time ... [we] had been accepted by them ... and they respected us." Maybe all of this is true, maybe not. I know it does not reflect my experience with journalists in Vietnam, and it goes straight to the place inside of me where all those bad feelings live.

From a different angle, but in an oddly similar vein, Just recalls the reaction of a soldier when informed that Just would be accompanying his patrol, writing that the soldier "became helpless with laughter. He doubled up, face shaking with mirth at the madness of it all." But was the soldier laughing "at the madness of it all," as Just says, or rather at the madness of taking an unarmed, untrained journalist on a dangerous platoon-sized patrol deep into enemy territory? The second interpretation seems not to have occurred to Just. Yet he himself subsequently writes that when the patrol was ambushed and nearly wiped out by the North Vietnamese, he was given a weapon that he did not know how to fire and in fact did not fire, made no attempt to reach a wounded man screaming for help, immediately began calling for a medic when he himself was wounded, yet noted later in the battle that while he had lost both his pack and the pistol he had been given, "I had my camera and my notebook."

What soldier or Marine in his right mind would willingly accept someone who could contribute nothing to the common defense while requiring protection and attention? Whose allegiance was not to the men around him, but to a camera and notebook? Who was, in the end—regardless of such worthy ideals and distant notions as upholding the traditions of a free press or keeping the American people informed—just excess baggage? Just dead weight. To those of us who had to do the dirty work, journalists were just men—and sometimes women—who had no relevance to us, except that occasionally they got in our way.

This carping, of course, is the 18-year-old kid talking again, the one who was armed to the teeth and scared down to the very marrow of his bones when he should have been sitting in sociology class or splitting a malt with Betty Lou. As you have long since surmised, it is not easy for me to write objectively or with detachment about journalists and the Vietnam War. At the same time, you should know that I have a higher opinion in my head of the better journalists who covered the Vietnam War than I do in my gut. In fact, my bad attitude aside, I am capable of recognizing that Laurence's 1970 documentary "The World of Charlie Company" is one of the most powerful and brilliant glimpses you will ever see of what it was like for the men who did the dirty work; that Staige Blackford's high opinion of Ward Just and Gloria Emerson's high opinion of John Laurence are fully justified by any reasonable measure; that the job of a journalist is not, cannot, and should not be the job of a soldier.

For the best journalists at least, their ultimate loyalty was to the truth, as nearly and accurately as they could determine that truth, and that is as it should be. If too few journalists in Vietnam could be included among the best, and if the entire system of information gathering and dissemination worked only very imperfectly during the Vietnam War, the coverage of our wars since 1975, as I have already mentioned, has given us all too many reasons to look back upon coverage of the Vietnam War and wish for the good old days. If, in retrospect, we realize that we can count the most disturbing images of the Vietnam War—the ones that made us feel like the war had been brought right into our living rooms—on one hand (a burning Buddhist monk, a Viet Cong suspect getting his brains blown out, a naked girl running down a road), try to conjure a single searing image from Grenada or Panama or Iraq. Whatever shocking images Americans have seen since the end of the Vietnam War—a collapsed barracks in Lebanon, the bruised face of a captured pilot in Iraq, a body dragged through the streets in Somalia—are all images of what is being done to us, not what we are doing to others.

Thus, *To What End* and *The Cat from Hue* have value both for what they have to say in and of themselves and because they remind us of who and what journalists used to be before the print media were gobbled up by multinational corporations, and the line between television journalism and entertainment ceased to exist, and the greater portion of those engaged in the profession of journalism, recognizing which side their bread is buttered on, became willing instruments of our very own Ministry of Propaganda.

That these two books should be looked at together stems from more than the obvious facts that both are memoirs of the Vietnam War written by journalists who covered the war, both are published by the same press, and both happen to have become available at roughly the same time (I refer here, of course, to Just's reprint, not the original). Both books also offer unusually vivid representations of the war, ranging widely from Saigon streets to jungle trails, from politics to combat. Moreover, Just actually makes a cameo appearance in *The Cat from Hue*, Laurence writing: "I began to understand what tough-minded journalists like David Halberstam, Neil Sheehan, Malcolm Browne, A. J. Langguth, Ward Just, Charles Mohr and others had been writing since the early 1960s: The first casualty of the Vietnam War was truth."

In fact, in another private letter, Laurence writes that Just's book "*To What End* was really the model for *The Cat from Hue*, or at least the inspiration. When Just's book was first published in 1968, I was struck by the similarity of the experiences he and I had, and the reactions we felt. I admired him at the time for making the effort to write about his experiences in Vietnam so honestly and so well that I never forgot his book." And the two books do often cover similar territory from a similar perspective, including striking descriptions of wartime Saigon, official American obfuscation of reality (the daily military briefings for the press eventually came to be dubbed "the Five O'Clock Follies"), the contrast between the tenacity and dedication of the Viet Cong with the ineptitude and lack of conviction among the Saigon forces, and the courage and fortitude of individual soldiers and Marines confronted with an absurd and unwinnable war, to mention but a few examples.

But the books are also very different from each other. Just, who covered the war for the *Washington Post* from December 1965 to May 1967, began working on his book immediately upon leaving Vietnam and published it the following year. Laurence did not first attempt to write his book until 1977, and did not succeed in completing it until another twenty-four years had passed. There is at least a veneer of journalistic detachment in Just's writing, while Laurence's book is, with few exceptions, straight experiential memoir from start to finish. Just's chapters are organized thematically, while Laurence's proceed for the most part chronologically, almost every chapter "title" being a specific date.

The main weakness in Just's book, in fact, is that it ends in mid–1967. It is only a brief snapshot of the war. Read from the perspective of 2002, it seems in many respects self-evident and obsolete. What must have been bold and controversial insights and observations in 1968 read like old news now. And so much happened after Just left Vietnam in May 1967 that the war he writes about seems almost quaint. He spends an entire chapter, for instance, on the government of Nguyen Cao Ky, who was prime minister of Vietnam from mid–1965 through the fall of 1967, while barely touching upon Nguyen Van Thieu, who displaced Ky and served as president from September 1967 until only a few days before the fall of Saigon almost eight years later. Just's account seems incomplete.

This, of course, is not Just's fault. He was not writing a history of the war, but only an account of what he saw and did and learned while he was there. And there is value in looking closely at that crucial period during which the war ceased to be a Vietnamese war and became an American war. As Just writes, "The Viet Cong had met the Saigon government in a reasonably fair test of arms and ideas and by 1964 by any reasonable standard had won the war. The Americans arrived in force in 1965 and 1966 and thereby upset all the calculations."

Moreover, reading Just is to be reminded of the deep fissures that existed in Vietnam not just between north and south, but in the south between Saigon and Hue, between Catholic and Buddhist, between urban and rural, between military and civilian. And one is treated time and again to vivid contrasts between theory and reality. Writing about the massive American aid program that was supposed to win the hearts and minds of the people of Vietnam, Just observes: "A school was built, but there were no books or teachers. Books were imported, and then sent to a village where there were no schools.... Funds were made available for a bridge and the bridge was never built but somehow the funds were spent." Of the war itself, commenting on Secretary of Defense Robert McNamara's attempts at "quantitative measurement," Just writes, "The death toll rises. All the indicators point to improvement, progress, victory. Yet victory does not come. It seems as far away now as it ever did." His account of "The Gook Dog That Hated Gooks," though apparently a true story, is a perfect allegory of the magnificent, breathtaking, delusional logic that infected the entire American chain of command right on up through the Pentagon and into the White House, and a brilliant way to end his book.

One of the more interesting aspects of Just's book is his barely disguised visceral hatred for the Communists. I said earlier that Just maintains "a veneer of journalistic detachment," and it is when writing about the North Vietnamese and Viet Cong that this veneer appears most thin. Noting that the fight between Americans and VC/NVA was not an equal contest, he cannot refrain from observing: "I have no doubt that the Communists, if they had possessed the aircraft and bombs, would have used them far more ruthlessly than the Americans used them," though it is hard to imagine an aerial campaign more ruthless than the one we waged for over a decade on South Vietnam. Official pronouncements from Hanoi, he writes with contempt, were "written with all the clarity and insight and candor that you might expect in a propaganda document prepared in Vietnamese by Marxists and translated into English by bureaucrats," as if the statements and press releases issued by the American military and government were any less bizarre. And after the rector of Hue University all but states that he would rather be subjugated by other Vietnamese, regardless of their political persuasions, than by Americans, Just calls it a "ploy" when the rector then asks, "What do you Americans want?" Surrounded by and apparently recognizing the futility of the American war, Just still cannot bring himself to accept that large numbers of Vietnamese would indeed rather be Red than dead.

All of this makes sense within the times in which Just was originally writing his book. What makes less sense is his foreword to the 2000 reprint. While he is willing to say explicitly that "of course the war was unwinnable. It was useless to fight the Vietnamese. They would have fought for a thousand years," even these many years later he still cannot understand why.

He seems still to think that what motivated those millions of Vietnamese who fought on relentlessly year after year against seemingly insurmountable odds was "the noble ideal of unification, and freedom to pursue their totalitarian dream" when in fact for most of them it was simply a desire to have the Americans stop killing them and go away.

Just, at least, did go away. In his foreword he writes, "The war had been my life, and I had no regrets, but it was time to turn to something else," which turned out to be a successful and still active career as a novelist and short story writer. Though his most recent novel (*Dangerous Friend*, 1999) returns to the Vietnam War, as do some of his other novels and stories over the years, he seems indeed to have left the war behind and with no regrets.

Not so Jack Laurence. After covering the war for nine months in 1965 and 1966, he returned to Vietnam for another nine months in 1967 and 1968, and then returned yet again for another four months in 1970, repulsed by the war yet unable to get free of it. And as his book makes abundantly clear, in all sorts of ways the Vietnam War has dogged his life ever since. Early on in the book, he says that writing it "revealed some secrets of survival, ways of escape from the trauma of past experience. This I hoped would be true not only for myself, but also for some of the people I know, for my country, for the Vietnamese, and for veterans and survivors of the war who have struggled as I have with the ghosts of Vietnam. By writing about the war I have learned how to survive it."

Unfortunately, though each of its many parts is intrinsically fascinating and often illuminating, the cumulative weight of the whole begins to press down heavily long before one reaches the end. I fear that only the most dedicated aficionado of the Vietnam War is likely to plow through its entire length, though I hope I am wrong because the book really is a wonderful piece of work, in its own way as insightful as Just's and in many ways more satisfying because it covers such a wide segment of the historical horizon—from soon after the arrival of American combat troops through the Tet Offensive of 1968 to the invasion of Cambodia.

Indeed, the one great failing of *The Cat from Hue* is its length. It goes on for nearly 900 pages. A more forceful editor at Public Affairs would have been doing Laurence and his readers a great favor by insisting that he cut the book by half, condensing many of the long conversations and summarizing events and experiences much more often than he does.

Nevertheless, Laurence writes with an earnest candor that is highly engaging, and one could spend an entire essay of this length trying and failing to touch upon all that is noteworthy. There is his account of Operation Piranha on the Batangan Peninsula, long a Viet Cong stronghold, in September 1965, during which the Marines encountered dozens of

Vietnamese villagers who had taken refuge in a large underground tunnel and refused to come out. The standoff lasted all day, and finally Laurence and his camera and sound men had to leave. The next day, the military issued a statement under the headline "66 VC Killed in Tunnel Complex in Operation Piranha." Mindful of the bad press resulting from the burning of Cam Ne earlier in the summer while Morley Safer recorded the whole scene, the Marines were not about to move against unarmed civilians with a TV camera crew watching. But as soon as Laurence left, the Marines had killed them all.

It was incidents like this—dozens of them, hundreds of them, day in and day out—that gradually forced Laurence to stop seeing the war as "an honorable cause" and himself as "a team player," though the transformation was neither rapid nor easy. "These military versions of events were reported by the press without judgment," he writes. "Truth and falsehood got equal weight. Editors called it 'balanced reporting.' … In the name of balance, all kinds of lies and distortions were reported." Moreover, he observes, even when he and some of the other reporters concluded that the war had become "an uncontrolled campaign of violence and pain, a runaway rampage of murder and mayhem—there was no way to say it to the public. No one would print it or put it on the air." (And this, remember, was the war that wasn't censored—not officially, at least.)

So why did Laurence keep going back? "The official organs of the U.S. government," he writes, "claimed that the allied war effort was rooting out the VC infrastructure, pacifying more and more villages, helping to train more aggressive South Vietnamese fighting forces, and building more democratic institutions of government. [Keith Kay, Laurence's cameraman at the time] and I didn't believe it. We thought what was happening on the battlefields of Vietnam was more urgent, more dramatic, more terrible than the news reports being broadcast on American television. We wanted to capture on film and sound the *horror* of the war. Our motivation was not high-minded or noble; there was nothing moral about it, not even political. Part of it was our empathy with the American troops. It seemed senseless for them to give up their lives for a war strategy that wasn't working."

Eventually, however, it became for Laurence a question both of politics and of morals. As he was preparing to return to Vietnam for the third time in 1970, another reporter accosted him, saying, "You can't go over there and try and stop the war. It isn't right. You can't cover the war if you're trying to subvert it."

"You mean it's okay to cover the war as long as you support it," Laurence replied.

"It's okay to cover the war as long as you're *objective*," his challenger countered. "It's *not* okay to go over with the intention of condemning it. That's not reporting, it's editorializing."

"How can you be objective about this war?" Laurence responded. "We've been killing people for five years for no reason other than to prop up a bunch of thieving Vietnamese generals who've made themselves rich on our money.... Communist menace, my ass.... It's madness. We're not going to win, everybody knows that. But we won't admit it and go home. So we go on killing people, thousands and thousands of people, including our own. And for what? For pride! For the egos and vanity of a bunch of old farts in Washington! How can you be objective about that?"

Good question, and Laurence raises a lot of good questions in *The Cat from Hue*. He also does some things I've never seen done anywhere else. For one thing, he's the only writer I can think of—combatant or journalist—who actually takes the time to consider the toll the war took on animals: "Meo [the cat from Hue that Laurence rescued and that gives the book its title] had a better chance of surviving than most animals caught by the war. Bombed, burned, shot at, starved, uprooted, displaced—animals suffered the whole vicious frenzy of violence that fate gave to living creatures in Vietnam." For another thing, his account of the so-called "Hue Massacre" is one of the very few to take into account that large numbers of civilians were killed not by Communist liquidation squads—though it is all but certain at least some people died in this manner—but by the accidental misfortune of getting caught in the midst of the savagely violent house-to-house street fighting that engulfed the third most populous city in South Vietnam for nearly a month.

Laurence's book is also fascinating for the occasional insights it gives into how some of our most visible and prominent journalists made their way to the top. At one point, for instance, Morley Safer—who was "anxious to get away" from the battlefield in any case—offered to get Laurence's crew's film footage and written text prepared and shipped to New York for broadcast. From the safety of Saigon, writes Laurence, instead of giving Laurence and his cameraman credit, Safer "wrote a single narration incorporating all the elements of the two stories that both of our teams had shot that day.... It was broadcast on the *CBS Evening News* and later won him many broadcast journalism awards for his skill and courage."

How do I sum up so rambling a discussion, part book review, part confessional (my own), part discourse on the nature of war and journalism? In the midst of working on this essay—the most difficult, I think, that I have ever attempted to write—I received a letter from a man named Edward Worman. I've never met Ed. Our connection is through his cousin Kenny, who was a childhood friend of mine and who died in Vietnam in May 1967. Ed Worman himself was a U.S. Army combat photographer in Vietnam. Included in his mailing to me was a copy of a letter to the editor he had written that was published in a Rochester, New York, newspaper. He was writing about *Requiem*, a powerful book of photographs from the Vietnam War, each one of which was taken by a journalist who was subsequently killed in the war. The editors had been war correspondents themselves, as had all of those who contributed essays to the book—including Jack Laurence, David Halberstam, Neil Sheehan, and Peter Arnett.

Quite remarkably, the editors thought to include photographs taken by Viet Cong and North Vietnamese Army combat photographers who had died in the fighting as well, along with civilian photographers from the United States, Japan, Thailand, France, Austria, and many other countries. But as Worman writes of U.S. Army and Marine Corps combat photographers in his letter, "The names of four of my friends and fellow photographers are on the Vietnam Memorial in Washington, D.C. Neither their work nor the work of Rochester native and Medal of Honor recipient Marine Corps combat photographer William T. Perkins Jr. is shown or mentioned in any way [in *Requiem*]. Another U.S. Army photographer, Verland Gilbertson, died in the battle of Ong Thanh, Oct. 17, 1968.... The editors of *Requiem*, Horst Faas and Tim Page, have been making money off the Vietnam War for 35 years. That's many more years than my friends had.... These soldiers deserve more than to be missing in action [in *Requiem*]."

I had been struggling for weeks to separate my heart from my head in order to be fair to Just and Laurence. When I realized I would either have to explain the feelings their books turned loose in me or not write about them at all, it made it a little easier. I would come clean up front, vent my spleen, and then get on with it. It almost worked. But then Ed Worman's letter arrived and reminded me all over again that those civilians with the notepads and the cameras could come and go as they pleased while we were stuck in the mud and madness to survive as best we could. That hurts. I can't help it. And if those two journalists from that long ago Thanksgiving showed up at my bunker again, I'd throw them out again just as quickly. God forgive me. And the journalists, too. The good ones, at least.

❖ ❖ ❖

Drawbridges on the Delaware

Ask Donna Norcross about the time the guy tried to jump off the Tacony-Palmyra Bridge and she'll tell you something like this:

One day a car stopped in the middle of the bridge's draw span and a man leaped out, ran to the railing, and climbed over, threatening to jump. Almost simultaneously, the driver leaped out and began pleading with his companion not to do it. A lively debate ensued as Norcross watched from the operator's tower of the bridge's draw span while awaiting the arrival of an inbound ship just coming into view downriver. For a few moments, she stood torn between the drama unfolding below her and the fact of the oncoming ship. Then she opened a window, leaned out, and hollered down, "Look, make up your mind, buddy. Jump or don't jump, but get off the bridge because I've got a ship coming."

Norcross, 37, is not hardhearted. It's only that if you operate a draw-bridge on a navigable waterway in the United States, the First Commandment is unambiguous: Thou shalt open the bridge when the ship gets there. You don't ask the ship to wait. You don't wait for the ship to hit your bridge. You open the bridge, period. The First Commandment is a matter of federal law: the Regulation of Drawbridges Act, passed in 1894, gives waterborn traffic right of way over highway traffic. It's also a matter of practicality: ships don't have brakes; it can take a mile or more to neutralize the inertial force of thirty thousand tons or so of moving steel.

It's just after midnight as Norcross tells the story of the wannabee jumper while awaiting the arrival of yet another ship, the *Areti*, presently docked upriver at Fairless Hills. Flying a Maltese flag and carrying a Filipino crew with Greek officers, *Areti* is still loading petrochemical machinery bound for Kuwait. Norcross and her coworkers know nothing about the ship except its name, nor do they particularly care. All they need to know is when the ship will reach their bridge.

Ships sail when they are ready, not a moment before, and seldom a moment later. Consequently, bridge openings can occur at rush hour or the midnight hour, Ted Mack Amateur Hour or the darkest hour before dawn. *Areti*'s sailing time was to have been 6 P.M., but that's been changed to 10 P.M., and then to midnight. Now the radio in the tower crackles as bridge dispatcher Dolores Leonard tells Norcross that *Areti*'s departure has been pushed back to 1 A.M.

Not a penny of taxpayers' money goes to the Burlington County Bridge Commission, which owns and maintains the Tacony-Palmyra Bridge—connecting Northeast Philadelphia with Palmyra, New Jersey—along with the Burlington-Bristol Bridge farther upriver, a tollfree drawbridge over Rancoccas Creek, and a number of smaller bridges in Burlington County, New Jersey. The commission's entire budget, including the salaries of all its employees, comes from its two toll bridges. Anything that reduces traffic over the bridge reduces revenue, and nothing discourages traffic like a bridge opening. Yet the bridge must open on demand for all commercial shipping, and even for pleasure boats too tall for the bridge's clearances (64 feet under the arch span, 54 feet under the adjacent draw span where the main channel flows).

"Tolls are our bread and butter," says chief engineer Sasha Harding, "We'd be happy if the bridge never opened." No chance of that, alas, so the trick is to get the bridge open and closed as quickly as safety allows. And that's quicker than you'd think. Says Leonard, a jovial woman who's worked for the bridge commission for 17 years, "I watch cars pull up to the toll plaza, see there's an opening, and hang a U turn, which is really dumb. By the time they get to the Betsy Ross Bridge [the next bridge downriver, owned by the Delaware River Bridge Commission], we're closed and traffic is moving again—and they pay $3 instead of $2."

Up at Fairless Hills, Delaware River pilot George Macintire has come aboard *Areti* and is preparing to bring the ship downriver. A third generation river pilot apprenticed in 1956 and licensed in 1960, Macintire, 59, will have complete command of the ship. Only when *Areti* reaches the Atlantic Ocean will the ship's captain take control.

Though Norcross has been an operator for seven years, and a tolltaker and backup operator for five years before that, she and Macintire have never met. Tonight, as always, they will be only disembodied voices identified to each other as "Tacony Bridge" and "*Areti*." On the ship-to-shore radio, Norcross can hear the Burlington operator asking *Areti* if the ship has left the dock yet, but the ship is too far away for her to hear *Areti*'s reply. She turns on a TV and begins to watch a murder mystery already in progress. It's 2 A.M.

Perched midriver, over a thousand feet from either bank, the operator's tower reminds one of a fortified turret guarding the only approach to some medieval castle. A windowless lower room contains an array of electrical panels. A steep iron stairway, almost a ladder, leads to the second floor, a room with windows 360 degrees around. This is the operator's station, containing the main control panel, various radios, a TV, two chairs, and assorted log books and procedural manuals.

The tower, rising some 80 feet above the river and 15 feet above the roadway, is a lonely and beautiful retreat. At night, much of the lesser developed New Jersey riverbank is dark, but the Pennsylvania side is all lights and color from well north of the bridge all the way down to Center City Philadelphia where the blue peaks of Liberty Place, the moving lights of the Philadelphia Electric Company Building, and the bright red letters of the Philadelphia Savings Fund Society Building stand out vividly from the myriad lesser lights among which they are nestled.

On ship-to-shore radio, Norcross can hear *Areti* calling the Burlington operator to say that the ship is just approaching the turnpike bridge

north of Bristol. It's still over an hour away from Tacony, but Norcross
uses the police band to let Leonard and the three bridge commission patrol
officers on duty know that the ship is moving.

At 2:35, the Burlington operator radios Norcross that *Areti* has cleared
his bridge. She hails the ship and asks to be informed when *Areti* reaches
Mud Island, about 20 minutes upriver from her. On *Areti*'s dimly lit bridge
high above the ship's main deck, Macintire feeds a steady stream of com-
mands to the helmsman—"starboard 10, starboard 20, midships, port 10,
midships, steady"—constantly fine tuning the ship's course as it travels
down the river.

Among the obstacles in the ship's way are the three drawbridges:
Burlington, Tacony, and the Delair railroad bridge. Burlington and Delair,
however, are lift bridges—their draw spans are each a single piece that rises
as if it were an elevator—and each offers ships an opening fully twice as wide
as Tacony's. Tacony is a bascule bridge, the bascule or draw span consisting
of two leaves that open upward. Touch your index fingers together, palms
flat and facing the floor, then swing your fingertips up toward the ceiling by
pivoting your hands at the wrists. That's how a bascule span opens. As *Areti*
passes through the bridge, the ship will have a maximum clearance on either
side of less than 85 feet. That may sound like a lot, but we're not talking
rack-and-pinion steering here; we're talking thousands of tons of floating
steel, and the passage is made trickier by the river's current and a prevailing
northwest wind, both of which can make major mischief.

Tacony-Palmyra Bridge spanning the Delaware River between the Tacony neighborhood of Northeast Philadelphia, Pennsylvania, and Palmyra, New Jersey. (Pho-
tograh provided by the Burlington County Bridge Commission)

"Tacony Bridge," Macintire radios, "this is *Areti*. I'm passing Mud Island." When Norcross hears this, she calls Leonard and asks for the backup operator. (There's no margin for error in this business. None. If a ship ever does hit the bridge, you're going to have bigtime damage, so there are backups for everything: backup operators, backup electrical systems, backup radios—there's even a pair of giant hand cranks, so you can crank the bridge open manually if it comes to that.) Tonight's backup operator is Cordell Washington, who's working lane two of the toll plaza. Acting Sergeant Glenn Entwhistle drives him out to the tower while patrolman Mark Brennan heads over to the Pennsylvania side and parks.

In the tower, Norcross powers up the control panel, automatically triggering one ring from a loud bell, then adjusts the power source (the drawbridge runs on electricity that can be drawn from either Philadelphia Electric Company on the Pennsylvania side of the river or Public Service Electric & Gas on the New Jersey side). When Washington reaches the tower, Norcross radios, "Signal Eleven," which tells the rest of the bridge staff to get into position for the opening, then fires one blast on a very loud siren. It's 3:13 A.M.

Peering upriver, she can barely make out *Areti* just north of the old Northern Metals plant. The ship is not easy to see because the only lights it shows are its running lights—one green, one red—and two white mast lights that Washington describes as "60-watt bulbs," exaggerating only minimally, but finally the darker black of the ship emerges from the shinier black of the river.

Aboard *Areti*, Macintire can see the bridge no better than Norcross can see the ship. The only lights on the bridge are some small red warning lights and the dull orange roadway streetlights, and these are utterly lost amid the brilliant array of lights that confront Macintire from his port quarter all the way around to his starboard beam. Macintire's not really watching the bridge, however. He's watching the various navigational lights on the river, and the small laptop computer he's brought with him. The computer is hooked into something called the Differential Global Positioning System, which gives the ship's position relative to the center of the river channel, accurate to within three feet.

As *Areti* draws closer, what Norcross sees are the two white mast lights lining up on each other until they appear as a single light. Norcross now knows the ship is heading straight for the bridge. "Signal 65," she radios over the police band, then fires another blast of the siren. It is 3:18.

On that command, all of the officers turn on their revolving lights. For motorists, this is the first warning that the bridge is about to open. Brennan drives his Jeep Cherokee out onto the bridge, checking the roadway and pedestrian sidewalks to make sure they are clear. On the other side of the river, Officer Jason Bowen blocks traffic while Entwhistle checks the bridge. Washington leaves the tower to check the roadway and sidewalks on the draw span.

Only when Washington returns and Norcross hears from Brennan and Entwhistle that the bridge is clear of all traffic, vehicular and pedestrian, does she release the drawbridge's brakes and turn the two brass handles that start the leaves up. From the tower, it appears at first as if Godzilla or King Kong is pushing the roadway up from below. Then the two leaves break apart and the Pennyslvania leaf seems to slide under the adjacent arch span, but the illusion is only momentary, quickly displaced by a feeling of vertigo as the roadway, sidewalk, handrails and streetlights travel inexorably from the horizontal to the nearly vertical.

Out on the roadway, Brennan is parked about 30 feet from the edge of the basule span. From this vantage point, only the Pennyslvania leaf is visible. As it rises ever higher, paper and debris on the roadway begin to tumble down, giving the eerie impression of a western ghost town, tumbleweed drifting on its only street, pushed along by a hardscabble breeze. A glass bottle bounces down the steel grating of the bascule span's road surface, banging loudly as it goes. Only then does one realize how quiet this has all been. There is only a barely perceptible electric hum. Though the leaves weigh two and half million pounds each, they are so well balanced that it requires only four 60 horsepower motors to raise and lower them, two to each leaf.

Aboard *Areti*, Macintire can now see the bridge's roadway lights and the warning lights marking the bridge piers. He can also see two red lights on the bascule span itself, the lights rising into the air and separating as the leaves go up. When the bridge is fully open, those two red lights will turn green, telling Macintire the bridge is ready.

In the tower, as the leaves reach the open position, the bell rings again. Norcross locks the brakes, then fires the siren twice, another signal to the ship that the bridge is fully open. The siren doesn't sound all that loud from inside the tower, but out on the roadway where Brennan is parked, it sounds as if someone has installed an air raid siren in the back seat of his Cherokee, which is not too far off the mark. "We all have relatives who complain about that siren," says Washington, grinning impishly.

Meanwhile, Macintire, intent upon guiding *Areti* safely through the narrow passage, doesn't hear the siren, which is meant largely for him, and pays scant attention to the green lights. He's focused on his various navigational aids, mentally calculating the effect of tonight's tide, current, and wind conditions, and calling constant course corrections to the helmsman. The ship's radio crackles: "*Areti*, this is Tacony-Palmyra. The bridge is fully open."

"*Areti*," Macintire replies, "Roger, Tacony, thank you very much." He has had *Areti* traveling at slow ahead, but once the bridge is open, he increases speed to half ahead. "It's safer to get through there as quickly as possible," he says, explaining that faster speed reduces the impact of wind and currents, provides better steering control, and minimizes the risk of power failure, either of the ship or the bridge, in mid-passage. As the ship bears down on the bridge, it seems to glide through the dark water in phantom-like silence, though if Brennan listens carefully, he can hear the low whine of the ship's diesel engines and the soft swish of the prop wash.

Macintire has positioned *Areti* a little toward the New Jersey bascule pier as he approaches the bridge because the current wants to push the ship toward Pennsylvania. As *Areti* slides through the narrow opening, Norcross can look down on the ship's main deck, which is covered with cargo containers and various large irregularly shaped objects impossible to identify in the poor light and the few seconds it takes the ship to glide by.

If Norcross leaned out of the window nearest to the channel and Macintire walked out onto *Areti*'s starboard bridge wing, they could have a conversation almost without raising their voices, but each has already turned to the next task at hand. As Norcross releases the brakes and starts the leaves back down, she can hear *Areti* calling the *First Coast*, a tugboat pushing a barge downstream; *Areti* is fast closing on the tug and barge, and Macintire needs to know to which side of the channel the tug will move as the ship overtakes it.

As *Areti* rapidly vanishes amid the lights of Philadelphia, Norcross stops the Pennsylvania leaf about five degrees from horizontal, then gently brings the New Jersey leaf down until they meet: "Working the handles," she calls it. Once the leaves are joined, she applies full power to the New Jersey leaf, driving both leaves down until they are fully seated. You can hear a deep *ca-thunk* as the leaves lock into place.

As soon as she sees the deck plates go flush on the sidewalk, she sets the brakes again, then turns on the overhead lane lights, a visual signal to Brennan that the bridge is ready for traffic. "4820 to all cars," says Brennan, using his radio call sign, "The red lights are on. Let 'em roll." It's 3:31 A.M. Traffic on the bridge has been halted for less than thirteen minutes. Norcross shuts down the control panel, then turns to her log books.

But what about that guy who was threatening to jump? "I didn't handle it very well," Norcross says sheepishly. Maybe not, but the jumper hesitated long enough for his companion to grab him and pull him back over the railing. Then both men got in the car and sped away. And the bridge was open when the ship arrived.

❖ ❖ ❖

Where Do We Go from Here?

Like just about everyone else in America, I am still reeling from the events of September 11th, the bloodiest day in American history. I am struggling to understand how our world has changed, and why, and how we are going to go on living in it. I do not believe there is anything good to be said about what happened on the morning of September 11th. It was a horror the likes of which I have never seen before and dearly hope never to see again.

But I have been almost as horrified by what has happened in our country since then: the thousands of acts of hatred and violence directed at Arab-Americans since September 11th; the flagrant, almost gleeful infringements on basic civil liberties; the massive bombing of Afghanistan resulting mostly only in the trading of one set of very bad rulers for another without resolving anything; all this and more, and apparently with the willing consent of huge numbers of my fellow Americans. I see and hear daily references to our war on terrorism, and I think of our war on drugs and our war on poverty and our war on crime and wonder if this new war against an equally elusive and spectral enemy will have a happier outcome.

I have heard few public officials or pundits wonder aloud why someone might hate this nation enough to do what was done on September 11th beyond self-serving and shallow explanations such as "these men hate freedom" or "you can't explain pure evil."

I expect those men were evil, or at least profoundly twisted. I don't imagine I would like to live in a world where they were in charge. But there are many ways to see the world and what happens in it. The great wonder to me is that such a small percentage of the world's population can dispose of so much of the world's resources year after year for decades and decades and then be shocked to discover that we have enemies.

Imagine for a moment how the world must appear to the tens of thousands of Palestinian refugees—many of them as old as me, and I am 53— who have never known any home but a crowded one-room cinderblock shack in a crowded U.N. refugee camp. Imagine for a moment how the world must appear to the thousands of Bosnian Muslims who were displaced, brutalized, maimed and murdered for four long years while the West stood around and wrung its collective hands. Imagine for a moment how the world must appear to the tens of thousands of Iraqi mothers whose children have died of malnutrition and disease resulting from an economic embargo kept in place by the United States of America for more than a decade in order to punish a people whose only crime is their failure to muster the resources and wherewithall to overthrow the brutal dictator who rules them with a lethal fist.

It is hard to imagine these things, especially at a time when we ourselves are still grappling with our own grief and pain. But we would do well to give some consideration to the sufferings of others, and who is responsible for that suffering, because if we think we can somehow make ourselves secure from the kind of attack this nation sustained on September 11th by sheer force of arms and military might, we have not put enough thought into the problem. And to imagine that we are a wholly innocent nation wantonly attacked by cowardly madmen for no sane reason will lead us nowhere useful. Millions of people hate the United States of America, and at least some of them have good reason to do so. It is not and will never be possible to find and kill them all, and the very effort will only create still more enemies.

So I think it is in our own best interests to ask ourselves why so many people hate us and what we might do about it. How many of us wear $80, $100, $120 sneakers? Have we ever seriously wondered who made those sneakers and how much they were paid to do so? Count up the number of telephones and television sets and CD players and computers you have in your house. Most of us have lives filled to overflowing with *things*. The most popular cars in America are three-ton gas-guzzling monsters. We have become, in fact and in name, not citizens but consumers.

I heard two very remarkable things on the radio only a week after September 11th, and within minutes of each other. First, a newscaster solemnly reported that 15,000 American sailors and Marines had put to sea to fight terrorism—as if the terrorists are out there on the ocean, bobbing around in boats, perhaps rowing to America. Then, only a short while later, an economist said that the best way America can recover from the devastating attack against us is to go shopping. He said we should get out there and go to the mall, buy things, spend money, get that old economy rolling again. Can you imagine how profoundly obscene that must sound to the many millions of people who cannot put clothes on their children's backs or bread in their children's bellies?

Historically and statistically speaking, most Americans have never had to face the horrors of war. September 11th changed all that. Now we are all combatants, or at least potential casualties, and all our high-tech wizardry is likely to be of little use against determined enemies with time on their side and nothing they are not willing to lose. Nor can we make ourselves more secure by taking fingernail clippers and crochet hooks away from airline passengers.

If the United States of America is ever to find real peace and security, we must start sharing with the rest of the world all the blessings and bounty this world has to offer. This will not be easy to do because it will mean that all of us will have to give up at least some of what we have, but it will be, in the end, easier to accomplish than any other option available to us. We need only look to the fate of the Greeks, the Romans, the Turks, or the Spanish for proof. We forget at our own peril that the sun never used to set on the British Empire.

MILITARY HISTORY
OF W. D. EHRHART

W. D. Ehrhart enlisted in the United States Marine Corps on 11 April 1966, while still in high school, beginning active duty on 17 June. He graduated from basic recruit training at the Marine Corps Recruit Depot, Parris Island, South Carolina, on 12 August, receiving a meritorious promotion to private first class, and completed basic infantry training at Camp Lejeune, North Carolina, on 12 September 1966. (While at Parris Island, he qualified as a rifle sharpshooter on 18 July 1966, subsequently qualifying as a rifle expert on 11 April 1968 and as a pistol sharpshooter on 24 April 1969.)

Assigned to the field of combat intelligence, Ehrhart spent 10 October to 15 December 1966 with Marine Air Group 26, a helicopter unit based at New River Marine Corps Air Facility, North Carolina, meanwhile completing a clerk typist course at Camp Lejeune in November 1966 and graduating first in his class from the Enlisted Basic Amphibious Intelligence School at Little Creek Amphibious Base, Norfolk, Virginia, in December 1966. He also completed a Marine Corps Institute combat intelligence correspondence course in December while at New River.

Before leaving for Vietnam on 9 February 1967, Ehrhart received additional combat training with the 3rd Replacement Company, Staging Battalion, Camp Pendleton, California, in January and February. Upon arrival in Vietnam, he was assigned to the 1st Battalion, 1st Marine Regiment, first as an intelligence assistant, later as assistant intelligence chief. In March 1967, he was temporarily assigned to the Sukiran Army Education Center, Okinawa, where he graduated first in his class from a course in basic Vietnamese terminology before returning to permanent assignment.

While in Vietnam, Ehrhart participated in the following combat operations: Stone, Lafayette, Early, Canyon, Calhoun, Pike, Medina, Lancaster, Kentucky I, Kentucky II, Kentucky III, Con Thien, Newton, Osceola II, and Hue

City. He was promoted to lance corporal on 1 April 1967 and meritoriously promoted to corporal on 1 July 1967.

Ehrhart was awarded the Purple Heart Medal for wounds received in action in Hue City during the Tet Offensive, a commendation from Major General Donn J. Robertson commanding the 1st Marine Division, two Presidential Unit Citations, the Navy Combat Action Ribbon, the Vietnam Service Medal with three stars, the Vietnamese Campaign Medal, a Cross of Gallantry Meritorious Unit Citation, and a Civil Action Meritorious Unit Citation.

Ehrhart was next assigned to the 2nd Marine Air Wing Headquarters Group at Cherry Point Marine Corps Air Station, North Carolina, from 30 March to 10 June 1968, where he was promoted to sergeant on 1 April. After a brief assignment with the Headquarters Squadron of Marine Air Group 15 based at Iwakuni Marine Corps Air Station, Japan, he was then reassigned to Marine Aerial Refueler Transport Squadron 152, Futema Marine Corps Air Facility, Okinawa, from 20 July to 30 October 1968, where he received a commanding officer's Meritorious Mast.

Ehrhart completed his active duty with Marine Fighter Attack Squadron 122, based alternately at Iwakuni and Cubi Point Naval Air Station, Philippines, from 31 October 1968 to 30 May 1969. While in the Philippines, he completed a field course on jungle environmental survival in February 1969.

On 10 June 1969, Ehrhart was separated from active duty, receiving the Good Conduct Medal. While on inactive reserve, he was promoted to staff sergeant on 1 July 1971. He received an honorable discharge on 10 April 1972.

ABOUT THE AUTHOR

W. D. Ehrhart was born in 1948 in Roaring Spring, Pennsylvania, and grew up in Lewisburg and Perkasie, both also in Pennsylvania. He holds an honorable discharge from the United States Marine Corps, a bachelor's degree from Swarthmore College, a master's degree from the University of Illinois at Chicago Circle, and a doctorate from the University of Wales at Swansea, where he was a research fellow in American Studies from 1997 to 2002.

Ehrhart is recipient of a Pew Fellowship in the Arts for poetry, Pennsylvania Council on the Arts fellowships in both poetry and prose, and a Mary Roberts Rinehart Foundation grant. He has been a poet-in-residence at the Downtown Detroit YMCA as part of the National Writer's Voice Project of the YMCA of the USA, a guest-in-residence at Unit One/Allen Hall of the

University of Illinois at Champaign–Urbana, and a writer-in-residence at the Washington Project for the Arts. In addition he has been visiting professor of war and social consequences at the University of Massachusetts at Boston and director of the Summer Writers' Workshop for High School Students at La Salle University.

Currently, Ehrhart teaches English and history at the Haverford School in Haverford, Pennsylvania. He lives in Philadelphia with his wife Anne and daughter Leela.

INDEX

Abrams, Creighton 81
Acheson, Dean 183
Adams, John 42
Alda, Alan 215
Alvarez, Everett, Jr. 90, 94–95
Anderson, Donald 136, 137, 141
Anderson, Doug 118–119, 127, 225
Apple, Jeff 32, 101
Appleman, Philip 226, 232
Arafat, Yasser 17
Armstrong, Neil 203
Arnett, Peter 255
Assad, Hafez 10
Axelsson, Arne 223

Baker, Kenneth 224
Balaban, John 31, 60, 62, 63, 64, 117,
    143, 212, 226, 230, 235, 237
Bao Dai 31
Barkley, Charles 129
Barry, Jan 160, 225, 230, 237
Barth, R. L. 117, 225, 232
Beidler, Philip 229
Benét, Stephen Vincent 225, 229
Benson, Elmer 183
Bentley, Steve 85
Biespiel, David 225
Bishop, John Peale 211, 226, 227
Black Kettle 68
Blackford, Staige 245, 246, 248
Blair, Clay 188, 207
Blesedell, Thomas 208
Blunden, Edmund 138, 227
Bly, Robert 226, 230
Bookheimer, Robert 199, 200

Borton, Lady 87–89
Bowen, Jason 260
Bowen, Kevin 120–121, 122, 127
Bowie, Thomas G., Jr. 134, 135, 136,
    137, 140
Bowman, Peter 237
Brady, James 189, 192–195
Brennan, Mark 259, 260, 261
Brisbane, Arthur 226
Brokaw, Tom 207
Brother Antoninus 225
Brown, D. F. 116, 122, 225, 230
Browne, Malcolm 246, 249
Bukowski, Charles 174, 177
Bursk, Christopher 232
Bush, George Herbert Walker 17, 29,
    75, 76, 77, 99
Butler, Robert Olen 62, 73, 143
Bylinowski, Mike 245

Callaway, Catherine 63
Caputo, Philip 143
Carruth, Hayden 143, 182, 213–214,
    224, 225, 232, 236
Carter, Jimmy 75, 76
Casey, Michael 225
Castan, Sam 245
Chamberlain, William 189
Chattarji, Subarno 223, 228, 229
Chiang Kai-shek 194
Childress, William 145, 146–150, 155,
    162, 163, 169, 182, 214, 221, 224, 232,
    233, 234, 236, 237
Chivington, John M. 68
Churchill, Winston 69

Ciardi, John 143, 205, 206, 223, 225, 228, 229
Clinton, William Jefferson 2, 51, 52, 53, 61, 77, 98, 131
Coan, C. Arthur 226
Cobb, Darien 233
Coleman, Horace 226, 235
Columbus, Christopher 96
Conein, Lucien 19
Connolly, David V. 121–123, 127, 226, 230
Coon, Gene 189
Cowley, Malcolm 211, 226, 227
Cox, Joseph T. 133, 134, 135, 138, 140
Crane, Stephen 2, 221
Crawford, William 192
Cumings, Bruce 188
cummings, e. e. 211, 223, 226, 227

Daly, James 94
D'Aubuisson, Roberto 69
Dengler, Dieter 94
Denton, Jeremiah 90
Dewald, Rev. Tim 37
Dickey, James 143, 225, 228
Dickinson, Emily 135
Diehl, John 198, 199, 200, 203, 204
Diem, Ngo Dinh 19, 31, 69, 89
Dong, Pham Van 81
Donovan 197
Dramesi, John 94
Dugan, Alan 143, 225, 228
Dulles, John Foster 171
Duncan, Donald 92
Dung, Le Tri 120
Dylan, Bob 197

Eberhart, Richard 143, 207, 223, 225, 228
Edwards, George 101–104
Edwards, Paul M. 145, 174, 225, 227, 229, 231, 232–233
Ehrhart, Anne Gulick 34, 36
Ehrhart, Evelyn M. 34
Ehrhart, Rev. John H. 33
Ehrhart, Leela G. 34, 36
Ehrhart, William D. 34, 36, 198, 201, 230
Eisenhower, Dwight D. 4
Eliot, T. S. 227
Emerson, Gloria 16–21, 23, 171, 244, 246, 248
Endicott, John 68

Entwhistle, Glenn 259, 260
Evans, George 117
Everson, William see Brother Antoninus

Faas, Horst 255
Fast, Howard 182–184, 224, 232, 234–235
Faulkner, William 150
Feld, Kenneth 97
Ferrizzi, Ron 63
Fish, Lydia 209
Fitzgerald, F. Scott 2
Floyd, Bryan Alec 27, 221, 226
Flynn, Sean 245
Foltz, Bob 106–116
Ford, Gerald 74
Forshe, Carolyn 144, 224
Frank, Pat 192
Frankel, Ernest 192
Franklin, H. Bruce 62, 70, 162, 163, 173, 219, 222
Friendly, Fred 247
Fulton, Len 161, 170–171, 173, 179, 219, 221
Furey, Joan 117
Fussell, Paul 23, 85, 144, 171, 223, 224, 226, 229, 230, 232

Gaffney, Gerry 245
Gandhi, Mohandas 28
Garwood, Robert 91
Gavin, Mike 106–107, 110–115
Geosits, Margaret 195, 196, 198, 199, 200, 203, 204
Geronimo 135
Giap, Vo Nguyen 81
Gilbertson, Verland 255
Gingrich, Newt 131
Ginsberg, Allen 226, 230
Glade, Jon Forrest 117
Godshall, Lynn 101
Goldwater, Barry 197
Gore, Albert, Jr. 77
Gotera, Vince 62, 117, 223, 225, 231, 232, 236
Graves, Floyd 242, 243, 245
Graves, Robert 227
Greenberg, Art 173
Gruner, Elliott 62, 90, 93–95, 134, 135, 136

Hackett, Sir John 216
Hager, Maynard 32, 204

Halberstam, David 188, 223, 246, 249, 255
Hammel, Eric 192
Harbaugh, James 221
Harding, Sasha 257
Harris, John Lee, Jr. 128
Hart, James 226
Hasford, Gustav 231
Hazo, Samuel 226
Hecht, Anthony 143, 225
Heinemann, Larry 60, 62
Hendricks, Debbie 101
Hendrix, Jimi 107, 203
Herr, Michael 215, 247
Hersch, Seymour 135
Hershiser, Orel 14
Hinojosa, Rolando 144, 145, 146, 150–155, 182, 223, 225, 232, 233, 237
Hitler, Adolf 11, 229
Ho Chi Minh 31, 67, 133
Hoffman, Daniel 226
Holmes, Oliver Wendell 42
Homer 79, 80, 82–83, 119, 142, 143
Hope, Bob 14
Howes, Craig 90–93, 95
Huddle, David 117, 226, 232
Hugo, Richard 143, 225
Hussein, Saddam 9, 12, 13, 15, 16, 29, 67, 76
Hussein bin Talal 10
Huston, John 149

Isaacs, Arnold R. 62, 63

Jacob, John 225
Jaeger, Lowell 230, 235
Jarrell, Randall 143, 206, 223, 225, 228
Jason, Philip K. 182, 183, 223, 237
Jeffers, Robinson 232
Jenkins, Andrea 101, 105
Johnson, Debbie 99
Johnson, Lyndon Baines 54, 81, 196, 198, 201, 242
Jones, James 143
Jones, Kevin E. 174, 181, 218, 220, 221
Jordan, June 226
Jordan, Michael 14, 129
Just, Ward 245, 246, 247, 248, 249, 250–252, 255

Kantor, MacKinlay 23, 85
Karlin, Wayne 70–74
Kay, Keith 244, 253

Keenan, William F. 97
Kees, Weldon 232
Kerin, James R. 143, 144, 145, 207, 223, 228
Kerin, Rick *see* Kerin, James R.
Kerrey, Bob 77
Kerry, John 79
Khomeini, Ruhallah al-Musavi 9, 75
Khrushchev, Nikita 197
Kilmer, Joyce 211, 223, 226, 227
King, Martin Luther, Jr. 28, 86, 128
Kinnell, Galway 226
Kipling, Rudyard 143
Kirstein, Lincoln 225
Kissinger, Henry 93
Knight, Etheridge 144, 145, 224
Komunyakaa, Yusef 117, 143, 226
Kovic, Ron 210–211
Kruk, John 14
Kubrick, Stanley 231
Ky, Nguyen Cao 250

Langguth, A. J. 249
Lattimore, Richmond 82
Laughlin, James 226
Laurence, John 244, 245, 246, 247–248, 249, 250, 252–254, 255
Layne, McAvoy 237
Leepson, Marc 62, 63
Leonard, Dolores 256, 257, 258
Levertov, Denise 226, 230
Lincoln, Abraham 2, 6, 68, 97, 99
Lind, Michael 207
Lindsay, Vachel 225, 226, 229
Little, Lloyd 61
Lowell, Amy 226
Lowell, Robert 225
Lowenfels, Walter 162, 173, 219, 224
Luce, Don 60
Lucie-Smith, Edward 174, 218, 219
Lynch, David 138, 139
Lynch, Tim 138, 139, 140
Lyons, Paul 61, 63

Maas, Roland 242
MacArthur, Douglas 193, 194
Macintire, George 257–261
MacLeish, Archibald 211, 225, 226, 227, 229
Magner, James, Jr. 145, 146, 155–158, 163, 172, 182, 225, 235
Maguire, Barrie 5; drawings 38, 41, 43, 46, 48, 96, 98

Mailer, Norman 143, 210
Manglesdorff, Rich 219
Mao Tse-tung 194
Marin, Pilar 60, 61
Mason, Bobbie Ann 3, 21–31
Mason, Patience H. C. 85, 221
Mason, Robert 61
Mason, Steve 117
Masters, Edgar Lee 226
Mather, Cotton 92
McAndrew, Mark S. 97
McCain, John 79, 90
McCarthy, Gerald 62, 117, 213, 226, 231
McCarthy, Joseph 169
McDonald, Walter 117, 226
McFarland, Keith D. 223
McGrath, Thomas 143, 182, 224, 225, 232, 236
McIntyre, Jay 58
McMahon, Marilyn 226
McNamara, Robert 198, 251
Melling, Phil 4, 144
Melville, Herman 2
Meredith, William 143, 145, 159, 225
Messick, Jill 99
Millay, Edna St. Vincent 225, 229
Miller, Jerome 236
Mitzna, Amram 18
Mohr, Charles 249
Molino, Joe 108–116
Monaghan, Patricia 225
Moore, Randy 200, 203
Morrison, Philip 183
Morrow, Vic 202
Moyer, Timothy 195, 197
Mozetic, Uros 64–67, 69
Murphy, Georgina 145, 182
Musto, Michelle 106–116
Myers, John 128

Nemerov, Howard 143, 211–212, 225, 228
Nguyen, Thanh T. 117
Nixon, Richard M. 69, 74, 81
Norcross, Donna 255–261
Norris, Chuck 70
North, Oliver 75

O'Brien, Tim 134, 142, 170
Olds, Sharon 226
Olson, Charles 236
Oppenheimer, Joel 226
Owen, Joseph 192

Owen, Wilfred 143, 227

Page, Tim 255
Palm, Edward F. 137
Paquet, Basil 226, 237
Pauling, Linus 183
Peleg, Tamar 19
Penn, William 41
Perkins, William T., Jr. 255
Perot, H. Ross 77, 89
Peters, Joan 20
Peters, Robert 163, 219, 222
Pierce, Edith Lovejoy 223
Pifer, John 204
Pino, Laurence J. 97
Poe, Edgar Allan 183
Pol Pot 75
Pound, Ezra 227
Powell, Colin 127, 135
Pratt, John Clark 60, 230, 231, 236
Purcell, Charles 230
Pyros, John 173, 181, 218, 219

Quayle, Dan 61
Quintana, Leroy V. 117

Rabin, Yitzak 17
Ramberg, Paal 236
Ray, David 226
Reagan, Ronald 70, 75
Reasoner, Harry 244, 245
Redford, Robert 95, 97
Rhee, Syngman 141
Ridenhour, Ron 135
Ridge, Lola 226
Rilke, Rainer Maria 166
Ritterbusch, Dale 62, 123–126, 127, 143, 226, 229
Rives, Tim 206
Rizzuto, Phil 133
Robinson, LeAnn 29
Rollins, Peter 63
Roper, Jon 4, 144
Rosenberg, Isaac 143, 227
Roskos, Dave 221
Rotenberg, Sam 99
Rottmann, Larry 62, 117
Royer, Eric 197, 199
Rush, Larry 199
Rusk, Dean 198
Russ, Martin 143, 189, 192

Safer, Morley 253, 254

Saldivar, Jose David 150
Sandburg, Carl 225, 226, 229
Saner, Reg 144, 145, 146, 158–161, 163,
    169–170, 182, 212, 213, 225, 232, 233,
    234, 236
Sang, Nguyen Quang 120
Sarid, Yossi 17
Sassoon, Siegfried 143, 149, 161, 227
Schafer, John C. 62
Schell, Jonathan 246
Schwarzkopf, Norman 13, 14, 135
Schwinn, Monika 94
Scott, Winfield Townley 232
Seeger, Alan 211, 223, 226, 227
Selleck, Tom 70
Shakespeare, William 43, 44
Shamir, Yitzak 17
Shapiro, Karl 225
Sharon, Ariel 17
Sharp, Rich 100–105
Shawa, Aoun 17
Shay, Jonathan 79–87
Sheehan, Neil 246, 249, 255
Shields, Bill 117
Sillitoe, Alan 2
Simmons, Edwin Howard 189–192
Simpson, Louis 143, 225, 228
Slabey, Robert 61, 62
Smith, George 92, 94
Smith, Lorrie 64, 209, 211, 230, 232
Smith, Ray 207
Snodgrass, W. D. 143, 225
Soldati, Joseph A. 214–215
Sorley, Charles Hamilton 227
Sourani, Raji 17, 19
Springsteen, Bruce 25
Stalin, Joseph 198
Stallone, Sylvester 60, 70, 209
Stallworthy, Jon 224
Steele, Daniele 25
Stephens, Michael 232
Steptoe, Lamont 117
Stevens, Wallace 226, 227
Stewart, Frank 232
Stockdale, James Bond 77, 89, 92
Stockdale, Sybil 92
Stokesbury, Leon 229
Stone, Dana 245
Styron, William 143, 189, 190
Summers, Harry, Jr. 19

Tennyson, Lord Alfred 143
Thieu, Nguyen Van 60, 250
Thomas, Dylan 4
Thomas, Ray 101–104
Thoreau, Henry David 27
Tiana (Thi Thanh Nga) 62
Truman, Harry S 169, 193
Tsemel, Leah 19

Van Devanter, Lynda 62, 117
Van Wienen, Mark 226

Walcott, Derek 159
Wallace, John 242, 245
Walker, Walton H. 154
Walsh, Jeffrey 171–172, 223, 226, 227,
    229, 231
Wantling, Ruth 175, 181, 218
Wantling, William 145, 161–164, 170,
    173–181, 182, 217–222, 224, 225, 232,
    236, 237
Washington, Cordell 259, 260
Washington, George 194
Wayne, John 59, 199
Weigl, Bruce 64, 117, 226, 230
Westmoreland, William 62, 81
Wharton, Edith 226
Whitman, Walt 135, 142
Wilbur, Richard 223, 225
Will, George 10
Williams, William Carlos 227
Willson, David A. 25, 60, 62
Wilson, Jean Morcroft 227
Wilson, Jim 192
Wilson, Keith 145, 146, 162, 164–169,
    182, 213, 224, 225, 232, 234, 235, 236,
    237
Wilson, Woodrow 68
Wimmer, Adi 60, 61
Winans, A. D. 174, 177, 218
Winsor, Ellen 226
Worman, Ed 254–255
Worman, Kenneth G. 203, 254
Wynn, Cheryl 101, 104

Yserman, Steve 98

Zaffiri, Samuel 173, 217, 218, 219
Zaquot, Naela 17